Faithful Inheritances

American Society of Missiology Monograph Series

Chair of Series Editorial Committee, James R. Krabill

The ASM Monograph Series provides a forum for publishing quality dissertations and studies in the field of missiology. Collaborating with Pickwick Publications—a division of Wipf and Stock Publishers of Eugene, Oregon—the American Society of Missiology selects high quality dissertations and other monographic studies that offer research materials in mission studies for scholars, mission and church leaders, and the academic community at large. The ASM seeks scholarly work for publication in the series that throws light on issues confronting Christian world mission in its cultural, social, historical, biblical, and theological dimensions.

Missiology is an academic field that brings together scholars whose professional training ranges from doctoral-level preparation in areas such as Scripture, history and sociology of religions, anthropology, theology, international relations, interreligious interchange, mission history, inculturation, and church law. The American Society of Missiology, which sponsors this series, is an ecumenical body drawing members from Independent and Ecumenical Protestant, Catholic, Orthodox, and other traditions. Members of the ASM are united by their commitment to reflect on and do scholarly work relating to both mission history and the present-day mission of the church. The ASM Monograph Series aims to publish works of exceptional merit on specialized topics, with particular attention given to work by younger scholars, the dissemination and publication of which is difficult under the economic pressures of standard publishing models.

Persons seeking information about the ASM or the guidelines for having their dissertations considered for publication in the ASM Monograph Series should consult the Society's website—www.asmweb.org.

Members of the ASM Monograph Committee who approved this book are:

Susan Maros, Affiliate Assistant Professor of Christian Leadership
Fuller Theological Seminary

Sue Russell, Professor of Mission and Contextual Studies
Asbury Theological Seminary

RECENTLY PUBLISHED IN THE ASM MONOGRAPH SERIES

George Shakwelele, *Explaining the Practice of Elevating an Ancestor for Veneration*
Peter T. Lee, *Hybridizing Mission: Intercultural Social Dynamics among Christian Workers on Multicultural Teams in North Africa*

Faithful Inheritances

A Study on the Role of Christianity in Shaping Second-Generation Latinos

Yamil Acevedo
Foreword by Elizabeth Conde-Frazier

American Society of Missiology Monograph Series

☙PICKWICK *Publications* · Eugene, Oregon

FAITHFUL INHERITANCES
A Study on the Role of Christianity in Shaping Second-Generation Latinos

Amerian Society of Missiology Monograph Series

Copyright © 2025 Yamil Acevedo. All rights reserved. Except for brief quotations in critical publications or reviews, no part of this book may be reproduced in any manner without prior written permission from the publisher. Write: Permissions, Wipf and Stock Publishers, 199 W. 8th Ave., Suite 3, Eugene, OR 97401.

Pickwick Publications
An Imprint of Wipf and Stock Publishers
199 W. 8th Ave., Suite 3
Eugene, OR 97401

www.wipfandstock.com

PAPERBACK ISBN: 979-8-3852-2083-0
HARDCOVER ISBN: 979-8-3852-2084-7
EBOOK ISBN: 979-8-3852-2085-4

Cataloguing-in-Publication data:

Names: Acevedo, Yamil. | Conde-Frazier, Elizabeth, foreword.

Title: Faithful inheritances : a study on the role of christianity in shaping second-generation latinos / Yamil Acevedo ; foreword by Elizabeth Conde-Frazier.

Description: Eugene, OR : Pickwick Publications, 2025 | Series: American Society of Missiology Monograph Series | Includes bibliographical references and index.

Identifiers: ISBN 979-8-3852-2083-0 (paperback) | ISBN 979-8-3852-2084-7 (hardcover) | ISBN 979-8-3852-2085-4 (ebook)

Subjects: LCSH: Hispanic Americans—Religious life and customs. | Hispanic American youth—Religious life and customs. | Hispanic Americans—Ethnic identity. | Christianity and culture—United States.

Classification: BR563.H57 .A35 2025 (paperback) | BR563.H57 .A35 (ebook)

VERSION NUMBER 04/25/25

All Scripture quotations, unless otherwise indicated, are taken from the Holy Bible, New International Version®, NIV®. Copyright ©1973, 1978, 1984, 2011 by Biblica, Inc.™ Used by permission of Zondervan. All rights reserved worldwide. www.zondervan.comThe "NIV" and "New International Version" are trademarks registered in the United States Patent and Trademark Office by Biblica, Inc.™

A Yare, mi amada esposa y admirable compañera de vida

Heritage is not just a thing of the past, it is the seed of the future.

—Author Unknown.

Contents

List of Tables | ix
Foreword by Elizabeth Conde-Frazier | xi
Preface | xv
Acknowledgments | xvii
List of Abbreviations | xix

1. Introduction | 1
2. Literature Review | 12
3. Research Methodology | 57
4. Familial, Cultural, and Personal Christian Orientations | 66
5. Findings on Sense of Belonging: Place, Culture, and Church | 87
6. Findings on Understanding and Participation in Mission | 110
7. Discussions of Findings, Missional Implications, and Conclusion | 122

Appendix A: Letter of Informed Consent | 147
Appendix B: Interview Protocol and Guidelines | 149
Appendix C: List of Participants | 153
Appendix D: Chronology of Content-Oriented Latino/a(s) Ethnic Identity Models | 156
Bibliography | 167
Index | 177

List of Tables

Table 1. Lifespan Model of Latinx Ethnic Identity Development | 19

Foreword

THE LATINO POPULATION IN the United States has more than doubled in the last forty years. From 14.5 million in 1980 to 63.6 million in 2022.[1] As this growth takes place, it is changing the composition of the population from first-generation immigrants to second and third-generation or children of immigrant parents born in the United States. While the number of immigrants will continue to rise, the number of births in the United States will increase significantly. The Latino population is also younger than the general population and is divided equally between males and females, with a more significant number being of school age. They will become a large part of the workforce of the United States.

The Pew Research Center reports on the generational differences between first, second, and third-generation Latinos. It shows that the second generation is less conservative on issues such as divorce and abortion and other social values; they have higher levels of education, and therefore, their household income is also higher, and a more significant percentage of them is bilingual while they are English dominant. Since they have a higher income ($50,000 on average), they also believe saving money for the future is essential. In contrast, the first generation thinks the future cannot be predicted. Regarding identity, the second generation will identify as Latino/Hispanic, and 38% will identify using their parents' country of origin. At the same time, 82% of second-generation and 81% of third-generation give precedence to family over friends.[2]

This last characteristic is essential when understanding identity as it relates to religion. Identity has been studied from the standpoint of physical, psychological, mental, moral, and ethnic development. However, when

---

1. Krogstad et al., "Key Facts about U.S. Latinos."
2. Pew Research Center, "2002 National Survey of Latinos."

looking at second-generation identity development, racial/ethnic identity has not been paired with religious development. How is it that the two interact with each other? How do they bring about self-awareness, confidence, and well-being?

Yamil Acevedo offers us a comprehensive discussion of the theories of identity. He compares, contrasts, and discusses the different development theories about identity formation, giving us a wonderful analysis of each in relation to the other. He also brings religious development into the conversation. This is not a discussion of stages of faith but a discussion about how identity is formed by religion and religious expression is influenced and shaped by the progressive development of identity. Thus, he creates a dialogue between these different aspects that helps us arrive at understanding the needs for including the need for religious self-understanding in the work of fashioning identity.

Identity is presented as a continuous process of meaning-making across one's lifespan as one interacts with and navigates contextual and environmental changes over one's lifetime. This includes the political and sociocultural context and the family ethos encompassing values. Acevedo argues that faith in God defines the frame of Latino culture and, on this basis, argues for its importance and inclusion in understanding worldview and how one finds one's place in the world.

Religious life in the Puerto Rican household helps create the daily routines that shape the outer rhythms of life and the inner rhythms of the soul, which form identity. Language or food alone are not the determinant factors. The rhythms create a beat of life ingrained in the psyche as a structure of the self. It comprises disciplines of daily life that repeat and reverberate, creating an inner voice and sense of an inner person. Religion offers this for Latinos on a weekly and daily level. These inner echoes form resilience patterns such as prayer, scripture, and community support necessary for survival and thriving. Their content informs daily conversation and values, which serve as the foundation for decision-making and a growing sense of self in relation to others. Behaviors are enforced or deterred based on these values. The values are grounded in relationships that take place in family, and for the immigrant, family means the church family where we call each other *hermana y hermano* (sister and brother), and we greet each other by offering each other a blessing rather than a polite "How are you?" Politeness is not sufficient for the full expression of religious values. Only the bond of a relationship will bring us into an intimacy that requires hospitality, respect,

Foreword

dignity, and support. Support is based on compassion, and compassion is expressed by committed service. The Puerto Rican second generation grows up in a church that instills in them a deep sense of responsibility for the wellbeing of the other through kindness and good works—"*haz el bien y no mires a quien.*"[3] We become responsible for sharing information, rides, food, medicine, prayer, money, and extending any favor or social capital to others. These deep relational routines of daily living create a sense of identity. We are servants as disciples of Christ as a church family. We derive a theology of justice from this compassion and service pattern. It is through this relational living that we gain a sense of belonging. Even though we may feel that we do not belong to the main or mother cultures entirely, we are nonetheless embraced. Acevedo points out that the "intersection of culture and belief points to community as the converging element."

The benefits of navigating identity through the lens of religion give one a way of critiquing colonial approaches to mission, particularly when participating in non-Latino religious communities. When taken seriously and reflected upon, these communities have the potential to bring about greater faithfulness to the mission of the church.

Acevedo's insights in this cross-reading of cultural identity and religion serve as an excellent indicator to Anglo-American religious communities, where second generations may come to worship, of how they are doing in becoming culturally sensitive and biblically grounded in growing in the area of racial and ethnic diversity.

To express myself as a second-generation Puerto Rican: I pray that as we read and reflect together, we may become more faithful as servant communities committed to the *basileia*.[4]

Elizabeth Conde-Frazier

---

3. Do good without exception of persons.
4. The reign of God.

Preface

THIS BOOK, *FAITHFUL INHERITANCES*, adapted from my dissertation, endeavors to bridge the academic rigor required for scholarly discourse with an accessibility that invites non-academic readers into a deep and engaging exploration. Over the past four decades, the field of social sciences has extensively documented the dynamics of constructing and maintaining Latino/a(s) ethnic and racial identities. This wealth of academic inquiry has fostered a diverse array of models explaining Latino/a(s) ethnic identity, broadly categorized into two streams: content-oriented models, which concentrate on behaviors and attitudes within the ethnic group, and process-oriented models, which delve into an individual's self-awareness of ethnic identity's role in shaping personal choices.

Despite the expansive dialogue surrounding ethnic identity, there remains a notable oversight concerning the influence of Christian beliefs on the formation and perseverance of ethnic identity among Latino/a(s) in the United States. Furthermore, while substantial attention has been devoted to ethnic identity in the context of group membership, the connection between ethnic identity and geographical belonging has been relatively understudied. With its primary aim to address these gaps, this book focuses on second-generation Puerto Ricans, examining how their Christian faith influences their understanding of ethnic identity and belonging within the broader landscape of being Latino/a(s) in the United States.

This study illuminates the concept of *faithful inheritances*, which refers to the dual legacies of faith and cultural heritage passed down through generations. These inheritances are not static relics of the past but dynamic forces that shape second-generation Puerto Ricans' identities, values, and community engagements. Through qualitative research involving twenty-seven participants across predominantly Protestant Anglo-American congregations and English-speaking Latino/a(s) congregations, this book

Preface

explores how these individuals integrate their cultural and religious identities. The findings underscore the role of Christian beliefs in shaping a distinctive ethnoreligious identity that guides second-generation Puerto Ricans in navigating their world, interacting with others, and fostering a sense of belonging.

Moreover, this investigation highlights the emergence of *comunidad* as a critical concept that threads through all stages of ethnic identity development as proposed in the Lifespan Model of Latinx Ethnic Identity Development. The depth of engagement with both Anglo-American and Latino/a(s) congregations significantly impacts the communal bonds and mission participation of second-generation Latino/a(s), with particular resonance for Puerto Ricans.

The value of this research extends beyond the specific context of second-generation Puerto Ricans. Many of the experiences and challenges faced by second-generation Puerto Ricans, such as navigating dual identities, cultural dissonance, and the integration of faith and ethnicity, are shared by other second-generation Latino/a(s) groups. This study's theoretical frameworks and models provide insights broadly applicable to understanding the complex identities of second-generation Latino/a(s) across different national backgrounds.

At the same time, it is crucial to acknowledge the unique cultural nuances and complexities within the broader Latino/a(s) community. Each subgroup—be they Mexican, Costa Rican, Venezuelan, or others—possesses distinct historical, sociopolitical, and cultural contexts that significantly shape their identity formation. Consequently, while this study's findings offer valuable insights that are broadly relevant, they must be applied with careful consideration and sensitivity to each group's specific circumstances to avoid overgeneralizations.

Faithful Inheritances adds a new dimension to scholarly discussions on ethnicity and mission within Christian contexts. It invites readers to reconsider the complex interplay of faith and ethnic identity in shaping community and individual lives across contemporary America's diverse Latino/a(s) spectrum. By understanding and honoring these faithful inheritances, we gain a deeper appreciation for the rich, multifaceted identities that second-generation Latino/a(s) bring to their faith communities and the broader society. This book contributes to the academic discourse and offers practical insights for church leaders, educators, and policymakers seeking to support the holistic development of second-generation Latino/a(s) within their communities.

Acknowledgments

First and foremost, I am wholeheartedly and forever grateful to the loving, mysterious, and highly meticulous Almighty God of the universe—his divine orchestration of thousands of experiences woven from eternity has formed, sustained, and given me a purposeful sense of being in him. Moreover, through him, hundreds of relationships and divine encounters bring support, inspiration, affirmation, challenge, and words of wisdom when needed to proceed one more step in the journey. These relationships are humbling, palpable evidence of God's grace. I can only mention a few on these pages, but I am grateful for every one.

I am forever grateful to my wife, Yaremí Alicea, for her support, friendship, encouragement, endurance, prayers, and unconditional love during my academic journey, research, and writing. Thanks to my children, Daniel and Rebeca, for making me laugh, asking questions, leaving encouraging notes on my desk, sharing a timely snack, and believing in me. I am thankful to my parents, Angel and Migdalia, for their interceding ministry and for being present.

I am grateful to the Intercultural Studies faculty at Trinity Evangelical Divinity School and to all my peers. I thank Dr. Tite Tienou for his patience in mentoring this emerging scholar during this long journey and Dr. Peter Cha for introducing me to some of this dissertation's themes and his pastoral-advisor role. Also, thanks to Dr. Craig Ott for his ongoing concern for my academic success and to Dr. Gustafson for opening the doors of his house for a week so I could do research and writing.

I thank all second-generation Latino/a(s) brothers and sisters who participated in this research. Your stories and experiences are worth listening to and sharing.

I appreciate the sisters of the Immaculate Conception Monastery in Ferdinand, Indiana, particularly Sister Jackie, whose remarkable hospitality

Acknowledgments

made my research and writing retreat memorable. Likewise, I am thankful to the Shunem House in Noblesville, Indiana, for providing a room for me and a cozy environment among missionaries so I could focus on writing in great company.

Lastly, I borrow the words from the Apostle Paul: "Now to him who is able to do immeasurably more than all we ask or imagine, according to his power that is at work within us, to him be glory in the church and in Christ Jesus throughout all generations, for ever and ever! Amen" (Eph 3:20–21 NIV).

List of Abbreviations

AAC	Anglo-American Congregation
ELC	English-speaking Latino/a(s) Congregation
LEIM	Latino/a(s) Ethnic Identity Model
LMLEID	Lifespan Model of Latinx Ethnic Identity Development
SGL	Second-generation Latino/a(s)
SGPR	Second-generation Puerto Rican
RQ	Research Question

1

Introduction

THIS STUDY PROBES THE role of Christian beliefs and values in constructing and maintaining ethnic identity and the sense of belonging for second-generation Puerto Ricans. It engages in a sustained conversation across various academic disciplines such as sociology, social psychology, geography, missiology, and theology to interpret and analyze stories and experiences of second-generation Puerto Ricans attending predominantly Anglo-American congregations or English-speaking Latino/a(s) congregations.

While this study focuses specifically on second-generation Puerto Ricans, the scope and findings offer valuable insights potentially transferable to the broader second-generation Latino/a(s) community in the United States. Many of the experiences and challenges faced by second-generation Puerto Ricans, such as navigating dual identities, cultural dissonance, and the integration of faith and ethnicity, are shared by other second-generation Latino/a(s) groups. The frameworks and models utilized in this research, including the Lifespan Model of Latinx Ethnic Identity Development, provide a comprehensive understanding of how second-generation Latino/a(s) individuals negotiate their cultural and religious identities within diverse contexts.

However, it is equally important to recognize the distinct cultural nuances and intricacies within the broader Latino/a(s) community. Each subgroup, whether Mexican, Dominican, Salvadoran, or others, brings unique historical, sociopolitical, and cultural contexts that influence their identity formation in specific ways. For instance, the colonial history and political relationship between Puerto Rico and the United States shape the

Faithful Inheritances

experiences of second-generation Puerto Ricans differently from those of other Latino/a(s) groups. Thus, while the findings of this study are broadly applicable, they must be interpreted with precision and sensitivity to these unique contexts to avoid overgeneralizations.

Understanding the specific cultural and historical backgrounds of different Latino/a(s) subgroups is crucial for developing targeted interventions and support systems that honor their distinct heritages. Church leaders, educators, and policymakers can benefit from this nuanced approach, creating more inclusive and supportive environments that recognize and celebrate the diverse experiences of all second-generation Latino/a(s). This study underscores the need for continued research that disaggregates data and focuses on individual national groups within the Latino/a(s) diaspora to capture these differences accurately.

This introductory chapter provides the problem context, research concern, research questions, scope, limitations, and significance. The next chapter explores, analyzes, and discusses relevant literature concerning the main scope of this research. Chapter 3 discloses the research methodology employed. Chapters 4 through 6 reveal the findings concerning Christian beliefs and ethnic self-understanding, sense of belonging, and understanding and participation in mission successively. Lastly, chapter 7 provides a discussion of the findings and a conclusion.

CONTEXT OF THE PROBLEM

In the United States, people born in or have heritage connected to Central and South American countries are known as Latino/a(s).[1] Currently, Latino/a(s) constitute the largest minoritized group in this country.[2] The social sciences have made significant contributions to understanding how Latino/a(s) develop their sense of membership and belonging in the United States.

Latino/a(s) academic conversations about self-understanding and belonging have mainly focused on ethnic identity. Over the last forty years, multiple ethnic identity models have been developed for Latino/a(s) children, adolescents, young adults, and adults, providing a growing understanding of the complexities surrounding ethnic development.[3] These

---

1. Comas-Diaz, "Hispanics, Latinos, or Americanos," 116–17.
2. "U.S. Census Bureau Quickfacts."
3. E.g., Bernal and Knight, *Ethnic Identity*; Bronfenbrenner, *Ecology of Human Development*; Torres et al., *Understanding the Latinx Experience*.

models acknowledge that multiple factors influence the construction and maintenance of Latino/a(s) sense of belonging over a lifetime. However, a significant gap in these previous studies seems to be an oversight regarding the influence of religious beliefs and practices in shaping Latino/a(s) ethnic identity. This oversight gains relevance when one takes into consideration that nine out of ten Latino/a(s) in the United States self-identify with a specific religious belief system.[4]

Furthermore, the need for more specificity concerning the country of origin also adds to the scholarship gap. For example, people from Central and South America have different traditions, customs, beliefs, and sociopolitical perspectives.[5] To that effect, the term Latino/a(s) seems to be imprecise to describe the religious belief systems and the intricate cultural distinctiveness corresponding to the country of origin influencing belonging and self-understanding for people such as Puerto Ricans.[6]

RESEARCH CONCERN

The case of Puerto Rican identity draws attention to the shortcomings of the current ethnic identity models. First, these models omit religious beliefs and social and cultural distinctiveness as part of the sense of belonging and ethnic self-understanding. Puerto Ricans account for 10 percent of all Latino/a(s) in the United States, and approximately 70 percent of them were born in one of the fifty states or Washington D.C.[7] Around 83 percent of island-born Puerto Ricans living in the United States self-identify as either Catholic or Protestant, as do 62 percent of mainland-born second and third-generation Puerto Ricans.[8] This indicates that seven out of ten Puerto Ricans are either acquainted with Christian beliefs or may appeal to them for ethnic self-understanding.

Chen and Jeung, when discussing Latino/a(s) and Asians in America, argue that religious beliefs shape behavior and the understanding of the self.[9] Orlando Crespo makes a similar argument as Puerto Rican and Latino/a(s) living in the US. He sustains that the Latino/a(s) spiritual

4. "Changing Faiths."
5. Torres, "Familial Influences."
6. The complexities of the terms Latino/a(s), Latinx, Latino, and Hispanic will be discussed in chapter 2.
7. Noe-Bustamante et al., "Facts on Latinos."
8. Krogstad et al., "Key Findings about Puerto Rico."
9. Chen and Jeung, *Sustaining Faith Traditions*.

journey is interconnected with the ethno-racial journey, so that when one learns something about God, their self-understanding grows, as well as the appreciation of others.[10] Chen and Jeung maintain that second-generation Latino/a(s) negotiate race, religion, and ethnicity through two trajectories: (1) religious primacy and (2) racialized religion. The authors, Gerardo Martí, Milagros Peña, and Carlos I. Hernández engage with these, respectively.[11][12]

Gerardo Martí suggests that Latino/a(s) in America participate in three types of communities: (1) ethno-specific, which are Christian communities composed of people sharing one particular ethnicity; (2) pan-ethnic, in contrast, move across nationalities and cultural differences, but sharing a Latino/a(s) American background, or (3) ethnic-transcendent, defined as Christian communities that transcend race and ethnicity, and become bounded by religion.[13] Martí elaborates, stating that context determines the adequacy of a particular Latino/a identity.[14] His proposal suggests a Latino/a(s) negotiation between race, ethnicity, and religion depending on surrounding circumstances and, most importantly, the composition of the community of faith. Martí concludes emphatically that religion influences one's identity.[15]

In turn, Peña and Hernández contend that racialized religion is also intrinsically connected to the Latino/a(s) ethnic identity.[16] The authors propose that Latino/a(s) converge and find unity in serving other Latino/a(s).[17] They suggest that Latino/a(s) remain identified with their ethnic heritage through service.[18] This claim implies that religious institutions are crucial in constructing and maintaining Latino/a(s) ethnic identity. Peña and Hernández assert that religious commitments are how ethnic groups manifest their identities.[19]

---

10. Crespo, *Being Latino in Christ*, 90.
11. Martí, "Diversity-Affirming Latino."
12. Peña and Hernández, "Second Generation Latin@."
13. Martí, "Diversity-Affirming Latino," 25–45.
14. Martí, "Diversity-Affirming Latino," 41.
15. Martí, "Diversity-Affirming Latino," 43.
16. Peña and Hernández, "Second Generation Latin@."
17. Peña and Hernández, "Second Generation Latin@," 93.
18. Peña and Hernández, "Second Generation Latin@," 93.
19. Peña and Hernández, "Second Generation Latin@," 110.

Introduction

Considering the two trajectories of religious primacy and racialized religion, one must conclude that Latino/a(s) ethnic identity models are missing a critical element by omitting religion. Religion appears to profoundly influence constructing and maintaining the Latino/a ethnic identity across generations. Therefore, not acknowledging it indeed represents a limitation. Because Christian beliefs have much to say about these subjects, the question arises: How and to what extent do Puerto Ricans' Christian-oriented beliefs influence their self-understanding? Latino/a(s) ethnic identity models cannot provide a definite answer to this question.

The second consideration in this issue is the limitation that the term Latino/a(s), as a category, brings to the understanding of the self. Although this matter will be discussed in more depth in the upcoming chapter, it is sufficient to recognize that national background helps to understand how the different histories and cultural elements have influenced the construction of a particular Latino/a(s) identity in the United States.[20] In the case of Puerto Ricans, the historical realities accumulated over time positioned them in a particular juncture of self-understanding and belonging that compares to no other Latino/a(s) group in the United States.[21] Therefore, the term Latino/a(s) limits recognizing national and cultural distinctiveness, creating a misunderstanding of the ethno-racial identity—a sense of belonging and self-understanding.

Puerto Ricans have been American citizens since 1917.[22] They are considered Latino/a(s) mainly because of the history of colonization by Spain. Puerto Rico shares that history, along with the Spanish language, with other Central and South American countries.[23] Puerto Ricans have non-restricted access to enter the United States and, therefore, move back and forth as a "commuter nation" and settle where they want.[24] Their cultural, ethnic, racial, and religious complexities go back to when the Taíno, Spaniards, and Africans began merging in 1493 on a 100-by-35-mile island in the Caribbean.[25][26] Considering these facts and acknowledging that as

---

20. Martínez, *Walk with the People*, 16–17.
21. Crespo, *Being Latino in Christ*; Ortíz, *Hispanic Challenge*.
22. "Puerto Rico."
23. Torres, "Familial Influences."
24. Torre et al., *Commuter Nation*.
25. Ortíz, *Hispanic Challenge*.
26. "A member of an aboriginal Arawakan people of the Greater Antilles and the Bahamas" ("Definition of TAINO," https://www.merriam-webster.com/dictionary/Taino).

the individual affinity to a particular place increases, the sense of belonging and membership also increases accordingly, one wonders: What does belonging mean for Puerto Ricans? What does belonging encompass? How does their sense of belonging relate to a place?[27]

Lastly, another shortcoming of the ethnic identity development models is how first and second-generation Latino/a(s) process the complexities of belonging and self-understanding in the United States. First-generation Latino/a(s) usually find affirmation of their traditions and heritage in churches where the Latino/a(s) presence is a majority.[28] In other words, churches with a Latino/a(s) majority play a preservative and adaptive role for the first-generation.[29] However, it is not the same for the second-generation, who often live in a liminal state, a state that Belmonte and Jao described as, "*No somos ni de aquí, ni de allá*" ("We are neither from here nor there").[30] Second-generation Latino/a(s) (SGL) find themselves seeking identity, not only in religious beliefs but also in race (i.e., physical attributes), ethnicity (i.e., sense of membership to a group), and cultural heritage.[31][32] How is the ethnoreligious identity of second-generation Puerto Ricans (SGPRs) constructed and maintained amid a predominant Anglo-American church?[33] How does this ethnoreligious identity compare to the experience of SGPRs in a predominant Latino/a(s) English-speaking congregation? How and in what ways do these two groups define themselves?

In summary, the three shortcomings of the Latino/a(s) ethnic identity models (how religion influences ethnic identity, the imprecise use of the term Latino/a(s), and how second-generation processes and maintains ethnic identity), this study analyzes and evaluates the influence of Christian beliefs on the ethnic self-understanding and sense of belonging of SGPRs. This book uses the stories of SGPRs to interpret the relationship between Christian beliefs and this group's social, cultural, and geographical awareness and how these beliefs shape their understanding and participation in the mission of God.

27. Trudeau, "Politics of Belonging."
28. Phinney, "Ethnic Identity"; Foley and Hoge, *Religion and the New Immigrants*.
29. Calvillo and Bailey, "Latino Religious Affiliation," 57.
30. Belmonte and Jao, "Nurturing the Next Generation," 75.
31. Chen and Jeung, *Sustaining Faith Traditions*, 3.
32. Race and ethnicity are discussed and analyzed in depth in chapter 2.
33. The term Anglo-American is used in this research as equivalent to White American.

Introduction

RESEARCH QUESTIONS

This study evaluates, analyzes, and interprets the stories of two groups of SGPRs self-identified as practicing Christians within the Protestant tradition.[34] One group attends predominantly Anglo-American congregations (AAC). The other group attends English-speaking Latino/a(s) congregations (ELC). It pays particular attention to (1) the ethnic composition of their ecclesial community, (2) prominent Christian beliefs that contribute to their sociocultural and geographical awareness, and (3) the relationship of their ethnic identity with their participation in the mission of God.

To conduct this evaluation and analysis, the following research questions (RQs) served as guidelines:

1. How do second-generation Puerto Ricans understand the relationship between their Christian beliefs and ethnic self-identification?

   - What are the participants' cultural and familial orientations toward Christianity?
   - What Christian beliefs are most prominent in the participants' lives?
   - How do Christian beliefs inform the participants' behavior, decisions, and actions?

2. How do Christian beliefs influence the way(s) second-generation Puerto Ricans perceive they belong in the continental United States?

   - What is the relationship between the participants' Christian beliefs and their identification with the place they live in the continental United States?
   - How do participants relate to the American mainstream culture and Puerto Rican culture?
   - What relationship exists between the participants' Christian beliefs and their identification with the church community?

3. How do second-generation Puerto Ricans understand their participation in the mission of God?

   - How do participants' sense of belonging—to a group and place—relate to their disposition toward the mission of God?

---

34. Protestant tradition was used as an exclusion marker of Roman Catholics, Jehovah's Witnesses, Later Day Saints, and other sects.

Faithful Inheritances

- How does ethnic identity affirmation in the ecclesial context relate to the participants' understanding of and contribution to God's mission?
- What Christian beliefs empower second-generation Puerto Ricans to participate in the mission of God?

RESEARCH SCOPE AND LIMITATIONS

This study focuses on the influence of Christian beliefs on the ethnic self-understanding and sense of belonging of SGPRs in Protestant congregations in the continental United States. However, three limitations must be acknowledged. First, this research utilizes a qualitative narrative inquiry and mode of analysis. Its findings cannot be generalized or considered statistically significant. While this study provides valuable insights into the experiences of SGPRs, it is important to acknowledge the variability within and other Latino/a(s) in general. Individual experiences can vary significantly based on factors such as personal background, level of acculturation, and the specific context of the congregations. This variability suggests that the findings may only apply universally to some SGPRs or Latino/a(s). However, it highlights essential information and questions that may apply to other Latino/a(s) and contexts.

A second limitation of this study is that it interviewed participants who self-identified as practicing Christians within the Protestant tradition. More explicitly, it excludes Roman Catholics, Jehovah's Witnesses, Later Day Saints, and other sects that may exhibit different dynamics.[35] Three in ten mainland-born Puerto Ricans self-identify as Protestants, while four in ten are Roman Catholics.[36] The slight statistical difference between Protestants and Catholics made no difference in the participation and significant data collection. Nevertheless, future research should aim to explore these variations to provide a more comprehensive understanding of Latino/a(s) and SGPRs' experiences across different religious contexts.

Lastly, the third limitation is the geographical regions where participants live. The original intention of this research was to focus on a specific area of the continental United States, the Midwest, and, more specifically, Illinois and Indiana. Other researchers on similar subjects, such as Denton and Sánchez, have used a narrow geographical focus to study Puerto Ricans

---

35. For more information on the interviewees Protestant traditions, see appendix C.
36. Krogstad et al., "Key Findings."

Introduction

in New York and Orlando, respectively.³⁷³⁸ The researcher acknowledges the value of these geographical limitations in academic writing. However, due to the realities of the COVID-19 global pandemic, the original proposed geographical restriction to the Midwest (Indiana and Illinois) had to change. Consequently, interviewees represent various regions of the continental United States, giving voice to a broader audience.³⁹

In addition, three delimitations of this study should also be acknowledged. First, this study focuses on two groups, one attending predominant AAC and the other attending predominant ELC. Although most first-generation Latino/a(s) participate in Spanish-speaking churches, SGLs tend to branch out and join English-speaking congregations.⁴⁰ By exploring the stories of these two groups, this research highlights significant differences and similarities in the influence and potential relationship between their Christian beliefs and ethnic understanding and belonging.

A second delimitation of this study lies in the definition of second-generation Puerto Ricans. Scholarship on migration has defined the second-generation mainly as those native-born—meaning born in one of the fifty states and Washington D.C.—with at least one foreign-born parent.⁴¹ However, Puerto Ricans born on the island of Puerto Rico are not considered native-born Americans—despite being American citizens.⁴² Therefore, this study considers SGPRs to be those who arrived in the continental United States in early childhood (ages zero to five), also known as the 1.75 generation.⁴³ This delimitation allows probing the experiences of two groups immersed in the Anglo-American culture since their earliest formative years and raised with some Puerto Rican cultural influence through at least one of their parents.

A third delimitation is age and education. This study interviewed people twenty years and older with some post-high school education. Although this delimitation excludes some younger people, research indicates that the second-generation undergoes a significant evaluation process and

---

37. Denton, "Hablo Español, You Know?"
38. Sánchez, "Puerto Rico's 79ᵗʰ Municipality?"
39. See appendix C for a detailed table of participants.
40. Chafetz and Ebaugh, *Religion and the New Immigrants*, 432; Orsi and Alba, "Passages in Piety."
41. Portes and Rumbaut, *Legacies*.
42. Farley and Alba, "New Second Generation."
43. Rumbaut, "Ages, Life Stages, and Generational Cohorts."

Faithful Inheritances

commitment to their ethnic and racial identity as young adults.[44] Puerto Ricans have the highest percentage of undergraduate completion among Latino/a(s) in the United States, with 19 percent.[45]

SIGNIFICANCE OF THE STUDY

Religious beliefs' influence on the sense of belonging and ethnic self-understanding must be comprehensively understood. The LEIMs developed over the last forty years fit into content-orientated and process-oriented models. Content-oriented models focus on behaviors and attitudes of the individual towards the in-group. In contrast, process-oriented models focus on self-understanding and how their ethnic and racial identity informs their decisions.[46] This study's significance is that it contributes to the growing knowledge of behavior, attitudes, and decisions through religious beliefs. More specifically, this research contributes to understanding how Christian beliefs inform human attitudes and decisions within social and cultural contexts.

In alignment with the contribution mentioned above, missiological implications are also anticipated. This study contributes to the discussions held within a theology of migration mainly centered on the other as the object of evangelistic efforts from an Anglo-dominant culture.[47] It provides a broader understanding of how and to what extent congregations with different ethnic compositions affirm the ethnic and racial identities of minoritized groups to co-labor in God's mission. It also contributes to understanding how Christian beliefs relate to the sense of belonging to a group that sometimes feels like marginal members of the national community despite being born and raised in the United States.[48] Finally, these findings benefit those serving minoritized groups by informing how the gospel message should resonate with the recipients' experiences.

The contributions of this study derive from its significance. Ethnic and racial identity complexities could not be circumscribed to process or content-oriented models. Instead, both—behavior and self-understanding—provide a valuable and complementary understanding regarding how

44. Ferdman and Gallegos, "Racial Identity Development"; Torres et al., *Understanding the Latinx Experience*.
45. Noe-Bustamante et al., "Facts on Latinos."
46. Phinney, "Three-Stage Model."
47. Acevedo, "Immigrant—גֵּר(Ger)."
48. Flores-González, *Citizens But Not Americans*.

identity is constructed and maintained and how and why it is reconfigured and negotiated over a lifetime. Therefore, the first significant element of this research is that it aids in understanding how these two are related through religious belief. It suggests additional perspectives on the role of salient Christian beliefs in constructing and maintaining particular ethnic and racial identities.

The second contribution of this study is how belonging and Christian beliefs empower a person to participate in God's mission. Amidst the increase in ethnic, cultural, and religious diversity in the American context, the question of who belongs and who is considered a stranger emerges. As previously stated, the theology of migration has mainly focused on evangelism and outreach, not including the minoritized other as a participant in God's mission. This approach perpetuates a binary perception of belonging. This research adds to the theology of migration by arguing that a sense of belonging and one's Christian faith relates to the agency of minoritized groups in sharing in the mission of God.

2

Literature Review

THE FOLLOWING LITERATURE REVIEW engages the theoretical framework that affects the most significant aspects of this study.[1] First, it examines the complexities of the terms Latino/a(s), Latinx, and Hispanic in the US. Then, it discusses the Latino/a(s) ethnic and racial identity as a salient concept within the social sciences. More narrowly, this section assesses the concepts of the Latino/a(s) sense of belonging and ethnic self-understanding. This review starts with background information on the concept of Latino/a(s) ethnic and racial identity. It analyzes significant studies in Puerto Rican ethnic and racial identity and ends with current applications in missiological works.

LATINO/A(S) ETHNIC AND RACIAL IDENTITY

Background Information

LATINO, LATINX, OR HISPANIC

Over the years, terms such as Latino and, more recently, Latinx have been used in the United States to describe people whose ancestry is connected to Central and South America and some islands in the Caribbean.[2] The term Hispanic has also been employed to categorize people who can trace their origins to either Spain or Latin America.[3] The debate concerning self-

---

1. Merriam and Tisdell, *Qualitative Research*.
2. Mochkovsky, "Who Are You Calling Latinx?"; Comas-Díaz, "Hispanics, Latinos, or Americanos."
3. López et al., "Who Is Hispanic?"

Literature Review

identification and social categorization of these terms has been extended to various circles in the United States.[4]

The background story of the terms Hispanic and Latino resides mainly in the history of the United States Census and its interest in tracking American residents' racial and ethnic composition.[5] The early beginnings of this categorization could be traced back to the inclusion of Mexican in the 1930 Census.[6] However, this categorization receded for several decades until 1975, when a task force was created to suggest an ethno-racial definition standard for all federal agencies.[7][8] After months of deliberation between the terms Latino and Hispanic, the task force recommended the latter, and its adoption paved its way into the 1980 Census.[9] According to Flores-Hughes, the primary consideration for selecting Hispanic was that the term Latino sounded like Latin, a word that could be related to Rome and its culture. It was also used derogatorily in certain regions in the United States.[10] Hispanic, in turn, suggests a lineage to "Western Hemisphere nations once colonized by Spain."[11] However, the term Latino was eventually added in the 2000 Census, recognizing it more as membership to a group and less as an origin.[12]

The Hispanic standardization suggested by the 1975 Ad Hoc committee was revised in 1997 by the Office of Management and Budget. The revisions created one definition for both Latino and Hispanic: "a person of Cuban, Mexican, Puerto Rican, South or Central American, or other Spanish culture or origin, regardless of race."[13] Unfortunately, the language used in this definition allowed both terms to be used interchangeably, generating more confusion and diverse opinions. Moreover, Michael Banton refers to this as a paradox that negates and affirms race, making the United States the

---

4. López et al., "Who Is Hispanic?"; Mochkovsky, "Who Are You Calling Latinx?"; Taylor et al., "When Labels Don't Fit"; Flores-Hughes, "Origin of the Term 'Hispanic'"; Comas-Díaz, "Hispanics, Latinos, or Americanos."

5. Gold and Manso, "Hispanic Origin," 1–2.

6. Gold and Manso, "Hispanic Origin," 2.

7. Flores-Hughes, "Origin of the Term 'Hispanic,'" 82.

8. A more in-depth exploration on Latino/a(s) ethnicity and race could found in the section Problematizing Ethnicity and Race.

9. Flores-Hughes, "Origin of the Term 'Hispanic,'" 83–84.

10. Flores-Hughes, "Origin of the Term 'Hispanic,'" 82.

11. Flores-Hughes, "Origin of the Term 'Hispanic,'" 82.

12. Gold and Manso, "Hispanic Origin," 4.

13. "Revisions to the Standards."

only country to use race as a practical categorization based on its history of blacks and whites.[14]

The terms Latino and Hispanics still generate bewilderment today. Some see the term Latino as an identifier of people with lineage from Central and South America, including Brazil, but excluding Spain.[15] Others prefer the term Hispanic as an identifier of a Spanish-speaking heritage connected to Spain, Central and South America, but excluding Portuguese and French-speaking countries, such as Brazil and French Guiana.[16] Furthermore, a 2019 survey from Pew Research revealed that 47 percent of Latino/a(s) prefer their family's country of origin to describe themselves over Latino or Hispanic.[17] Regarding the terms Latino and Hispanic, 27 percent prefer the former, and 18 percent prefer the latter.[18]

In recent years, Latinx has emerged as an alternative within certain circles, such as the academy and social media.[19] Latinx proposes an alternative to Hispanic and Latino binary options by branching out of the ethnoracial implications and adopting a more progressive stance of gender inclusivity and neutrality. More specifically, Latinx is perceived to cater to the LGBTQ community and reflect a more unbiased form toward masculinity—a concept known as gender-expansive.[20] However, according to Pew Research, Latinx has not gained enough traction among Latino/a(s), with only 3 percent of Latino/a(s) actively using it.[21]

Nevertheless, despite its perceived slow acceptance in the broader Latino/a(s) community, Latinx has gained more acceptance within the academy. For example, Cristobal Salinas, Jr. asserts that students feel comfortable using Latinx at higher education institutions rather than with their families.[22] An example of this is Elizabeth Conde-Frazier's 2021 book titled *Atando Cabos: Latinx Contributions to Theological Education*, which

14. Banton, *What Do We Know*, 2.

15. López et al., "Who Is Hispanic?"; Comas-Díaz, "Hispanics, Latinos, or Americanos."

16. López et al., "Who Is Hispanic?"; Comas-Díaz, "Hispanics, Latinos, or Americanos."

17. Gonzalez-Barrera, "Ways Hispanics."

18. López et al., "Latinos Now More Negative."

19. de Río-González, "To Latinx or Not to Latinx"; López et al., "Who Is Hispanic?"; Mochkovsky, "Who Are You Calling Latinx?"

20. de Río-González, "To Latinx or Not to Latinx."

21. Noe-Bustamante et al., "Latinx Used by Just 3%."

22. Salinas, "Complexity of the 'X.'"

acknowledges its value for our current United States context yet submits to a particular audience.

The complicated history of the terms Hispanic, Latino, and Latinx suggests the need for terminology that validates the individual's sense of belonging and self-understanding. It seems that none of the three main terms completely satisfy the increasingly diverse and accelerated growing community of Latino/a(s) in the US. This study uses the term Latino/a(s) as an alternative to identify people whose ancestry is connected to Central and South America and the Caribbean, so far as the individual recognizes and embraces this lineage. By using the term Latino/a(s), this book aspires to be female and male-inclusive and simultaneously mindful of the individual and the community. However, it does not intend to engage with or imply a position concerning the current social and cultural gender issues and discussions in the United States.

Ethnic and Racial Identity Theories

Within the social sciences, three significant theories inform the concept of Latino/a(s) ethnic and racial identity: (1) the social identity theory, (2) the ego identity theory, and (3) the acculturation theory. First, Henri Tajfel and John C. Turner's social identity theory states that people derive a positive self-understanding through their sense of belonging to a group.[23] This sense of belonging provides an identity for the individual in the larger society and becomes a source of self-esteem and well-being.[24]

It is at this point where the crux of the theory resides. In order to increase their self-esteem, in-group members look at the negative aspects of the out-group.[25] In the social theory, a person's self-understanding is perceived to be built upon a constant tension of contrasts between groups.[26] More specifically, it is built on the personal value given to one's group significance, power, influence, and status in society compared to others.[27] Within the social identity theory, a person's sense of who they are is dependent on their group(s) membership(s).

---

23. Tajfel and Turner, "Integrative Theory."
24. Tajfel and Turner, "Integrative Theory"; French et al., "Development of Ethnic Identity."
25. Tajfel and Turner, "Integrative Theory."
26. Hogg et al., "Tale of Two Theories."
27. Deaux, "Surveying the Landscape"; Stets and Burke, "Identity Theory."

Faithful Inheritances

The social identity theory contrasts with the second foundational identity theory, Erik H. Erickson's ego identity theory. In the former, identity is constructed and maintained through a person's self-perception of belonging to a group with a harmonious set of beliefs and behaviors. In contrast, in the latter, individual identity formation requires several elements, such as psychic, environmental, and familial.[28] Understanding who one is, in this theory, does not depend on a sense of belonging to a group but on a series of cognitive processes that gain coherence over a lifetime influenced by relationships and places.[29]

Erickson suggests that individuals continuously evaluate their identity after processing outside social, environmental, and familial impositions.[30] This leads to another difference in the social identity theory. In the ego identity theory, self-understanding is constructed and maintained as a personal resolution to internal and external tensions. In other words, the individual possesses the agency to commit to a specific orientation of the self.[31]

A third theoretical foundation related to ethnic and racial identity is the acculturation theory, credited to Robert Redfield, Ralph Linton, and Melville J. Herskovits.[32] Like the social identity theory, the acculturation theory deals with the interaction between groups. However, it focuses on the relationship sustained with the group. Individuals' self-understanding abides in the relationship with their group as part of the society rather than in their sense of belonging or feelings towards it.[33]

The acculturation theory states that groups sustain different attitudes, values, and behaviors that cause changes when in contact with other groups.[34] This is better understood in the relationship between minoritized and dominant groups.[35] Members of minoritized groups will be influenced by those of the dominant group, causing a reevaluation that could lead to (1) adopting the mainstream culture, (2) maintaining their culture, (3)

---

28. Ashforth and Mael, "Social Identity Theory"; Erickson, *Identity: Youth and Crisis*.

29. Marcia, "Ego Identity" and Marcia, "Identity and Psychological Development."

30. French et al., "Development of Ethnic Identity."

31. Phinney, "Ethnic Identity."

32. Redfield, "Memorandum for the Study of Acculturation."

33. Redfield, "Memorandum for the Study of Acculturation"; Phinney, "Ethnic Identity."

34. Redfield, "Memorandum for the Study of Acculturation"; Berry et al., "Assessment of Acculturation."

35. Torres et al., *Understanding the Latinx Experience*, 31.

Literature Review

negotiating a bicultural orientation, or (4) retreating into a marginal state that rejects both.[36] These four dimensions provide a sense of well-being and self-understanding of the person concerning society.[37] Moreover, among the three foundational theories, acculturation is the only one that deals explicitly with cultural identity within plural societies.[38]

These theoretical frameworks try to explain the dynamics between groups and their members as society participants. They all deal with a person's sense of belonging and self-understandings to different degrees and measures, giving ground to developing ethnic and racial identity concepts. Generally defined as a subjective self-identification with a group or culture, ethnic and racial identity responds to "Who am I?" as part of the larger society.[39] Ethnic identity models address this question by examining the elements influencing ethnic and racial orientation and individual development.

Recent Developments of Ethnic Identity Models

Before discussing the recent development of the ethnic identity model, a brief chronology seems adequate to introduce the discussion.[40] The chronology of content-oriented ethnic identity models for young adult Latino/a(s) started in 1981 with the Mexican-American to Chicanismo model, created by Carlos H. Arce.[41] Six years later, Susan E. Keefe and Amado E. Padilla published the Chicano Ethnicity Model, including two primary factors that shape the identity of Mexican descent in the United States: cultural awareness and ethnic loyalty.[42] In 1994, María Felix-Ortiz, Michael D. Newcomb, and Hector Myers presented the Multidimensional Model, nuancing a measure of cultural identity that includes language, attitudes (or values), behaviors, and familiarity with both the American and Latino/a cultures.[43] In 1997, Vasti Torres and Rosemary E. Phelps introduced the Bicultural Orientation Model (BOM), which considers the relationship between acculturation and ethnic identity and assumes that when one

---

36. Berry, "Ethnic Identity in Plural Societies"; Berry et al., "Assessment of Acculturation."
37. Schwartz and Zamboanga, "Testing Berry's Model of Acculturation."
38. Berry, "Ethnic Identity in Plural Societies."
39. Bernal and Knight, *Ethnic Identity*.
40. See Appendix D for a more detailed chronology of content-oriented LEIMs.
41. Arce, "Reconsideration."
42. Keefe and Padilla, *Chicano Ethnicity*.
43. Felix-Ortíz et al., "Multidimensional Measure."

aspect increases, the other decreases.[44] Finally, in 2001 and 2012, Bernardo Ferdman and Plácida Gallegos introduced a Racial Identity Orientation Model, arguing that although ethnicity and culture are essential, race was still very significant for Latino/a(s).[45] However, the more recent development in ethnic identity models was rendered in 2019 by Vasti Torres, Ebelia Hernández, and Sylvia Martínez. This section will discuss their proposal.

The Lifespan Model of Latinx Ethnic Identity Development (LMLEID) is perhaps one of the most complex and elaborated process-oriented models for Latino/a(s) in emerging adulthood and adulthood.[46] The findings are based on a mixed-method longitudinal study between 2000 and 2011. The study included over 500 college students from four colleges and 80 adults between twenty and fifty-eight years old with different educational achievements ranging from high school to doctoral degrees.[47] In addition, the research included surveys and multiple interviews over time—in many cases with the same individual—to understand better their experiences and choices and how these relate to their ethnic identity.[48]

Vasti Torres, Ebelia Hernández, and Sylvia Martínez present a holistic model that consists of a progression through three statuses, where the individual moves from an external definition of self to an internal one.[49] Two critical movements or transitions connect these stages, generally described as moments of reflection on particular life experiences, called borderlands.[50] Lastly, the authors suggest an open window of re-evaluation after the final status, called looping.[51] The looping process implies a cyclical and continuous reformulation of the individual's sense of self throughout life.[52]

The statuses suggested starting with defining the self externally. In this first status, the individual's definition of self and ethnicity derives from their location, demographics, and familial influence.[53] For example, the ethnic identity assumed will depend on whether the upbringing location

---

44. Torres and Phelps, "Hispanic American Acculturation."
45. Ferdman and Gallegos, "Racial Identity Development."
46. See Table 1.1.
47. Torres et al., *Understanding the Latinx Experience*, 11–14.
48. Torres et al., *Understanding the Latinx Experience*, 11–14, 28.
49. Torres et al., *Understanding the Latinx Experience*, 36.
50. Torres et al., *Understanding the Latinx Experience*, 36.
51. Torres et al., *Understanding the Latinx Experience*, 44–46.
52. Torres et al., *Understanding the Latinx Experience*, 45.
53. Torres et al., *Understanding the Latinx Experience*, 36.

has a high or low concentration of Latinos/a(s), if the diversity varied, and the influence of family instruction. The authors sustain that the individual's first status is not contested.[54] In other words, the early formation of the Latino/a(s) ethnic identity is informed by the person's environment and finds no resistance or questioning from the individual.

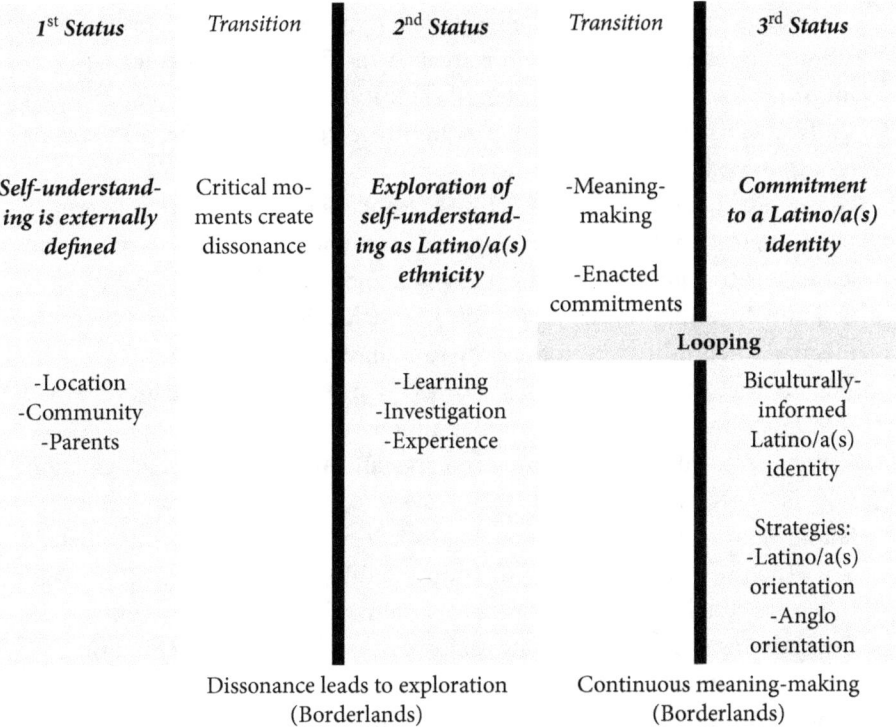

Table 1.1 Lifespan Model of Latinx Ethnic Identity Development[55]

The next step of the process is a transition called critical moment caused by dissonance.[56] This transition is always caused by external events such as a change in environment, entering into contact and relating with other Latinos/a(s), or experiencing racism.[57] These events trigger a period

---

54. Torres et al., *Understanding the Latinx Experience*, 36–37.
55. Adaptation of Torres et al.'s work in *Understanding the Latinx Experience*.
56. Torres et al., *Understanding the Latinx Experience*, 38.
57. Torres et al., *Understanding the Latinx Experience*, 38.

of questioning the peripheral understanding of the self and propel a deeper understanding of the self amid two cultures.[58]

After this transition, the individual enters the second status, exploring Latino/a(s) ethnicity.[59] In this status, the individual must find a supportive entity to learn more about their culture or connect with other Latino/a(s) groups.[60] If new positive ideas and behaviors are found within these supportive networks, the individual moves forward in their development progress; if not, they will retreat to the first status of external definitions.[61] The formation of internal definitions begins in this status and leads towards an ethnic identity commitment; however, the duration of this status is uncertain.

Once the individual internalizes new ideas and behaviors concerning their ethnic identity, it is time to process them and decide what to retain and leave; this transition is called exploring choices and meaning-making.[62] It will be where individuals loop back after achieving a committed Latino/a identity when it becomes necessary to refine previous concepts. It is considered part of the final status. Torres, Martínez, and Hernández assert that this borderland becomes a continuous meaning-making process for Latinos/a(s), where commitments emerge and are enacted in participation with Latino/a(s) organizations, new ways to cope with family and other relationships develop, and individuals advocate for other in-group members.[63]

The third and final status is committed Latino/a(s) identity.[64] Within this stage, the individual embraces a system of negotiation that integrates the Latino/a(s) and United States cultures; the authors call it a biculturally-informed Latino/a(s) identity and describe it as a supporting "strategy" to cope with the challenges encountered at the stage.[65] Although the authors recognize that some individuals may lean more toward one culture, this does not change private and constant engagement with both cultures.

---

58. Torres et al., *Understanding the Latinx Experience*, 38.
59. Torres et al., *Understanding the Latinx Experience*, 38.
60. Torres et al., *Understanding the Latinx Experience*, 38.
61. Torres et al., *Understanding the Latinx Experience*, 39.
62. Torres et al., *Understanding the Latinx Experience*, 41.
63. Torres et al., *Understanding the Latinx Experience*, 42–43.
64. Torres et al., *Understanding the Latinx Experience*, 43–44.
65. Torres et al., *Understanding the Latinx Experience*, 43.

Furthermore, this status provides space to refine behaviors and ideas if tested by new experiences.[66]

The last component of this process is looping.[67] Latino/a(s) may return to the borderlands of meaning-making when their environment changes or a new event changes their life season. This meaning-making is considered more of a refinement in response to life's changes than a probing.[68] The looping frequency is uncertain, but the meaning-making of their socially constructed identity becomes a part of daily life.

The LMLEID makes a new contribution to the evolution of tools that aid understanding Latino/a ethnic identity development. The crux of the model is that the Latino/a identity is under constant evaluation, even throughout adulthood.[69] Other models have stated movement across orientations, but the LMEID proposal differs. It suggests that environment and context play a crucial role in the linear development of the Latino/a ethnic identity by causing reevaluation in response to new experiences. Development does not change orientation but the perception of the self. This perception changes in response to racism, stereotypes, politics, and history.[70] In other words, this model of Latino/a ethnic identity development hinges on an individual's continual meaning-making process, enabling them to cope with contextual and environmental changes (e.g., political, sociocultural) over life.[71]

However, although the LMLEID proposes a robust framework for understanding the Latino/a ethnic identity development, it does not account for religion or race substantially (apart from experiencing racism in the dissonance stage). This is particularly important considering that ethnicity, race, and religion are observed as critical to identity and belonging.[72] Engaging in an exploration of these would have significantly strengthened the model. Additionally, the LMELID has a general interpretation of ethnic identity that does not consider the particularities of the different cultures that comprise the Latino/a(s) community in the United States.

---

66. Torres et al., *Understanding the Latinx Experience*, 43.
67. Torres et al., *Understanding the Latinx Experience*, 44–46.
68. Torres et al., *Understanding the Latinx Experience*, 45.
69. Torres et al., *Understanding the Latinx Experience*, 46.
70. Torres et al., *Understanding the Latinx Experience*, 103.
71. Torres et al., *Understanding the Latinx Experience*, 103.
72. Chen and Jeung, *Sustaining Faith Traditions*.

Faithful Inheritances

Observations on the LMLEID

Considering some observations about the LMLEID model, it is essential to address some general critiques process-oriented models have encountered over time. The first criticism of the status models is that they misrepresent Erickson's theory.[73] Erickson's theory proposes that identity is transactionally constructed between the environment (context) and the individual. However, Côté and Levine maintained that process-oriented models focus on individual choices and disregard the role of context.[74] For example, imitation and internalization of values from authority figures, such as parents, is natural for particular groups.[75] This imitation of beliefs negatively affects the identity development model status.[76]

Moreover, this imitation is what the socialization model suggests for Latino/a(s) families. The main argument against this model is that the social ecology of Mexican-American families creates specific exchanges, familial and non-familial, which influence the self-concept of ethnic identity.[77] Within the socialization model, context plays a crucial role in forming ethnic identity, encompassing self-identification, constancy, role behaviors, ethnic knowledge, preferences, and feelings.[78] These five components collect information about ethnic group members and their ethnic identity through different means within society, such as school, family, and community.[79] The process-oriented models, particularly the LMLEID, only partially address these context-oriented components and represent limitations.

Another observation is the strictly linear progression of process-oriented models. Wim Meeus, reviewing ethnic identity longitudinal studies from the first decade of the twenty-first century, suggests a progressive identity development and even change in status throughout life.[80] In other words, changes in ethnic identity status should be expected over time but not linearly. Meeus sustains that sequential models do not provide the fluidity that identity development necessitates.[81] He maintains the linear models

---

73. Erikson, *Identity: Youth and Crisis*; Côté and Levine, "Critical Examination."
74. Côté and Levine, "Critical Examination."
75. Cheng and Berman, "Globalization and Identity Development."
76. Schwartz et al., "Identity in Emerging Adulthood," 98.
77. Knight et al., "Social Cognitive Model"; Bernal et al., *Ethnic Identity*.
78. Knight et al., "Social Cognitive Model," 106.
79. Knight et al., "Social Cognitive Model," 107.
80. Meeus, "Study of Adolescent Identity," 83.
81. Meeus, "Study of Adolescent Identity."

Literature Review

that assert a stage of exploration before commitment.[82] Meeus suggests that transitions could be (1) progressive but non-linear, (2) regressive toward previous commitments, or (3) stable in adolescence or adulthood.[83] This means that people do not have a blank slate or linear progression regarding their ethnic identity. Furthermore, Meeus finds no evidence of an ethnic identity crisis that leads exclusively to exploration during adolescence.[84] Meeus concludes that identity development is more fluid and complex than linear process-oriented models suggest.

This critique opens a possible exchange between process-oriented models and content-oriented models. More research is needed in this area, where ethnic orientations also become part of fluid progression in constructing, re-constructing, and maintaining ethnic identity. However, to some extent, the LMLEID does account for reconstruction by suggesting a looping reevaluation process. This looping is limited, though, to the committed state. One wonders if the individual could loop back in the process to previous stages of exploration.

Turning to the LMLEID in particular, among all the LEIMs, it is the only one that follows a sequential progression of ethnic identity development. One possible reason for this is because it seems to draw from Phinney's theoretical framework of three-stages of ethnic identity development—unexamined stage, exploration stage, and achievement stage.[85] It also integrates the possibility of an evolving or reconfiguring factor. The model leans on the ego-identity theory, which argues for a lifespan approach to human development.[86] This indeed responds to the observation about a fixed achievement status, but it does not have an answer for the non-linear fluidity problem raised by Meeus, Schwartz et al., and Knight et al.[87]

Another observation of the LMLEID is that it contends biculturalism as a strategy to cope with life in a committed identity stage rather than a person's orientation. The authors' argument suggests that the individual could opt in or out of a bicultural mode depending on the circumstances without necessarily being a bicultural person. This contrasts with other scholarships

---

82. Meeus, "Study of Adolescent Identity," 75.
83. Meeus, "Study of Adolescent Identity," 82–83.
84. Meeus, "Study of Adolescent Identity," 84.
85. Phinney, "Ethnic Identity."
86. Torres et al., *Understanding the Latinx Experience*, 29.
87. Meeus, "Study of Adolescent Identity"; Schwartz et al., "Identity in Emerging Adulthood"; Knight et al., "Social Cognitive Model."

such as Felix-Ortíz et al. and Phinney.[88] Felix-Ortíz et al. assert that most Latino/a(s) have a bicultural orientation—or state—and not a bicultural selective coping tool.[89] One could not help but wonder if both arguments are necessarily mutually exclusive or could complement each other. Moreover, although outside of the scope of this research, one wonders how cultural hybridity could form part of ethnic identity development as well.

Elaborating on bicultural identity, Phinney asserts that individuals need to secure—and achieve—ethnic identity and understand themselves as part of a group and its relation to the mainstream.[90] Therefore, if biculturalism is a strategy and not a settled state, how will individuals of minoritized groups process their self-understanding and sense of belonging concerning mainstream culture? The LMLEID has to provide more clarity on this matter.

Ethnic Identity Models Major Concepts

Over the last forty years, several Latino/a(s) ethnic and racial identity models have focused on childhood and adolescence,[91] and adulthood[92] to explain how Latino/a(s) gain a conscious understanding of self and their surroundings. The most salient concepts found in these Latino/a(s) ethnic identity models (LEIMs) are discussed here to frame the review on Puerto Rican self-understanding and sense of belonging. These salient concepts found in the LEIMs are (1) race and ethnicity and (2) self-awareness and well-being.

RACE AND ETHNICITY

Race and ethnicity have been the object of considerable research in various academic fields, such as history, psychology, sociology, and politics.[93] Sometimes, race and ethnicity have been used and applied interchangeably.[94]

88. Felix-Ortíz et al., "Multidimensional Measure"; Phinney, "Ethnic Identity."
89. Felix-Ortíz et al., "Multidimensional Measure."
90. Phinney, "Ethnic Identity," 126.
91. E.g., Bernal et al., *Ethnic Identity*.
92. E.g., Ferdman and Gallegos, "Racial Identity" and "Latina and Latino Ethnoracial Identity"; Torres et al., *Understanding the Latinx Experience*.
93. E.g., Banton, "Vertical and Horizontal" and *What Do We Know*; Hughes, "Correlates of African American and Latino"; Rumbaut, "Pigments of Our Imagination"; Grosfoguel, "Race and Ethnicity."
94. Cokley, "Racial (Ized) Identity"; Phinney, "Ethnic Identity."

Literature Review

Nevertheless, both terms have been central to the LEIMs scholarship. In this sub-section, some of the complexities of race and ethnicity will be evaluated in terms of this study's scope.

Michael Banton analyzes race from a historical perspective. One of his first arguments is that words have meanings that change over time and context.[95] He argues that that has been the case with race, which has been employed in various spheres, such as literature (i.e., Paradise Lost, 1667), as well as in scientific categorizations (i.e., Carl Linnaeus' categorization of animals, vegetables, and minerals in 1775).[96] The author seems to be pointing out how elastic and shapeable the definition of race is.

Ruben G. Rumbaut seems to agree with this, suggesting that race has a malleable meaning.[97] Rumbaut quotes a study in which 41 percent of second-generation youths checked the box for "Other" under the question on race and wrote down "Hispanic" or "Latino" as their race; 19 percent wrote down their nationality.[98] The study also revealed that the parents of these children gave a different to the same question of race.[99] He interprets these findings to maintain that "Latinos" and "Hispanics" are not racially homogeneous, not only because their countries of origin are different but also because of generational differences that exist between them and their parents.[100] With this last remark, Rumbaut seems to indicate the existence of various elements influencing the meaning of race across Latino/a(s) generations.

A second and more extended argument Banton makes is that race has always had a vertical and a horizontal dimension throughout history.[101] The vertical dimension, according to Banton, "identified the historical origins of what made a set of persons distinctive, emphasizing heredity and genealogy . . . [and the] sharing of a common ancestry."[102] The horizontal dimension "identified the nature of that distinctiveness."[103] How Banton uses the word "nature" in his definition has to do with the inner disposition, an

---

95. Banton, "Vertical and Horizontal Dimensions" and Banton, *What Do We Know*.
96. Banton, *What Do We Know*, 11–13.
97. Rumbaut, "Pigments of Our Imagination."
98. Rumbaut, "Pigments of Our Imagination," 14–16.
99. Rumbaut, "Pigments of Our Imagination."
100. Rumbaut, "Pigments of Our Imagination."
101. Banton, "Vertical and Horizontal Dimensions" and Banton, *What Do We Know*.
102. Banton, *What Do We Know*, 11.
103. Banton, *What Do We Know*, 11.

Faithful Inheritances

inherent character, or essence. Banton argues that although the two dimensions have always been present, the horizontal dimension has taken more preponderance over the vertical in recent years.[104] With this, the author intends to point out that the use and applications of race vary according to the issuers, receivers, cultures, and historical contexts. It seems to suggest that it is somewhat subject to external forces.

Additionally, Banton contends that race has theoretical and practical understandings.[105] He explains his point by borrowing the terms etic and emic from anthropology.[106] Emic constructs are concepts and categories that carry meaning for the members of a community.[107] On the other hand, etic constructs are concepts and categories that hold meaning for the scientific community members.[108] Banton sustains that emic constructs change over time, while etic constructs are transferable and transcultural.[109]

Connecting both illustrations, it could be argued that the vertical dimension of race is emic, while the horizontal dimension is etic. The author states that both dimensions are necessary to properly understand and use the word race. The vertical dimension—emic—helps understand the practical side of race. The horizontal dimension—etic—informs the theoretical knowledge. Each dimension has its purposes and, therefore, its vocabulary. Banton cautions that academic writing must be mindful of this.

Banton's arguments are informative for this discussion because they give us the vocabulary and a reference point to analyze the different conversations on race. Moreover, it helps distinguish between theoretical and practical—and when it confuses. Banton explains that an example of this confusion was the conflict generated by using the word race in the 2000 Census.[110] When the American Sociological Association (ASA) was asked to respond to this issue, they faced a political and intellectual dilemma.[111] Banton states that their final response was paradoxical, failing to recognize its educational use and origin and defending its use in the Census.[112]

---

104. Banton, *What Do We Know*, 12.
105. Banton, "Vertical and Horizontal Dimensions" and Banton, *What Do We Know*.
106. Banton, "Vertical and Horizontal Dimensions."
107. Banton, "Vertical and Horizontal Dimensions," 131.
108. Banton, "Vertical and Horizontal Dimensions," 131.
109. Banton, "Vertical and Horizontal Dimensions," 131.
110. Banton, *What Do We Know*, 1–3.
111. Banton, *What Do We Know*, 1.
112. Banton, *What Do We Know*, 2.

Literature Review

Race researchers have not always maintained a clear definition of race. For example, Katherine A. Ocampo, Martha E. Bernal, and George P. Knight wrote about racial constancy—the knowledge of permanent properties on self or the other—and stated that there is a "genetic transmission of race that is apparent through physical cues."[113] Immediately, the authors added that people from the same ethnic group share cultural values and traditions even if they are from a "pure or mix[ed] race."[114] They conclude by stating that "one may recognize another's ethnicity through both physical cues and more subtle behavioral cues."[115] But, one must wonder what the authors meant by suggesting that the physical attributes, previously linked to race, signal a particular ethnicity.

Another example is Ferdman and Gallegos' Latino/a(s) Racial Orientation Model.[116] In the model, the authors assert that Latino/a(s) culture values race and ancestry, alongside ethnic and cultural identifiers, as part of their group membership requisites.[117] Ferdman and Gallegos suggest a racial identity model with diverse orientations that respond to the realities Latino/a(s) face in the United States.[118] The factors used by the authors to define a Latino/a(s) individual's orientation towards their identity are (1) the "lens" toward identity, (2) the personal self-identification preference, (3) perception of the group from the outside, (4) how "Whites" are seen from the inside, and (5) how race is perceived.[119][120] Again, however, their argument is unclear and seemingly contradictory. It states that race and ethnicity are group membership requisites, yet the outsider's perception of race also factors their orientation. Banton expressly contends against this, saying that racial theories create controversies when trying to make an etic construct out of an emic scheme.[121] In this case, one wonders about the theoretical and practical consistency of the term race.

---

113. Ocampo et al., "Gender, Race, and Ethnicity," 15.

114. Ocampo et al., "Gender, Race, and Ethnicity," 15.

115. Ocampo et al., "Gender, Race, and Ethnicity," 15.

116. Ferdman and Gallegos, "Racial Identity Development" and Ferdman and Gallegos, "Latina and Latino Ethnoracial Identity."

117. Ferdman and Gallegos, "Racial Identity Development," 44–47.

118. Ferdman and Gallegos, "Racial Identity Development."

119. Ferdman and Gallegos, "Racial Identity Development," 49–50.

120. See appendix D for a more detailed explanation of the Latino/a(s) Racial Orientation Model.

121. Banton, "Vertical and Horizontal Dimensions," 131.

Faithful Inheritances

More recently, Torres, Hernández, and Martinez concede race a place in the LMLEID, but only as an element of dissonance that may trigger a season of Latino/a(s) ethnic exploration (i.e., an experience with racism).[122] By adopting this approach, the authors initiate a relationship between race and ethnicity that was left underdeveloped in the rest of LMLEID. Moreover, at the last stage of their model, the authors suggest that the Latino/a(s) Biculturally-informed identity learns to manage its complexities by leaning into Latino/a(s) or Anglo orientations.[123] Although their use of "Anglo" in this instance refers to a culture and a set of behaviors, it also carries a racial meaning. Nevertheless, the difference and relationship between the two remain unclear.

The lack of clarity and understanding of race has had severe implications in the United States. It has created categorizations and superior/inferior hierarchies based on biological features, ancestry, and culture.[124] The theoretical and practical complexities of race are apparent in Rumbaut's declaration that "'Race' is a social status, not a zoological one; a product of history, not of nature; a contextual variable, not a given."[125] With this statement, Rumbaut argues that race is a social construct, just as other scholars have previously and recently articulated, and as such, prone to create "ideas of social worth and stigmas."[126][127] Advancing this conversation further into LEIMs, the question of how Latino/a(s) respond to such notions becomes pressing.

Many researchers have written about how the racial socialization process operates among Latino/a(s) in response to the cultural stereotypes created by race in the United States.[128] Racial socialization explains how cultural values, heritage, and history are transferred amid family members of minoritized groups in two main dimensions: cultural socialization and preparation for bias.[129] In particular, Diane Hughes conducted a study

122. Torres et al., *Understanding the Latinx Experience*.

123. Torres et al., *Understanding the Latinx Experience*, 41–47.

124. Rumbaut, "Pigments of Our Imagination"; Banton, "Vertical and Horizontal Dimensions" and Banton, *What Do We Know?*; Grosfoguel, "Race and Ethnicity?"

125. Rumbaut, "Pigments of Our Imagination," 1.

126. E.g., Gómez, *Manifest Destinies*; Hughes, "Correlates of African American."

127. Rumbaut, "Pigments of Our Imagination," 1.

128. E.g., French et al., "Development of Ethnic Identity"; Umaña et al., "Longitudinal Examination"; Chavez et al., "Learning to Value the Other"; Hughes, "Correlates of African American."

129. Hughes, "Correlates of African American"; Araujo Dawson and Quiros, "Effects

among Puerto Ricans, Dominicans, and African-American families on the prevalence and frequency of these dimensions.[130]

Hughes explains that the first dimension of racial socialization, cultural socialization, consists of the transfer, by family members, of messages that carry ethnic pride, history, and heritage through traditions, values, music, language, and food.[131] Her study observed Latino/a(s) parents accentuate their ethnic identity to their children more than African-American parents, especially during adolescence.[132] The author concurs with other scholars that this intense cultural socialization is, in part, resistance to the racialization systems in the United States, for example, emphasizing certain ethnic distinctives to avoid discrimination based on skin color.[133][134] Hughes concludes that this cultural socialization is the way Latino/a(s) families use to "ensure adolescents' positive group identification as they exert their independence and become oriented toward the larger world of peers."[135]

It is important to note that race and ethnicity play a part in racial socialization. They are not used interchangeably as in other instances previously mentioned but are used in tandem. Thus, this suggests that race and ethnicity inform the construction of the individual self-understanding and sense of belonging as a sign of group membership and a coping mechanism in the United States.

The second dimension of racial socialization is preparation for bias, and it encompasses racial discrimination and cultural biases.[136] This dimension deals with the messages and dialogues about potential racial and social dispositions. Hughes found that Latino/a(s) parents do not sustain conversations on racial discrimination and biases with the same frequency and intensity as cultural socialization.[137] The author suggests that this is due to an understanding that (1) these themes might be detrimental to the well-being of their children and (2) more challenging to address.[138] In a similar

---

of Racial Socialization"; Phinney and Chavira, "Ethnic Identity and Self-Esteem."

130. Hughes, "Correlates of African American."
131. Hughes, "Correlates of African American."
132. Hughes, "Correlates of African American," 29.
133. Urciuoli, *Exposing Prejudice*; Pessar, *Visa for a Dream*.
134. Hughes, "Correlates of African American," 29.
135. Hughes, "Correlates of African American," 30.
136. Hughes, "Correlates of African American."
137. Hughes, "Correlates of African American," 30–32.
138. Hughes, "Correlates of African American," 30.

study, Beverly Araujo Dawson and Laura Quiros shared that adult Latinas reported being exposed to racial socialization during their upbringings in themes such as "anti-Black sentiment, marginalization of facial features, and elevation of whiteness," yet not through preparation bias.[139] The participants reported that cultural racialization and preparation for bias informed a lasting and positive ethnic and racial identity.[140] Araujo Dawson and Quiros' study supports Hughes in that Latino/a(s) parents are (1) less likely to prepare for bias than other minority groups and (2) more likely to accentuate ethnic identity.[141]

Araujo Dawson and Quiros, and Hughes' contributions are relevant, in various ways, to the discussion of race and ethnic identity.[142] First, it suggests that race influences Latino/a(s) the ethnic sense of belonging to their cultural and social environment.[143] Second, it indicates that ethnic self-understanding encompasses a racialization process.[144] Lastly, it suggests that both dimensions of social racialization transferred by family and other social institutions during childhood and adolescence become part of constructing the ethnoracial identity and meaning-making process.[145]

Race and ethnicity are prominent in these discussions. Race and ethnicity have a history in the United States. Kathleen Neils Conzen and David E. Gerber narrate that the invention of ethnicity took place during the second quarter of the nineteenth century.[146] Then, the United States was receiving a large number of immigrants. The authors sustain that Americans were defining their national identity while processing the newcomers' identity.[147] Conzen and Gerber argue that the ethnicity category was initially called nationality, and it was created to distinguish these new

---

139. Araujo Dawson and Quiros, "Effects of Racial Socialization," 209.

140. Araujo Dawson and Quiros, "Effects of Racial Socialization," 209.

141. Araujo Dawson and Quiros, "Effects of Racial Socialization"; Hughes, "Correlates of African American."

142. Araujo Dawson and Quiros, "Effects of Racial Socialization"; Hughes, "Correlates of African American."

143. Flores-González, *Citizens but Not Americans*.

144. Quintana and Scull, "Latino Ethnic Identity"; Chavez et al., "Learning to Value the Other."

145. Christerson et al., *Growing Up in America*; Grosfoguel, "Race and Ethnicity"; Nelson and Hiemstra, "Latino Immigrants."

146. Conzen and Gerber, "Invention of Ethnicity."

147. Conzen and Gerber, "Invention of Ethnicity."

groups with different traditions, behaviors, and customs.[148] However, the creation of ethnicity was a process that also required the re-invention of the immigrants in a new context, a process that the authors refer to as "dialogue between majority and minority cultures."[149]

Concerning the scope of this research, it is essential to note that not all newcomers were considered part of an ethnic group. Conzen and Gerber state that English immigrants who exhibited different behaviors, traditions, and customs were not seen as an ethnic group.[150] Although the authors reject the idea that the invention of ethnicity was biological or cultural, for them, it was an "interactive behavior . . . between immigrants' groups and the ethnocultural mainstream," the question of what constitutes an ethnic group remained unanswered from their part.[151]

In 1970, Nathan Glazer and Daniel Patrick Moynihan suggested that ethnicity mobilized groups after socioeconomic issues concerning their larger society. For Glazer and Moynihan, polyethnic societies will face a scarcity of resources; therefore, ethnic groups are formed to help upward mobility.[152] Later, anthropologist Clifford Geertz popularized the idea that ethnicity has a primordial character stemming from group identity.[153] For Geertz, individuals have a sense of belonging that could be traced back to their ancestors and cultures.[154] Nearly two decades later, Jean S. Phinney defined ethnicity within the American context from the social sciences perspective.[155] According to Phinney, ethnicity consists of set cultural values, attitudes, behaviors, sense of membership, and experiences as a minority group, such as powerlessness, discrimination, and prejudice.[156] Phinney's contributions to ethnic identity studies are foundational to many LEIMs.

Phinney's definition of ethnicity shares many elements with the cultural racialization dimension from the racial socialization theory, such as ethnic

---

148. Conzen and Gerber, "Invention of Ethnicity."
149. Conzen and Gerber, "Invention of Ethnicity."
150. Conzen and Gerber, "Invention of Ethnicity."
151. Conzen and Gerber, "Invention of Ethnicity."
152. Glazer and Moyniham, *Beyond the Melting Pot.*
153. Geertz, *Interpretation of Cultures.*
154. Geertz. *Interpretation of Cultures.*
155. Phinney, "When We Talk."
156. Phinney, "When We Talk," 919.

pride, values, and traditions. Race and ethnicity are also considered a social construct transferred by in-group socialization and familial heredity.[157]

However, how and on what grounds race and ethnicity share similar attributes and still differ is debated. Scholars such as Jane A. Helms argue in favor of the influence of context in ethnoracial development.[158] Helms suggests that race and ethnicity are contingent on the social environment.[159] Complementary, Stephen A. Quintana and Nicholas C. Scull believe that culture provides racial and ethnic identity development grounds. Quintana and Scull comment: "Culture is the context in which people interact with each other, bound by a set of shared values, beliefs, norms, lifestyles, identity, and developmental patterns."[160] Moreover, later works of Jean S. Phinney and Anthony D. Ong assert that the commonalities between race and ethnicity may vary in gravity, depending on the context where these are evaluated.[161] In sum, context appears to mediate the construction and maintenance of the ethnoracial identity, yet it is unclear how it affects self-understanding and sense of belonging.

Another aspect of the definition of ethnicity rendered by Phinney is that it shares shared experiences with Glazer and Moynihan.[162] Phinney's proposal differs from Glazer and Moynihan's on ethnicity's formulation, nature, and purpose.[163] However, the sense that ethnic groups have shared experiences that bind them is an unexpected similarity. In particular, other scholars have also pointed out this element as a bonding element between individuals and groups that helps construct self-understanding and belonging.[164] These two, ethnic self-understanding and belonging, are vital pieces of ethnic identity.

Within the social sciences, it is generally accepted that ethnic identity is one's self-perception of belonging to a minority group.[165] More broadly,

---

157. Quintana and Scull, "Latino Ethnic Identity"; Ontai-Grzebik and Raffaeli, "Individual and Social Influences."
158. Helms, "Some Better Practices."
159. Helms, "Some Better Practices."
160. Quintana and Scull, "Latino Ethnic Identity," 214.
161. Phinney and Ong, "Conceptualization and Measurement," 271–74.
162. Phinney, "Three-Stage Model"; Glazer and Moynihan, *Beyond the Melting Pot*.
163. Phinney, "Three-Stage Model"; Glazer and Moynihan, *Beyond the Melting Pot*.
164. Roehling et al., "Immigration Debate."
165. French et al., "Development of Ethnic Identity"; Bernal and Knight, *Ethnic Identity*.

ethnic identity is a conscious identification with a particular group's cultural traits, values, expected behaviors, language, beliefs, and traditions.[166]

Over the years, LEIMs scholarship has coursed different views of ethnic self-identification and self-understanding. LEIMs such as Arce 1981, Keefe and Padilla 1987, and Phinney 1993, all understood that conscious identification reached a settled state or permanent ethnic achievement. However, at the turn of the century, other LEIM scholars started to question this achievement stage with new research that suggested that individuals could question, challenge, re-evaluate, and re-interpret their commitments to ethnic identity multiple times over their lives.[167]

Additional discrepancies arise on issues of the ethnic identity elements previously conceived as markers of ethnic commitment. Phinney and Ong suggest that behaviors, values, and beliefs should not be considered ethnic identity markers.[168] According to the authors, this is because, first, behaviors are mainly perceptions—an innate understanding of specific actions.[169] They claim that a person could retain a healthy self-concept of belonging to an ethnic group without necessarily exhibiting the behavior.[170] Second, the authors contend that how values relate to the sense of belonging depends on commitment to the group.[171] Hence, when commitment is low or challenged, values are compromised.

Phinney and Ong's arguments on behaviors, values, and beliefs are potentially problematic.[172] On the one hand, the cultural racialization dimension of the racial socialization theory inherently transfers behaviors, values, and beliefs related to ethnic identity. Therefore, discrediting these as ethnic identity markers is potentially debunking the racial socialization theory as a whole. On the other hand, if a person can maintain a strong sense of belonging to an ethnic group yet remain disconnected from the behaviors that characterize the group, then that person is exhibiting a form of affiliate ethnic identity. Tomás R Jiménez proposes that affiliate ethnic

---

166. Romanucci-Ross et al., *Ethnic Identity*; Yip, "Ethnic Identity in Everyday Life"; Ocampo et al., "Gender, Race, and Ethnicity"; Rogler et al., "Intergenerational Change."

167. Torres et al., *Understanding the Latinx Experience*; Torres et al., "Identity Development Theories"; Marcia, "Identity and Psychological Development."

168. Phinney and Ong, "Conceptualization and Measurement."

169. Phinney and Ong, "Conceptualization and Measurement," 272.

170. Phinney and Ong, "Conceptualization and Measurement."

171. Phinney and Ong, "Conceptualization and Measurement."

172. Phinney and Ong, "Conceptualization and Measurement."

identities are "rooted in knowledge, regular consumption and deployment of an ethnic culture that is unconnected to an individual's ancestry."[173] What is interesting about Jiménez's thesis is that individuals may or may not be regarded by others as part of the ethnic group. Still, as long as they consider themselves members, they have created an affiliate ethnic identity. Phinney and Ong's claim does not meet all of Jiménez's identifiers of an affiliate ethnic identity but still raises the question of how sustainable belonging is without enacted beliefs or behaviors.[174]

Self-awareness and Well-being

Proponents of the relationship between ethnic and racial identity and well-being argue that conscious identification is indispensable. During childhood and early adolescence, Latino/a(s) self-understanding and sense of belonging are external, informed by the family.[175] The family becomes the main in-group in transferring and mediating racial and ethnic elements according to their experiences, historical background, and environment.[176] During this stage, individuals enjoy high levels of self-esteem and well-being, and their ethnic and racial awareness is understood to be in an uncontested stage.[177] Their self-understanding and sense of belonging are closely connected to those manifested within kin and family.[178]

As the individuals move into further stages in life, their ethnic and racial self-understanding passes from being externally defined to internally defined, consequently affecting their well-being. Self-awareness becomes more relevant as Latino/a(s) experience what process-oriented models call "dissonance," an unsettling event that clashes against their racial and ethnic identity.[179] This event could result from a change in the environment or context, an act of racism, or a perception of social injustice against the individual.[180] Because well-being is linked to the individual's conscious un-

---

173. Jiménez, "Affiliative Ethnic Identity," 1757.

174. Phinney and Ong, "Conceptualization and Measurement"; Jiménez, "Affiliative Ethnic Identity."

175. Arce, "Reconsideration of Chicano Culture"; Bernal and Knight, *Ethnic Identity*; Torres et al., *Understanding the Latinx Experience*.

176. Knight et al., "Social Cognitive Model"; Keefe and Padilla, *Chicano Ethnicity*, 48.

177. Phinney, "Ethnic Identity"; Torres et al., *Understanding the Latinx Experience*.

178. Keefe and Padilla, *Chicano Ethnicity*.

179. Phinney, "Ethnic Identity"; Torres et al., *Understanding the Latinx Experience*.

180. Phinney, "Ethnic Identity"; Torres et al., *Understanding the Latinx Experience*.

Literature Review

derstanding of self, well-being will be compromised until a new racial and ethnic understanding is forged through personal exploration.[181] Exploration leads to an internal definition and self-awareness, belonging, and well-being.

Vasti Torres, Ebelia Hernández, and Sylvia Martinez observe that Latino/a(s) self-awareness undertakes a meaning-making process.[182] According to Torres, Hernández, and Martinez, meaning-making is how individuals gather new ideas and behaviors and decide what to retain and leave as part of their racial and ethnic identity.[183] For Torres, Hernández, and Martinez, meaning-making is perceived as a necessary process of self-awareness that generates belonging and the strategies to make sense of the world.[184]

However, despite all the dialogue on well-being and self-esteem, Adriana J. Umaña-Taylor, Marcelo Diversi, and Mark A. Fine assert that the relationship between a committed ethnoracial identity and well-being and self-esteem is uncertain.[185] The authors analyzed twenty-one studies on ethnic identity and self-esteem and, after comparing the ethnic conceptions and methodologies, could not conclude a relationship between them. Furthermore, the authors had problems answering the following questions: "Does one's ethnic identity determine the coping strategies one will use, and will those strategies influence one's self-esteem? Or does one's self-esteem determine both one's ethnic identity and the strategies that one will employ"?[186] Finally, Umaña-Taylor, Diversi, and Fine suggest that a more robust LEIMs scholarship by (1) indicating the theoretical perspective used, (2) accurately articulating the Latino/a(s) population and its geography, and (3) a more nuanced approach of stereotype and discrimination knowledge that considers social classes and lighter skin colors.[187]

Umaña-Taylor, Diversi, and Fine raise essential questions for future LEIMs research. In particular, the importance of geography. As observed, context plays a central role in ethnic and racial identity development. Therefore, themes such as geographical awareness, local contextual factors, and how these influence ethnoracial identity development could help advance the conversation. A second observation made by the authors is that

---

181. Phinney, "Ethnic Identity"; Torres et al., *Understanding the Latinx Experience*.
182. Torres et al., *Understanding the Latinx Experience*.
183. Torres et al., *Understanding the Latinx Experience*, 41.
184. Torres et al., *Understanding the Latinx Experience*.
185. Umaña-Taylor et al., "Ethnic Identity."
186. Umaña-Taylor et al., "Ethnic Identity," 324.
187. Umaña-Taylor et al., "Ethnic Identity."

well-being and self-esteem are not thoroughly explored nor explained. It appears to be subjective and limited to specific demography and socioeconomic sectors.

Another critique of LEIMs scholarship is that it has maintained ethnic and race separate even though both are prominent and consistent factors in research. For example, researchers Chelsea Derlan Williams, Christy M. Byrd, Stephen M. Quintana, Catherine Anicama, Lisa Kiang, Adriana J. Umaña-Taylor, Esther J. Calzada, María Pabón Gautier, Kisa Ejesi, Nicole R. Tuitt, Stefanie Martinez-Fuentes, Lauren White, Amy Marks, Leoandra Onnie Rogers, and Nancy Whitesell recently published "A Lifespan Model of Ethnic-Racial Identity" (ERI).[188] In their research, Williams et al. acknowledge that ethnic heritage and racial background comprehend an individual's self-understanding.[189] They do not equate ethnicity and race as one but see them factoring together into five dimensions: awareness, affiliation, attitudes, behaviors, knowledge, and enactments of a person's identity.[190] The group's goal was to develop an integrated model to explore a person's ethnic and racial development through these dimensions from childhood to adulthood while also considering contextual factors. ERI does not suggest that a person acquires self-esteem and well-being through their ethnic and racial identity development. Instead, ERI focuses on the individual's movement and progression in each dimension. LEIMs research could benefit from this type of framework.

Considering the discussion in this section and its alignment with the topic of this study, the following questions could be raised: First, how do ethnic and racial exploration look through Christian values? Second, how and to what extent do Christian beliefs factor into the individual's conscious ethnic and racial identification? Third, how do Christian beliefs relate to their meaning-making process and well-being? After attending to the most salient LEIM concepts, the following section discusses the academic research concerning Puerto Ricans and ethnoracial identity.

WORKS ON PUERTO RICAN ETHNIC AND RACIAL IDENTITY

Much has been written on Puerto Rican identity.[191] The diverse academic research (i.e., sociological, political, ethnographical, and historical)

188. Williams, "Lifespan Model."
189. Williams et al., "Lifespan Model."
190. Williams et al., "Lifespan Model."
191. E.g., Daniel, "Migration and the Reconstruction"; Cruz, *Identity and Power*;

comprises a growing collection of valuable information. However, there is limited academic work on Puerto Rican ethnic and racial identity, particularly addressing self-understanding and a sense of belonging. This section discusses a selection of the most notable contributions.

Geographical Belonging

Research suggests that having self-awareness of one's racial and ethnic identity provides a sense of belonging and positive self-esteem. This sense of belonging is particularly crucial for minoritized groups as it creates, among other things, a sense of unity that helps group members make sense of their environment and face adversity.[192] Using Angel 'Monxo' López Santiago's spatial research on Puerto Ricans, this section evaluates three areas of geographical belonging: (1) geography, (2) community, and (3) politics.

Applying a spatial reading to *The Memoirs of Bernardo Vega*, a historical autobiography of the political activist and journalist Bernardo Vega, Angel 'Monxo' López Santiago states that Puerto Ricans gain a sense of belonging by claiming geographic ownership for their community.[193] By spatial reading, López Santiago means extracting key information to re-create places, context, and the environment to understand the author's arguments and motives.[194] More specifically, through a spatial reading of the text, López Santiago intends to explore "the constructed nature of [A]place, the social dynamics of place-making, and the diverse and unique ways in which people create community."[195]

First, López Santiago observes Vega's arrival in New York as a movement of geographical awareness, from dislocation to belonging.[196] Vega's memoirs read, "[I was] kept afloat only by the confidence I felt in the presence of my friend."[197] López Santiago says that Vega was making New York his city.[198] In this statement, the author suggests that this dynamic of place-making and belonging corresponds to a combination of elements: the city,

---

Flores, *Divided Borders*; Giles et al., "Social Identity."
  192. López, "'But You Don't Look,'" 102.
  193. López Santiago, "Geography of Bernardo Vega's Memoirs," 154.
  194. López Santiago, "Geography of Bernardo Vega's Memoirs," 153–54.
  195. López Santiago, "Geography of Bernardo Vega's Memoirs," 174.
  196. López Santiago, "Geography of Bernardo Vega's Memoirs," 161.
  197. Vega, "Memoirs of Bernardo Vega," 74.
  198. López Santiago, "Geography of Bernardo Vega's Memoirs," 161.

the friend, and the meaning bestowed. This triad finds plausible support in Robert Sack's paradigm.[199]

Sack's paradigm claims that these three realms—meaning, social relations, and nature—provide a place's basic structure and elements[200] Furthermore, Sack asserts that transformation happens through a relational system in which human culture and social relations and meanings connect with nature.[201] Comparing López Santiago's triad with Sack's realms, it can be observed that Vega's sense of belonging and place-making was possible because of a city or location (in the function of nature realm), a friendship (in the function of social relations realm), and a reason for the movement (in the function of the realm of the meaning).[202] However, neither Sack's paradigm nor López's spatial reading provides a clear understanding of the nature of Vega's belonging or its relationship with his ethnic or racial identity. On this account, Luis Sánchez's research advances the discussion.[203]

Sánchez studied the process making of "Puerto Ricanness" in Metro-Orlando, Florida.[204] Sánchez declares that "Puerto Rican identities are based on language, race, ethnicity, religion, sexuality, gender, class, nationalism, they are predominantly based on place of origin."[205] Sánchez intentionally utilizes identities in the plural to highlight his point that there is no homogeneous Puerto Rican identity.[206] He suggests that "Puerto Ricanness" is contextual and means something different to different people in other places.[207] How people process, give meaning, and interpret their environment or context is connected to the identity construction process.[208]

Sánchez's research suggests an ethnoracial identity process contingent on a localization, based on places of origin, and open for negotiation.[209] The Puerto Rican mix in Metro-Orlando of island-born and mainland-born seems to be causing a process of continuous ethnic and racial re-inventions.

199. Sack, *Homo Geographicus*.
200. Sack, *Homo Geographicus*, 61–63.
201. Sack, *Homo Geographicus*, 60.
202. López Santiago, "Geography of Bernardo Vega's Memoirs."
203. Sánchez, "Puerto Rico's 79th Municipality?"
204. Sánchez, "Puerto Rico's 79th Municipality?"
205. Sánchez, "Puerto Rico's 79th Municipality?" 8.
206. Sánchez, "Puerto Rico's 79th Municipality?" 130.
207. Sánchez, "Puerto Rico's 79th Municipality?" 71.
208. Denton, "Hablo Español, You Know?"; Sánchez, "Puerto Rico's 79th Municipality?"
209. Sánchez, "Puerto Rico's 79th Municipality?"

In her study on mainland and island-born Puerto Ricans at Syracuse University, Margarette Moore reached similar conclusions.[210] She maintains that despite the ethnic pride, there was no agreement on being Puerto Rican.[211] Like Sánchez, Moore's work suggests that the differences in the place of origin affect self-understanding and sense of belonging.[212] She concludes by stating that the Puerto Ricans at Syracuse University are not homogeneous self-identities.[213] Lastly, Rachel Ann Denton's research supports that geography influences the construction and maintenance of ethnic self-understanding.[214] She observed how Puerto Ricans living in New York and on the island articulate their identity based on their places of birth while maintaining ethnic and cultural pride.[215] Sánchez, Moore, and Denton all seem to nuance López Sanchez's observations on geography in that location relates to belonging and separate ethnic and racial identity developments.[216]

A second spatial observation López Vega made in Vega's Memoirs concerns the community. López Santiago observes that Vega acknowledges a developing Puerto Rican enclave years before it was called *El Barrio* (a Puerto Rican neighborhood in Harlem).[217] Vega accounts for only 150 Puerto Ricans at that location and refers to them as the first settlers of "our barrio."[218] López Santiago states that this was Vega's effort to "claim part of the city's geography on behalf of the Puerto Rican diaspora."[219] López's observation suggests that despite the size of this Puerto Rican community, a geographical awareness process took place, providing a sense of ethnic and racial proprietorship on the location.

Both Sánchez and Moore noted nuancing findings on this spatial observation of community.[220] For example, Sánchez observes that Central Florida has no *barrios* in which a compacted Puerto Rican population

---

210. Moore, "Puerto Rican and Proud."
211. Moore, "Puerto Rican and Proud," 64–66.
212. Sánchez, "Puerto Rico's 79th Municipality?"; Moore, "Puerto Rican and Proud."
213. Moore, "Puerto Rican and Proud," 65.
214. Denton, "Hablo Español, You Know?"
215. Denton, "Hablo Español, You Know?"
216. López Santiago, "Geography of Bernardo Vega's Memoirs"; Sánchez, "Puerto Rico's 79th Municipality?"; Moore, "Puerto Rican and Proud"; Denton, "Hablo Español, You Know?"
217. López Santiago, "Geography of Bernardo Vega's Memoirs," 164.
218. Vega, "Memoirs of Bernardo Vega," 76.
219. López Santiago, "Geography of Bernardo Vega's Memoirs," 164.
220. Sánchez, "Puerto Rico's 79th Municipality?"; Moore, "Puerto Rican and Proud."

could cultivate and transfer culture as a community.[221] Instead, relationships are dispersed, causing Puerto Ricans to have less frequent contact with each other and more interactions with Anglo-American spaces.[222] Sánchez concludes that this lack of community due to dispersion and quotidian access to the Anglo-American mainstream is "producing a notion of hybridization."[223] Sánchez's research differs from López Santiago's observations on community building. Puerto Ricans in Metro-Orlando are not claiming a place or creating cultural enclaves; they are experiencing the opposite.[224] Nevertheless, Sánchez and López Santiago seem to agree, although in different ways, that each Puerto Rican community, despite its size, promotes culture and ethnic pride.[225]

Moore observed two dynamics concerning community.[226] First, mainland-born and island-born Puerto Ricans at Syracuse University, when choosing a place to live, they decided after neighborhoods in which they were a minority group.[227] This first dynamic could suggest a potential normalization of a minoritized status informed in part by a cultural racialization process. Second, mainland-born and island-born Puerto Ricans, although sharing a desire to create community, when enacted, excluded each other.[228] According to Moore, this second dynamic has to do with an us-versus-them mentality based on the different cultural markers of each group, such as dress code and ways of talking.[229] Moore suggests that although both groups have a strong cultural identity as Puerto Ricans, their self-understandings are different, therefore making community-making challenging. This perspective also seems to conflict with López Santiago's spatial reading of community.

A third spatial observation from López Santiago is politics. The author observes how Bernardo feels "at home" because of the economic, cultural,

---

221. Sánchez, "Puerto Rico's 79th Municipality?" 131–33.

222. Sánchez, "Puerto Rico's 79th Municipality?" 107.

223. Sánchez, "Puerto Rico's 79th Municipality?" 107.

224. Sánchez, "Puerto Rico's 79th Municipality?"; López Santiago, "Geography of Bernardo Vega's Memoirs."

225. Sánchez, "Puerto Rico's 79th Municipality?"; López Santiago, "Geography of Bernardo Vega's Memoirs."

226. Moore, "Puerto Rican and Proud."

227. Moore, "Puerto Rican and Proud," 43–45.

228. Moore, "Puerto Rican and Proud," 46–49.

229. Moore, "Puerto Rican and Proud," 48–49.

Literature Review

and political venues.[230] Vega states, "[A]ll kinds of political, economic, social, and philosophical issues were discussed there; every night, speakers aired their views."[231] López Santiago sees how Vega values the liberty to participate in these events and to have a specific place to gather, create networks, and have generative discussions as a community.[232] For this Puerto Rican community, the freedom to participate in political and intellectual expressions forms part of their sense of belonging, not only to a group but to a place.

Sánchez and Moore agree that the historical-political relationship between Puerto Rico and the United States influences Puerto Ricans' sense of belonging and ethnoracial self-understanding.[233] Sánchez observes how island-born and mainland-born Puerto Ricans living in Metro-Orlando have different interpretations of Puerto Ricanness based on political and cultural incorporation.[234] Sánchez's findings appear to be paradoxical in the sense that these two groups argue over authentic Puerto Ricanness while at the same time believing they are part of the same community.[235] According to Sánchez, this seems to reflect the island's Commonwealth status.[236] He sustains that in some instances, the United States treats Puerto Rico as domestic, others as foreign.[237] In the same way, "Puerto Rican identities" are "something different from 'American,' but at the same time as 'also-Americans.'"[238] This behavior also differs from López Santiago's interpretation of Vega's Memoirs in that politics does not necessarily create belonging bonds.

Moore observed that the island's political status influences Puerto Ricans' cultural identity.[239] The most salient aspects of this political influence over cultural identity are the tension between Puerto Rican and American mainstream cultures and the concern that the latter could absorb the

---

230. López Santiago, "Geography of Bernardo Vega's Memoirs," 167–70.
231. Vega, "Memoirs of Bernardo Vega," 77.
232. López Santiago, "Geography of Bernardo Vega's Memoirs," 170.
233. Sánchez, "Puerto Rico's 79th Municipality?"; Moore, "Puerto Rican and Proud."
234. Sánchez, "Puerto Rico's 79th Municipality?" 134.
235. Sánchez, "Puerto Rico's 79th Municipality?" 134.
236. Sánchez, "Puerto Rico's 79th Municipality?" 43–45.
237. Sánchez, "Puerto Rico's 79th Municipality?" 43.
238. Sánchez, "Puerto Rico's 79th Municipality?" 44–45.
239. Moore, "Puerto Rican and Proud."

former.[240] In addition, Moore reported that mainland-born and island-born Puerto Ricans had difficulties explaining the political status of Puerto Rico to Anglo-Americans and their American and Puerto Rican identities.[241] A plausible explanation of this difference with López Santiago is the historical context of these stories. *The Memoirs of Bernardo Vega* takes place in 1955, right after the approval of the Commonwealth of Puerto Rico. Moore's study took place over fifty years after Vega's autobiography.[242]

López Santiago asserts that *Bernardo Vega's Memoirs* invites Puerto Ricans to make New York their new space.[243] New York becomes a unique geography where the Puerto Rican racial, ethnic, and political identity thrives. The author highlights in his closing remarks that Puerto Rico, as a space, is absent from Vega's autobiography but not its sociopolitical colonial issues.[244] This observation accentuates the relationship between place—where community thrives—and the sense of belonging through people's everyday problems across space and time.

Like López Santiago, Mérida Rúa's ethnographic research of Puerto Ricans living in Chicago argues for the ethnoracial complexities of identity and space.[245] In her book, *Grounded Identidad*, Rúa states that Puerto Ricans in Chicago evoke the past belonging or loss of belonging to their place to make sense of their present.[246] Furthermore, the author suggests that memories of belonging and community are transferred from generation to generation and are directly connected to their context.

According to Rúa, locality defines identity negotiation.[247] Therefore, Puerto Ricans represent and refine their ethnic and racial identity through social relationships with others.[248] As their network borders decrease, the ethnic identity negotiation increases, and vice-versa. An example of this relationship will be the tradition and cultural blend between Puerto Ricans, Mexicans, and Dominicans, depending on the ethnic and racial

---

240. Moore, "Puerto Rican and Proud," 60–63.
241. Moore, "Puerto Rican and Proud."
242. Moore, "Puerto Rican and Proud."
243. López Santiago, "Geography of Bernardo Vega's Memoirs," 170.
244. López Santiago, "Geography of Bernardo Vega's Memoirs," 172.
245. López Santiago, "Geography of Bernardo Vega's Memoirs"; Rúa, *Grounded Identidad*.
246. Rúa, *Grounded Identidad*, 53.
247. Rúa, *Grounded Identidad*, 53.
248. Rúa, *Grounded Identidad*, 90.

Literature Review

concentration of the group; and the diasporic *puertorriqueñidad* expressed in 2001 solidarity of Puerto Ricans living in the United States with those in the island, protesting the United States Navy practice playground in Vieques (one of the islands comprising the archipelago of Puerto Rico).[249]

Problematizing Ethnicity and Race

In general, findings on Puerto Rican ethnicity and race are aligned with the major concepts discussed in previous sections. Nancy S. Landale and R.S. Oropesa conclude that for Puerto Ricans, race and ethnic identity are almost inseparable.[250] Along with that same thought, Rogers Brubaker emphatically contends that the lines between race and ethnicity are unclear.[251] "'Racial' differences are in some instances based on ancestry, way of life, or even class rather than on phenotype; conversely, phenotypical differences are often implicated in 'ethnic' categorization."[252] Moreover, cultural elements, the Spanish language, and visiting family from Puerto Rico are associated indistinguishably with ethnicity and race.[253]

This apparent exchange of attributes and characteristics between race and ethnicity is the crux of the Puerto Rican dilemma. For example, when Puerto Ricans are asked to identify their race on the United States Census, they tend to use their place of origin, Puerto Rico, and not the black or white categories.[254] Since Puerto Rican is not a race, this constitutes a problem of ethnicity and race among Puerto Ricans. The following are discussions on the problematization of ethnicity and race for Puerto Ricans.

Ramón Grosfoguel argues that whatever sense of ethnic and racial self-understanding Puerto Ricans have is under the idea of "coloniality of power."[255] By this notion, Grosfoguel means that people whose ancestry comes from a United States colonized country—such as Puerto Rico in 1898—are under a hierarchal structure that privileges white Euro-Americans

---

249. Rúa, *Grounded Identidad*, 90–102.

250. Landale and Oropesa, "White, Black, or Puerto Rican?" 248.

251. Brubaker, "Ethnicity, Race, and Nationalism."

252. Brubaker, "Ethnicity, Race, and Nationalism," 26; Jenkins, *Rethinking Ethnicity*; Cornell and Hartman, *Ethnicity and Race*.

253. Landale and Oropesa, "White, Black, or Puerto Rican?"; López, "'But You Don't Look Puerto Rican'"; Duany, *Puerto Rican Nation*.

254. Rumbaut, "Pigments of Our Imagination"; Landale and Oropesa, "White, Black, or Puerto Rican?"; Duany, *Puerto Rican Nation*.

255. Grosfoguel, "Race and Ethnicity," 321.

Faithful Inheritances

over the inhabitants and descendants of such country.[256] Furthermore, he asserts that issues of race have a historical continuity.[257] As a result, the identities of groups such as Puerto Ricans and African Americans are ascribed negative racial stereotypes in the United States.[258]

For Grosfoguel, Puerto Ricans have a "colonial/racialized ethnicity" within the United States.[259] However, Grosfoguel asserts that Puerto Ricans often encounter less discrimination and an affirmative acceptance outside the United States.[260] This assertion may imply that, in the United States, ethnic and racial identity is disconnected from citizenship. Furthermore, it assumes a non-equal status ascription by the majority culture.[261]

Frederik Barth maintains that ethnic groups are perceived in two ways. On one level, there is self-ascription, which is how individuals perceive themselves as members of a group and as part of society.[262] On the other hand, ascription concerns how others perceive the individual.[263] Grosfoguel's observations deal with ascription and self-ascription, suggesting that the Puerto Rican ethnic and racial self-understanding and sense of belonging are problematized politically, historically, and geographically.[264]

Jaime Gerardo Lluch analyzes this issue through a political identity lens and focuses on race, ethnicity, and nationhood.[265] Lluch's research question was: "How is racial identity represented in Puerto Rico itself and Puerto Rican communities in the United States, and how do racial categories shift as Puerto Ricans cross the cultural border between the Island and the continental United States?"[266] Lluch's findings revealed that Puerto Ricans who moved from the island to the United States would be forced to look for ways to reconcile ethnic and racial identities relatively absent in Puerto Rico.[267] Second, the location where they move in the United

---

256. Grosfoguel, "Race and Ethnicity," 321.
257. Grosfoguel, "Race and Ethnicity," 326.
258. Grosfoguel, "Race and Ethnicity," 322–23.
259. Grosfoguel, "Race and Ethnicity," 323–28.
260. Grosfoguel, "Race and Ethnicity," 328, 332.
261. Flores-González, *Citizens but Not Americans*.
262. Barth, *Ethnic Groups and Boundaries*, 13.
263. Barth, *Ethnic Groups and Boundaries*, 13.
264. Grosfoguel, "Race and Ethnicity."
265. Lluch, "Unpacking Political Identity."
266. Lluch, "Unpacking Political Identity," 17.
267. Lluch, "Unpacking Political Identity," 12.

States and their skin pigmentation will make them more or less prone to prejudice and segregation.[268] Third, they will be ascribed a new Hispanic or Latino category rather than Puerto Rican.[269] Fourth, their cultural practices will be potentially racialized and stereotyped depending on the location's demographics.[270]

Lluch's final observations are that when Puerto Ricans move to the continental United States and face these realities that challenge their self-understanding as Puerto Ricans, they tend to resist, negotiate, or adapt, favoring their preference.[271] "Puerto Ricans reject the White/Black paradigm of race and are forging ahead with another racial schema."[272] This other racial schema is negotiated in their respective contexts in the United States. However, within these racial schemas, Lluch concludes, culture, language, and sentiments of belonging are "the most totalizing and all-encompassing."[273] This point contributes that "in contrast with the importance placed on cultural practices and linguistic characteristics, aspects of identity such as race and nationality seemed of much less importance in the participants' construction of their individual identities."[274]

Landale and Oropesa studied racial self-identification among Puerto Ricans on the island and mainland.[275] Their study found that mainland Puerto Ricans exhibit more rejection of the United States' notions of race than Puerto Ricans living on the island. According to the authors, this is due to the differences between the United States and Puerto Rico concerning the meaning of race and its repercussions within the larger society.[276] Landale and Oropesa put it this way: "[In Puerto Rico]" physical characteristics that suggest a mixed heritage do not generally result in placement at the bottom of the racial hierarchy."[277] Rumbaut affirms this, saying that context gives meaning.[278]

268. Lluch, "Unpacking Political Identity," 15.
269. Lluch, "Unpacking Political Identity," 15.
270. Lluch, "Unpacking Political Identity," 15.
271. Lluch, "Unpacking Political Identity," 20.
272. Lluch, "Unpacking Political Identity," 20.
273. Lluch, "Unpacking Political Identity," 20.
274. Denton, "Hablo Español, You Know?" 87.
275. Landale and Oropesa, "White, Black, or Puerto Rican?"
276. Landale and Oropesa, "White, Black, or Puerto Rican?" 250.
277. Landale and Oropesa, "White, Black, or Puerto Rican?" 250.
278. Rumbaut, "Ages, Life Stages," 14.

Faithful Inheritances

Ethno-religious Identity

As previously noted, scholars agree that religion and ethnicity are intertwined in Central and South American countries and Puerto Rico.[279] For Puerto Ricans, religion and culture are expressed through traditional festivals and carnivals.[280]

Max Harris asserts that the *Fiestas de Santiago Apóstol* ("The Festival of the Apostle James," personal translation) in the town of Loíza, Puerto Rico, is not only among the best known and crowded on the island, but also full of social, cultural, and theological meaning.[281] Harris argues that the festival "appear[s] to be rooted in the mixed soil of local tensions, Carnival, and Christianity."[282] During the processions, an image that depicts the heads of two beheaded Moors at the feet of Santiago is carried around town.[283] Harris explains that Santiago, known in Spain for his re-conquests, appeals to the people's sentiments of oppression.[284] This is significant for the town of Loíza because, during Spanish colonization, it was an enclave of enslaved people.[285] This first element of local social tensions is exemplified through a series of events during the fiestas, such as the return of the Loizan diaspora and the joyful celebration that leaves the town of Loíza and travels on to Medianía.[286] Although plantation owners later populated Loíza, leaving Loíza to the adjacent sector of Medianía symbolizes liberation—a celebration motif that challenges the hierarchical powers.[287]

The festivity is also known for the colorful costumes and coconut masks featuring exaggerated facial expressions known as *vejigantes* (little devils).[288] One interpretation of these costumes is that the little devils fight the Apostle Santiago until he finally overcomes them.[289] However, Harris asserts that

279. Chafetz and Ebaugh, *Religion and the New Immigrants*; Díaz-Stevens and Stevens-Arroyo, *Recognizing the Latino Resurgence*; Yang and Ebaugh, "Religion and Ethnicity."

280. Harris, "Masking the Site" and Harris, *Carnival and Other Christian Festivals*.

281. Harris, "Masking the Site," 358.

282. Harris, "Masking the Site," 367.

283. Harris, "Masking the Site," 360.

284. Harris, "Masking the Site," 360–361.

285. Harris, "Masking the Site," 360–361.

286. Harris, "Masking the Site," 364–67.

287. Harris, "Masking the Site," 366–67.

288. Harris, *Carnival and Other Christian Festivals*, 40.

289. Alegría, "La Fiesta de Santiago Apóstol."

its true meaning is that these masks mock the white colonial perception of the dark-skinned people associated with the demonic.[290] Although different, Harris and Alegrías' proposals indicate how Puerto Ricans make sense of their world through ethnic, cultural, and religious elements.

Harris finally observes that the festival is also rooted in the Christian belief that no one is excluded from God's festivities.[291] At *las fiestas*, the Spanish colonizer has no exclusive access to God; all ethnicities and races are welcome as equals. In this sense, the *Fiestas de Santiago Apóstol* moderates cultural, religious, and political expressions as part of the Puerto Rican identity.

The discussion in this subsection provides an example of the mix between culture and religion. *Las fiestas* do not represent a standardized cultural enclave for all Puerto Ricans. Yet, they point to the transferred cultural intricacies that possess deeper and more complex meanings influencing ethnic, racial, and religious identity formation.

Spanish Language Identity

Language is perceived as a critical identity value.[292] The Spanish language, mainly, is esteemed within Latino/a(s) in the United States. Pew Research reported that 95 percent of Latino/a(s) think it is very important—or somewhat necessary—for the next generation to speak Spanish.[293] For most Latino/a(s), the Spanish language is crucial to maintaining and transferring traditions and cultural capital.[294] Ilan Stavans asserts: "*Hablar español* [to speak Spanish] is to reclaim the past."[295] The Spanish language seems to become a conduit of the Latino/a(s) ethnic and racial identity, heritage, and history across generations.

Orlando Crespo observes that as a Puerto Rican living in the United States, the Spanish language was a catalyst for culture and a way to intimate with family.[296] However, the weakening of Spanish language proficiency

---

290. Harris, "Masking the Site," 362.
291. Harris, "Masking the Site," 367.
292. Chen and Jeung, *Sustaining Faith Traditions*, 84.
293. Taylor et al., "When Labels Don't Fit."
294. Ebaugh and Chafetz, "Dilemmas of language," 432; Orsi and Alba, "Passages in Piety."
295. Stavans, *Hispanic Condition*, 163.
296. Crespo, *Being Latino in Christ*, 34–35.

meant distancing from the Puerto Rican culture and family.[297] Similarly, Amilcar Antonio Barreto observes a cultural and economic tension between Puerto Ricans on the island who speak the Spanish language and those who live in the mainland United States.[298] English is perceived as an out-group marker for the former group, a political and social status statement, yet a means of upward mobility and social esteem due to the many American-owned companies that operate on the island and the opportunity to study in the United States.[299] These observations suggest a complex relationship between Spanish and English languages, the Puerto Rican ethnic self-understanding that implies family, politics, and upward mobility. As expected, these three are affirmed and contested by other contributors to the conversation on Spanish as an ethnic identity marker among Puerto Ricans.

Proposers of the relationship between the Spanish language and family note that cultural reproduction occurs via family closeness.[300] For first-generation Latino/a(s), identity and culture are constructed and maintained through speaking Spanish. The loss of Spanish proficiency represents a loss of Latino/a(s) identity and culture.[301] A failure of later Latino/a(s) generations to maintain the Spanish language is perceived as a turning away from cultural heritage.[302]

However, Sarah Nieves-Squires posts the following valid questions: "So if the language that we speak defines us, who are the true Puerto Ricans?[303] Who validates us? Who[m] are we associated with?"[304] Nieves-Squires sustains that second and third-generation Puerto Ricans who have lost their Spanish language proficiency often find themselves without systems or networks that can validate their self-understanding as Puerto Ricans.[305] The author challenges the notion of the Spanish language as a marker of a "true Puerto Ricans."[306] Rachel Ann Denton and Brenda Domínguez-Rosa-

---

297. Crespo, *Being Latino in Christ*.

298. Barreto, "Speaking English in Puerto Rico."

299. Barreto, "Speaking English in Puerto Rico," 5–7.

300. Ebaugh and Chafetz, "Dilemmas of Language"; Portes and Rumbaut, *Legacies*; Wood, "Do Latino Covenant Churches."

301. Wood, "Do Latino Covenant Churches."

302. Portes and Rumbaut, *Legacies*.

303. Nieves-Squires, "Cultural Identity and Bilingualism."

304. Nieves-Squires, "Cultural Identity and Bilingualism," 43.

305. Nieves-Squires, "Cultural Identity and Bilingualism."

306. Nieves-Squires, "Cultural Identity and Bilingualism," 43.

Literature Review

do elaborate in their respective works that maintaining cultural traditions is a more legitimate Puerto Rican identity marker than language.[307] Denton asserts that third, fourth, and fifth-generation Puerto Ricans feel connected to their origins even when they do not speak Spanish.[308] Denton suggests that language is not necessarily a cultural link nor a marker of self-understanding formation as Puerto Ricans, such as attitudes, behaviors, music, food, and family life.[309] She concludes that "certain aspects of identity take on greater significance at times, and less importance (sic) in other moments."[310] Similarly, Domínguez-Rosado maintains that following even Americanized versions of Puerto Rican cultural traditions and customs is a significant factor in establishing identity.[311]

Other scholars, such as Leeman and Flores-González, argue that Spanish language proficiency directly influences the Latino/a(s) self-understanding and sense of belonging.[312] For example, Jennifer Leeman asserts that the English language is linked to an Anglo-American identity, while the Spanish language is to an "un-American."[313] In addition, Nilda Flores-González asserts that second-generation Latino/a(s) that use Spanish outside of their in-group are prone to racial aggression, silencing, or banning despite being American citizens.[314] Therefore, according to the LEIMs scholarship, it could be argued that these types of events Flores-González describes may expedite an exploration stage or a looping into meaning-making.[315]

Nieves-Squires seems to be aligned with Barreto on the relationship between the Spanish language and upward mobility.[316] Nieves-Squires states that the English proficiency acquired by second and third-generation Puerto Ricans in the United States has no positive influence on their

---

307. Denton, "Hablo Español, You Know?"; Domínguez-Rosado, *Unlinking of Language*.

308. Denton, "Hablo Español, You Know?" 87.

309. Denton, "Hablo Español, You Know?" 87.

310. Denton, "Hablo Español, You Know?" 88.

311. Domínguez-Rosado, *Unlinking of Language*, 76–80.

312. Leeman, "Racializing Language"; Flores-González, *Citizens but Not Americans*.

313. Leeman, "Racializing Language," 524.

314. Flores-González, *Citizens but Not Americans*.

315. Flores-González, *Citizens but Not Americans*.

316. Nieves-Squires, "Cultural Identity and Bilingualism"; Barreto, "Speaking English in Puerto Rico."

socioeconomic status.[317] She uses Blacks to illustrate that 200 years of speaking English has limited their upward mobility.[318] With this, the author seems to contend that other elements at play, such as ethnicity and race, contribute to the general socioeconomic stagnancy of Puerto Ricans in the United States. Her observation, although well-received, is perceived with animosity and on the anecdotal side since she did not provide facts or figures to support it.

Lastly, Joann Marie Camacho Escobar further explores the relationship between the Spanish language as an identity marker and politics.[319] In her historical account of how language and culture were linked to Puerto Rican cultural nationalism, Camacho Escobar proposes that Puerto Rican politics have a fair share of responsibility, equating the Spanish language with *puertoriqueñidad* (Puerto Ricanness).[320] One of the historical facts presented is Luis Muñoz Marín's (first elected Governor by the people) *Operación Serenidad* (Operation Serenity), which intended to balance culture and education. According to the author, since Muñoz Marín was the leading advocate of the Commonwealth, his *Operación Serenidad* ultimately cemented the colonial status by simultaneously creating a mainstream cultural identity.[321] The project successfully defended the Spanish language but at the same time politized it.[322] Later, when pro-statehood governor Ferré advocated for having English and Spanish as equal, he claimed the former as the one of the state and the latter as the *patria* (nation).[323]

Furthermore, Camacho Escobar argues that in the 1980s, Governor Rafael Hernández Colón used the Spanish language as a political strategy to "connect Puerto Rico to the world" by having a pavilion at Seville's World Fair 1992 and the Regatta Columbus in the same year.[324] Camacho Escobar concludes that participating in these events "confirmed the superiority of the Spanish cultural heritage over the African and Taíno cultures, and even over the United States American. In that context, the Spanish language was

---

317. Nieves-Squires, "Cultural Identity and Bilingualism," 44.
318. Nieves-Squires, "Cultural Identity and Bilingualism," 44.
319. Camacho Escobar, "Aquí Se Habla Español."
320. Camacho Escobar, "Aquí Se Habla Español," 91, 190–91.
321. Camacho Escobar, "Aquí Se Habla Español," 2, 190.
322. Camacho Escobar, "Aquí Se Habla Español," 149.
323. Camacho Escobar, "Aquí Se Habla Español," 184–85.
324. Camacho Escobar, "Aquí Se Habla Español."

Literature Review

the cornerstone of the Puerto Rican *personalidad*."[325] Camacho Escobar's language of "superiority" could be nuanced; nevertheless, her argument is clear, Puerto Rican politics have contributed to making the Spanish language a cultural identity marker.

As observed, the Spanish language is affirmed and contested in various ways as an identity marker. It adds to the complexities of Puerto Rican ethnic and racial identity formation. Moreover, it raises questions of belonging and self-understanding across generations and geographies.

The works assessed in this section suggest that for Puerto Ricans, the creation and maintenance of ethnoracial identity is multi-faceted and complex. As a result, several questions emerge: How do SGPRs understand belonging when (1) Spanish and English proficiency and (2) the sociopolitical heritage effect of geography are perceived as salient in—out—markers? How do Puerto Ricans relate to their geographical contexts, United States and P.R.? What religious and second-generation Puerto Ricans maintain cultural traditions to inform their ethno-racial identity? Why?

The following section advances the discussions on ethnic and racial identity through the voices of several theologians and missiologists.

SELECTED THEOLOGIANS AND MISSIOLOGISTS ENGAGING LATINO/A(S) ETHNORACIAL IDENTITY

Orlando Crespo

In his book, *Being Latino in Christ*, Puerto Rican missiologist Orlando Crespo shares his research on the journey of ethnic self-understanding and belonging of many Latino/a(s) in the United States. Two significant themes found in the book will be discussed here: (1) the creation of a new Latino/a(s) identity and (2) the influence of Christian beliefs.

Early in his book, Crespo sustains the liminality state of the Latino/a(s) ethnic identity in the States.[326] Although this claim has also been made by other researchers, such as Conde-Frazier and Lee and Martínez, his focus is on how Latino/a(s) should "thrive in it, instead of being debilitated by it."[327] Crespo observes that the in-between state of ethnic identity could harm the individual's ethnic self-understanding and sense of belonging as

---

325. Camacho Escobar, "Aquí Se Habla Español," 190–91.

326. Crespo, *Being Latino in Christ*, 32.

327. Conde-Frazier and Lee, "Intergenerational and Intercultural Issues"; Martínez, *Walk with the People*; Crespo, *Being Latino in Christ*, 32.

Faithful Inheritances

Latino/a(s) without the support networks of other second and third-generation Latino/a(s).[328] He suggests that the definition of a Latino/a(s) ethnic and racial identity changes from first to later generations and that a new membership emerges to help them make sense of their world.[329]

Crespo indicates that acquiring a self-understanding and sense of belonging from other second and third-generation Latino/a(s) helps to navigate the clashing of the cultural values learned at home and the dominant culture's values to embrace both.[330] For example, Ed Morales, using Spanglish as a metaphor—mixing and adapting two languages—comments: "Spanglish is what we speak, but it is also who we Latinos are . . . a fertile terrain of negotiating a new identity."[331] Crespo fleshes out this concept by sharing from his own experience that some values and Christian beliefs learned at home, such as humility, familial, and God's providence, had to be negotiated in other contexts with self-confidence, the inclusion of other believers in Christ and owning decisions as influencers of personal destiny.[332] Crespo asserts that this negotiation process is a constant in constructing and maintaining the Latino/a(s) ethnic and racial identity and that in connection to a support system of other Latino/a(s), wholeness and well-being are achieved.[333]

Crespo connects various concepts from the Scriptures to his calling for Latino/a(s) ethnic and racial identity. First, from the story of Moses, Crespo states that God used his [Moses'] ethnic awareness to bring hope and justice to advocate before Pharaoh for the Israelites.[334] Next, perusing the story of Esther and Mordecai, Crespo observes how God's faithfulness operated through their sense of belonging to save a group of people.[335] Lastly, Crespo points out how the gospel advanced across Jews and Gentiles because of Paul's dual identity—Jew and Roman citizen.[336] Crespo concludes that by embracing and affirming their ethnic and racial identity, Latino/a(s)

---

328. Crespo, *Being Latino in Christ*, 32.
329. Crespo, *Being Latino in Christ*, 32–34.
330. Crespo, *Being Latino in Christ*, 33–37.
331. Morales, *Living in Spanglish*, 3, 7.
332. Crespo, *Being Latino in Christ*, 35.
333. Crespo, *Being Latino in Christ*, 52–53.
334. Crespo, *Being Latino in Christ*, 68–69.
335. Crespo, *Being Latino in Christ*, 70–73.
336. Crespo, *Being Latino in Christ*, 76–77.

can accomplish God's work in the world as these biblical characters did as mediators between cultures in the United States of America.[337]

The author explains that a robust ethnic affirmation stems out of obedience to Jesus' commandment of love ourselves (implied in Mark 12:31b, "Love your neighbor as yourself").[338] Ethnic and racial identity are not idolized.[339] Instead, Crespo emphasizes embracing one's ethnicity and "love of yourself, your people, your culture and the culture of others."[340] An adequate self-understanding is subordinated to God to participate in his mission.[341]

Crespo challenges Latino/a(s) Christians to speak more openly about ethnicity and race.[342] The author argues that the Latino/a(s) experience as a minoritized group can contribute to racial healing in the country.[343] Using Puerto Ricans as an example, Crespo advocates for open discussions on racial integration and particular cultural gifts, such as hospitality and relational harmony, that can bless all ethnicities and races in American society.[344] In summary, Crespo contends for wholeness in Latino/a(s) ethnic and racial identity through God, as individuals, community, and co-laborers of his mission in America and among the nations.

Manuel Ortiz

Second-generation Puerto Rican Manuel Ortiz emphasizes the Christian ministry development of second and third-generation Latino/a(s) in the multi-cultural context of the United States.[345] Ortiz pointedly observes that the Latino/a(s) participation in the mission of God, in and outside the United States, needs better communication between first and later generations that celebrates the first-generation achievements and empowers the second and third generation to do ministry.[346] On the one hand, the Latino/a(s) ethnic and racial identity of the first generation should provide the historical and cultural awareness that gives a base and foundation to

337. Crespo, *Being Latino in Christ*, 77, 142.
338. Crespo, *Being Latino in Christ*, 92.
339. Crespo, *Being Latino in Christ*, 145.
340. Crespo, *Being Latino in Christ*, 92.
341. Crespo, *Being Latino in Christ*, 145.
342. Crespo, *Being Latino in Christ*, 108–23.
343. Crespo, *Being Latino in Christ*, 108.
344. Crespo, *Being Latino in Christ*, 100–112.
345. Ortíz, *Hispanic Challenge*.
346. Ortíz, *Hispanic Challenge*, 114–15.

the next generation.[347] On the other hand, Ortiz points out that second and third-generation Latino/a(s) have a better sense of direction regarding the current sociocultural environment in America, which includes justice and racial reconciliation.[348]

Ortiz's observations speak of the ethnic identity tensions between Latino/a(s) generations within the church. The author suggests that these tensions could be caused mainly by a fear of changes in religious traditions related to first-generation ethnic and racial identity.[349] As previously observed, first-generation Latino/a(s) find, in the church, a place where culture and traditions are preserved.[350] Meanwhile, second-generation Latino/a(s) are looking for an affirmation and a place to express their ethnic and racial identity far from their parents.[351] The author advises that perceptions of a superiority or inferiority definition or expression of Latino/a(s) ethnic identity are detrimental to the church's growth and the spreading of the gospel and should be prevented.[352] In other words, the ethnic self-understanding and sense of belonging across Latino/a(s) generations are not only different. Still, they require intentional accommodation for these groups to work together to advance the mission of God.

Martínez and Elizondo

Juan Francisco Martínez and Virgilio Elizondo are not Puerto Rican.[353] Still, their contributions to the relationship between Christian beliefs and the Latino/a(s) self-understanding and sense of belonging in the United States are worth capturing here. Martínez argues that Latino/a(s) are missionaries, not in formal commissioning, but through their sense of responsibility to share the gospel wherever they go.[354] The author notes that Latino/a(s) churches' proliferation is evidence of their sense of mission.[355]

---

347. Ortíz, *Hispanic Challenge*, 115, 124.
348. Ortíz, *Hispanic Challenge*, 112–13, 124.
349. Ortíz, *Hispanic Challenge*, 82–87.
350. Calvillo and Bailey, "Latino Religious Affiliation."
351. Ortíz, *Hispanic Challenge*, 82–87.
352. Ortíz, *Hispanic Challenge*, 115.
353. Martínez, *Walk with the People*; Elizondo, "Jesus the Galilean Jew."
354. Martínez, *Walk with the People*, 51.
355. Martínez, *Walk with the People*, 51.

Martínez observes faith and hope as two salient characteristics of Christian beliefs related to the Latino/a(s) ethnic and racial identity.[356] Martinez boldly claims that "faith in God is part of the frame that defines the Latino culture."[357] Most Latino/a(s) believe God is active daily in their lives.[358] This faith is manifested through religious devotion, such as prayer and church attendance, and an expectation of listening to God when reading the Bible.[359] This Latino/a(s) worldview of God's daily intervention reflects a cultural and religious awareness of the spiritual world operating in the physical, an environment where faith is pivotal.[360]

Hope stems from this faith in God's proximity, particularly amidst the challenges Latino/a(s) endure.[361] Martínez observes that Latino/a(s) are willing to make personal sacrifices and endure difficult circumstances for long periods because of their hope in God.[362] Moreover, hope unifies Latino/a(s) to support each other and creates a sense of community.[363] Therefore, it could be concluded that according to the author, the Latino/a(s) behaviors and choices are closely related to their religious beliefs, more narrowly, to their faith in God and hope for a better future.

For the Catholic priest and theologian Virgilio Elizondo, a second-generation Mexican American, the issues of racial and ethnic identity and belonging are at the root of his *mestizo* theology.[364] Elizondo observes that the second-generation Latino/a(s) experience of cultural in-betweenness resembles that of the inhabitants of the land of Galilee.[365] Galilee was a place where multiple ethnicities collided, marginalized, and negatively stereotyped.[366] However, Jesus made Galilee his home, consequently becoming a participant in the alienating experience of ethnicity and place of origin from dominant groups.[367] Living as a Galilean, Elizondo asserts,

---

356. Martínez, *Walk with the People*, 56–58.
357. Martínez, *Walk with the People*, 57.
358. "Changing Faiths"; Martínez, *Walk with the People*.
359. Martínez, *Walk with the People*, 57–58.
360. Martínez, *Walk with the People*, 57.
361. Martínez, *Walk with the People*, 57, 83–86.
362. Martínez, *Walk with the People*, 57, 83–86.
363. Martínez, *Walk with the People*, 57, 83–86.
364. Elizondo, "Jesus the Galilean Jew," 263–66.
365. Elizondo, "Jesus the Galilean Jew," 271–73.
366. Elizondo, "Jesus the Galilean Jew," 271–72.
367. Elizondo, "Jesus the Galilean Jew," 274.

Faithful Inheritances

could be seen as Jesus' preparation to usher in the kingdom of God and inaugurate the new humanity.[368]

For Elizondo, the experience of Jesus the Galilean provides a new mission paradigm and calling for second-generation Latino/a(s). The in-between identity becomes "a new, more universal identity, a new source of belonging . . . a painful but creative mediating role in processes of intercultural encounter."[369] In *mestizo* theology, the racial and ethnic self-understanding and sense of belonging of second-generation Latino/a(s) are understood as instrumental to co-laboring in the mission of God. It is a calling of mediation and reconciliation as followers of Jesus from the margins.

The works previously addressed heighten several questions that concern this study. First, how do second-generation Puerto Ricans perceive themselves as participants in the mission of God? Second, how do Christian beliefs, conveyed in different ecclesial contexts, affirm the ethnic and racial identity of second-generation Puerto Ricans and influence their relationship with God's mission? Third, how do Christian beliefs inform how second-generation Puerto Ricans perceive and relate to the dominant culture? Finally, how do second-generation Puerto Ricans process and connect to the current sociocultural tensions of race in the United States, and what role do they take as Christians?

---

368. Elizondo, "Jesus the Galilean Jew," 274.
369. Elizondo, "Jesus the Galilean Jew," 279.

3

Research Methodology

INTERVIEW METHODOLOGY

THIS STUDY UTILIZED A qualitative research method consisting mainly of semi-structured interviews with follow-up questions and a narrative inquiry.[1] The semi-structured interview provided the direction and flexibility to allow participants to share their stories. For instance, personal stories could go in a different direction and sometimes detour the main topic under scrutiny. In those cases, the interview guideline was very beneficial to staying on topic. In addition, the semi-structured interview guideline prompted stories in an organized conversational manner.[2] Its design had a logical and progressive organization, starting with the participants' upbringings and ending with their participation and understanding of the mission of God.

The interview protocol intended to compile a series of personal stories around eight main topics and seasons of the participant's life. A list of questions was created under each topic, which served as guidelines to stay focused on the research questions. Necessary flexibility was employed according to the interview dynamics. Depending on the development of the conversation, the participants' stories, and the information gathered, the order of the questions was altered, and some were omitted.

---

1. Merriam and Tisdell, *Qualitative Research*; Freeman, *Modes of Thinking*; Clandinin, "Narrative Inquiry"; Clandinin et al., "Negotiating Narrative Inquiries."

2. See appendix B.

Faithful Inheritances

It is important to note that the interview guidelines underwent a few modifications during the first five interviews. The main reason for these subtle changes was to articulate better questions and clarify the objectives.

Using a narrative inquiry and focusing on the participants' stories, this research collected essential data to address its questions.[3] Also, the narrative mode of analysis helped bring coherence to the data and understand how the participants give meaning to their beliefs, behaviors, relations, and surroundings.[4] However, early in the interview phase, a particular challenge emerged—not all participants were storytellers or could not remember stories to tell. In these cases, follow-up questions were raised to probe deeper into particular topics related to the research within the participant's story.

As anticipated, the narrative inquiry method required more time than other qualitative research methods.[5] Participants were informed that the interview could last between sixty and ninety minutes. On average, interviews lasted approximately eighty-five minutes. At the end of the interviews, both parties' experiences, interviewee and interviewer, were one of gratitude and expectation. Most interviewees expressed gratitude for giving them a voice and helping them process and think deeper about their ethnic and Christian journey.

All of the interviews were conducted in English, with seldom interjections of Spanish. However, participants often recurred to Spanish to describe Puerto Rican traditions, dishes, festivities, and other cultural elements. In those cases, the researcher assumed the responsibility of translation into English.

Before the interview, all participants received an email disclosing the interview process and expectations, the research aim, and the fact that all participation was voluntary and confidential. In addition, participants were given an electronic copy of the informed consent form to read and sign before the interview.[6] All participants completed the form, either signing it or orally acknowledging it. When participants verbally acknowledged participating, the researcher read the consent form to the participant, and they were asked to reply, "My name is [participant's name], and I agree to

3. Clandinin, "Narrative Inquiry"; Clandinin et al., "Negotiating Narrative Inquiries."
4. Freeman, *Modes of Thinking*.
5. Clandinin et al., "Negotiating Narrative Inquiries"; Suárez-Ortega, "Performance, Reflexivity, and Learning."
6. See appendix A for the Letter of Informed Consent.

Research Methodology

participate in this research." Instead of the consent form, the video recording of the oral acknowledgment served as the signed informed consent. To maintain confidentiality, the names mentioned in this research are pseudonyms given by the researcher. Same with age; only an approximate will be shown instead.

As previously stated, interviews were conducted in 60 to 90 minutes. No participant was asked to terminate or withdraw during the interview. Only one participant had a last-minute schedule conflict and asked in advance to complete the interview in sixty minutes. In addition, two other interviews were interrupted for several minutes due to connectivity issues, resulting in split-video recordings. Nevertheless, all interviews were completed successfully.

RESEARCH POPULATION AND SELECTION

Thirty individuals participated in this research. However, only twenty-seven participants were considered part of the study: fourteen from majority Anglo-American Protestant congregations and thirteen from predominantly English-speaking Latino/a(s) Protestant congregations.[7] Despite receiving and signing the consent form, the three participants were excluded from the research as they needed to meet all the selection criteria. This information was discovered during the interviews. The researcher thanked the participants for their willingness to contribute and kindly communicated that their profile needed to meet all the research criteria. The researcher terminated the interview after ensuring the participants understood their unmet criteria.

Although the original number of research interviews was forty, the researcher was aware that the narrative inquiry method generates a significant amount of data and that fewer participants might be sufficient to achieve depth and breadth of the information. This proved to be true. After conducting twelve interviews, no new insights emerged for each group, and the information received started to confirm what had already been found redundantly. Nevertheless, the researcher conducted three more interviews to ensure that the study had unearthed its potential and reached its saturation point; no more interviews were conducted.[8]

The selection criteria were the following: (1) participants must be second-generation Puerto Ricans, meaning that at least one parent was born in Puerto Rico and raised there at least until the age of eighteen and

7. See appendix C for a detailed list of participants.
8. Suárez-Ortega, "Performance, Reflexivity, and Learning."

was born in one of the fifty States, or Washington D.C., or moved to live on the mainland before the age of six; (2) participants must be eighteen years or older and have some post-secondary education, such as undergraduate degree (completion is not necessary), associate degrees, technical studies, or certificates;[9] (3) participants must self-identify as practicing Christians within the Protestant tradition (not Roman Catholic, Jehovah's Witnesses, Later Day Saints, or member of a sect); and (4) finally, participants must attend a predominant Anglo-American congregation (AAC), or a predominant English-speaking Latino/a(s) congregation (ELC).

The fourth criterion discriminates by participants who attend two types of church settings, AAC and ELC. Therefore, other settings, such as Spanish-speaking Latino/a(s) congregations and multi-ethnic and multi-racial congregations, are excluded. This criterion is because the original research plan contemplated a specific geographical area in the Midwest United States: Illinois and Indiana. According to the researcher's observations, research, and understanding, AAC and ELC were the two primary church settings that second-generation Puerto Ricans commonly attended within this geographical area. However, due to the unexpected COVID-19 pandemic, the researcher broadened the geographical research area to the contiguous forty-eight states but decided to keep the church's settings as planned to make the data collection more manageable and the findings more significant.

Purposeful sampling was used to identify the participants who met the abovementioned criteria. Four search methods were used. The first search method was personal, ministry colleagues, and acquaintance contacts. Second was the snowball method, where participants shared the names of other individuals interested in being interviewed.[10] The third search method was through Christian organizations, colleges, and universities in the United States. Lastly, open invitations were made through Facebook and Twitter.

All of the search methods employed rendered results to different degrees. The search methods that rendered most participants were personal relationships and snowball—approximately 65 percent of the participants connected through these two.

---

9. This criterion of "some post-secondary education" was necessary because research demonstrate that ethnic identity is particularly challenged or entered into a process of serious evaluation, definition, and articulation when the individual leaves the family and immerse him or herself in a majority culture environment for an extended period of time (Phinney, "Ethnic Identity in Adolescents and Adults"; Torres et al., *Understanding the Latinx Experience*).

10. Merriam and Tisdell, *Qualitative Research*.

Research Methodology

Gender distribution was reasonably balanced, with fifteen female and twelve male participants. In ecclesial contexts, five males and eight females represented the Latino/a(s) English-speaking congregations, and seven for the predominant Anglo-American group. The average age for both groups was 37.5, slightly over 30, the median age of Puerto Ricans in the United States.[11]

RESEARCH LOCATIONS

Due to the unprecedented worldwide health situation concerning the COVID-19 virus, all interviews were held via Zoom on September 10, 2020, and November 14, 2020. As anticipated, connecting through the Zoom platform provided significant participation from around the country rather than a geographical delimitation. Hence, participants came from nine different states: Texas (2), Virginia (1), New York (3), New Jersey (2), Indiana (1), Illinois (6), Tennessee (1), Florida (5), Massachusetts (4), and Wisconsin (2).

Interview dates and times were coordinated with each participant. The researcher adapted his schedule to fit the participants. The researcher provided the Zoom link and password to the participant as soon as the agreed date. As expected, interview cancellations occurred, but they were promptly rescheduled for the same week or the next at the most.

As previously stated, the original plan contemplated Indiana and Illinois as the primary research locations. The researcher acknowledges that an unintended consequence of broadening the geographical research area is the regional nuances from one location to another, such as differences in ethno-racial diversity, Latino/a(s) communities, and concentration of particular church traditions. These regional differences pose an additional challenge in comparing and contrasting analyses. As mentioned in the scope and limitations section, the researcher acknowledges the value of other research on similar subjects, such as Denton and Sánchez, who focused on New York and Orlando, respectively, creating some boundaries to regionalism.[12] However, despite the regional nuances across the nine states where participants live, this research brings value to the current academic conversation through the experiences and voices of a broader sample of second-generation Puerto Ricans (SGPRs) across the continental United States. These interviewees' stories provide a more ample understanding of the dynamics of SGPRs and their churches—a vantage point of a larger landscape.

11. Noe-Bustamante et al., "Facts on Latinos."
12. Denton, "Hablo Español, You Know?"; Sánchez, "Puerto Rico's 79th Municipality?"

DATA COLLECTION AND ANALYSIS

A three-step process was implemented to secure and back up all interviews. First, all interviews were recorded and saved in the Zoom cloud. Second, Zoom's digital audio and video files immediately following the interview were copied to a local computer for coding and analysis. Lastly, the computer was backed up on an external disk each day.

In addition to the recordings, another means of data collection was personal handwritten notes. The researcher took notes during and after the interviews with the participants' permission. These notes were used to record personal impressions, thoughts, self-memos, ideas, questions, and visual observations, such as body language, gestures, and dress. These notes were taken in two notebooks and saved in the researcher file cabinet.

After each interview, the researcher added key takeaways, ideas, and questions using a different ink color, usually red. This helped distinguish between the notes taken during the interview and afterward and identified meaningful preliminary notes.

During the first five interviews, the researcher conducted several data analyses. This was done to adjust the research methods and evaluate and refine the interview questions. As a result, some questions were modified to articulate their aim and intent better, notably, the questions related to belonging (questions four to six Interview Guideline). In addition, the researcher was prepared to point to and read from Mathew 28:18–20 during questions eight to ten in case participants asked for clarification on what is commonly known as the Great Commission. The decision to do so emerged from researching how to inquire about the participants' engagement at church and their understanding of co-laboring with the mission of God.

Interview audio files were transcribed using two software programs: NVivo's Transcription Module and Trint. This allowed the researcher to compare transcripts and select those whose transcription was more adequate for coding (i.e., formatting and accuracy). Transcripts from both services were ultimately uploaded into the qualitative data analysis software.

NVivo was the primary tool for data coding, querying, and analysis. Later in the process, Microsoft Excel was used to organize the findings. With the use of this software, meaningful patterns were identified and organized.

It is essential to understand that finding a plot was instrumental for the data analysis to connect behaviors and actions to their unique significance.[13] The coding methods described below were carefully selected to give

---

13. Freeman, *Modes of Thinking*, 36–37.

the individual's story agency in this analytic phase to reveal how humans enact their interpretations of beliefs and meaning-making process.[14] When analyzing participants' stories, the researcher followed Freeman's suggestion of Narrative thinking, identifying the plot (what happens in the narrative) and its four components: (1) action—sequencing of events; (2) theme—an event or issue connected to the action; (3) context—a particular time, place, and location; and (4) point of view—one or more vantage points.[15]

For the first coding cycle in NVivo, the researcher used four different coding methods from Saldaña's *The Coding Manual for Qualitative Researchers*: (1) Structural, (2) Values, (3) Narrative, and (4) In Vivo.[16] The first coding method used was Structural. This method helped categorize the data into the three research questions guiding this study. Questions one through three are mainly connected to the first RQ, four through seven to the second RQ, and eight through ten to the third RQ. The structure coding provided organization and the ability to compare, contrast, and find commonalities in the data.[17]

The second coding method employed was Values. This method explored the "participant's values, attitudes, and beliefs, representing his or her perspectives."[18] The benefit of using this coding method was that it helped analyze critical elements of this research, such as self-understanding, meaning-making, and decisions.

The third coding method used was Narrative. This coding method has gained traction within the social sciences because it allows the researcher to explore the human condition through stories.[19] In particular, narrative coding is used to inquire about "identity development; psychological, social, and cultural meanings and values."[20] Furthermore, for this research, this coding method helped find the dimensions of the general plot (theme, point of view, action, and context) for each main category.[21]

---

14. Freeman, *Modes of Thinking*, 41.
15. Freeman, *Modes of Thinking*, 32–37.
16. Saldaña, *Coding Manual*.
17. Saldaña, *Coding Manual*, 98.
18. Saldaña, *Coding Manual*, 131.
19. Saldaña, *Coding Manual*; Freeman, *Modes of Thinking*.
20. Saldaña, *Coding Manual*, 155.
21. Freeman, *Modes of Thinking*, 35–37.

Faithful Inheritances

The last coding method used in the first cycle was In Vivo. In Vivo gave the participants a voice using their own words.[22] The In Vivo coding lens last looked at the participants' stories and experiences within the categories created through previous coding methods.

Although the data was organized and categorized after the first cycle of coding methods, the researcher applied a second cycle using Elaborative coding.[23] Although this coding is used mainly to interact with "a major theoretical finding [of previous research]," Saldaña continues, "[it] can support, strengthen, modify, or disconfirm the findings from previous research."[24] Since this study elaborates on ethnic identity models, notably the Lifespan Model of Latinx Identity Development, implementing the Elaborative coding was appropriate.[25]

A database was created in Microsoft Excel to easily manipulate, arrange, and rearrange the analyzed data. This database allowed the researcher to try different ways to organize the data. For example, one meaningful way this database benefited the research was to discriminate between participants attending predominantly Anglo-American congregations and those attending Latino/a(s) English-speaking congregations.

The computer that stored the NVivo and the Excel database was frequently backed up into an external disk and cloud storage. As a result, the research experienced no security breaches or data loss.

VALIDITY

According to Maxwell, all qualitative researchers must identify their validity threats, biases, and reactivity.[26] For this study, the researcher is aware of his potential biases as a Puerto Rican male. In particular, (1) his preconceived ideas on how Puerto Ricans relate to their cultural heritage within the Anglo-American context, and (2) his theological understanding of Christian beliefs. The researcher has stayed alert and mindful of these biases so as not to impose his ideas and understandings on the participants or the research findings. There were two ways in which the researcher prevented these threats. First, the researcher reviewed his interviews and tried to find potential leading questions or comments that could cause a

22. Saldaña, *Coding Manual*, 105.
23. Saldaña, *Coding Manual*, 255–60.
24. Saldaña, *Coding Manual*, 256.
25. Torres et al., *Understanding the Latinx Experience*.
26. Maxwell, *Qualitative Research Design*, 124.

participant's reactivity. When a leading question or comment was found, and the participant response seemed to be influenced, such answers were not considered. Second, the researcher cautiously evaluated his conclusions when analyzing the data. If the findings were too close to the researcher's perspectives, these were subjected to further analysis.

Another threat to the validity of this study resides in the narrative mode of thinking itself. Freeman observes that researchers using this method must be aware of memory issues and the perception of past events from the vantage point of the present.[27] The researcher paid attention to the consistency of the participants' stories and immediately clarified any discrepancy or dissonance perceived. Also, Freeman warns of the tendency to align with the norm rather than resist it.[28] Here, the researcher kept an open mind and observed the interconnectedness against the status quo without forcing it.

The researcher followed three additional strategies to improve validity. First, during the interviews, the researcher kept his advisors informed of any critical development, personal biases, and compromised analysis. There were no issues of this matter during the research phase. Second, the participant's feedback.[29] The researcher validated some of his preliminary findings and observations with some of the first participants as a way of cross-checking the data. The researcher shared an abridged version of the early findings via email, phone call, or video call according to the data collected and asked them for feedback. This helped determine the integrity of the data analysis. The third and final strategy implemented was triangulation.[30] To reduce systematic biases, The researcher ensures that the information gathered comes from diverse ages, genders, contexts, education, locations, and social statuses.[31] Also, interview questions were subjected to the researcher's advisor's scrutiny to probe their neutrality and generality assessment during the research proposal phase.

---

27. Freeman, *Modes of Thinking*, 41–42.
28. Freeman, *Modes of Thinking*, 42–43.
29. Maxwell, *Qualitative Research Design*, 126–27.
30. Maxwell, *Qualitative Research Design*, 128.
31. Maxwell, *Qualitative Research Design*, 128.

4

Familial, Cultural, and Personal Christian Orientations

To understand how second-generation Puerto Ricans see the relationship between their Christian beliefs and their ethnic self-understanding, this study examines (1) the participants' familial upbringings, (2) the Christian beliefs and values that the participants consider close to their Puerto Rican culture, and (3) the salient Christian beliefs that inform participants' behaviors, decisions, and actions. This is the primary concern of the first research question and how this chapter is organized. As noted previously, interviewees were grouped as attending AAC and ELC. The findings address the corresponding distinctions when these groups differ or share tenets. The contributions and answers to this research question emerge from the information provided by the participants.

PUERTO RICAN FAMILY UPBRINGINGS

As expected, participants from both groups had some related and unrelated upbringing. Although the frequency, consistency, and expression varied in degree from one family to another, most interviewees reported growing up in a household with many Puerto Rican traditions, customs, symbols, and values. Conversely, only a few respondents mentioned that they grew up in an American assimilated household, meaning an environment with seldom expressions of the Puerto Rican culture (i.e., traditions, music, food, and language) and numerous expressions of the majority culture.

Familial, Cultural, and Personal Christian Orientations

Most participants reported growing up surrounded by a robust family network and a predominantly Latino/a(s) Christian community. From New Jersey and now in her fifties, Jessica shared that she grew up surrounded by a Puerto Rican family and a neighborhood, church, and shops. "Everybody was connected," Jessica continued, emphasizing the Puerto Rican cultural influence in her upbringing by quoting a line from the poem, *Ode to the Diasporican*, "*yo no nací en Puerto Rico . . . Puerto Rico nació en mi*" (I was not born in Puerto Rico . . . Puerto Rico was born in me).[1] Bryan, who grew up in Ohio and is also in his early fifties, remembers living close to his cousins, grandparents, uncles, and aunts. He remembers how there was always a family member around the house and that the demographics of the surrounding community were Latino/a(s), but predominantly Puerto Ricans. In Bryan's household, attending church was non-negotiable; it was a predominant first-generation, Spanish-speaking Latino/a(s) church. In her twenties, Sonia moved around different states with her family. Her dad was a church planter. Everywhere her family moved, they ended up living in a community with an elevated Latino/a(s) presence, not necessarily Puerto Ricans. She shared that despite the distance, her family remained very close. They frequently traveled to Puerto Rico to visit relatives, and some came to live with them in the States for some time.

Visiting the island of Puerto Rico was also a common denominator among most of the interviewees. Some visited the island with their parents yearly and spent the summer or Christmas vacations with relatives there. Others only went once during their upbringings. Some decided to pursue their undergraduate studies in Puerto Rico to learn more about the culture and develop their Spanish. Only a few participants have yet to visit the island of Puerto Rico but expressed desire and plan to visit soon. Nevertheless, all participants expressed having relatives and families living in Puerto Rico with whom they still connected.

Participants who grew up in a predominantly Latino/a(s) church referred to church members as extended family and a place that helped preserve their culture. Many described them as a warm, inviting, and welcoming familial environment. Victoria, a worship leader in her twenties, still attends the church where she grew up. The church is located in Florida, and she describes it as a Hispanic church, but mainly Puerto Rican. She is pleased that her church has adapted and changed over time to care for the

---

1. Jessica quoted a line of the poem, "Ode to the Diasporican," by María Teresa Fernández, a second-generation Puerto Rican born in the Bronx.

second generation. She says, "[my church] is one of the biggest blessings in my life, and I'm so very grateful . . . , a lot of them are like grandparents to me, like older aunts and uncles to me." Victoria went through a difficult season of depression that she overcame with the help of her family and church. She expressed feeling known, understood, and not judged by any.

Jessica also shared how her home church helped her follow through and overcome some challenging seasons early in her life concerning racism. She remembered attending a football game and observing a manifestation of the KKK and feeling completely "astonished and unsettled." She could not understand how members of the Anglo-American churches around her community were actively engaged with it. At her school, she was shunned for her accent and withheld from some access. Although she had many unanswered questions before God concerning these events, her family and church were critical in providing her with a safe space and strong Christian faith to process these experiences. Jessica reported that the Latino/a(s) church had given her "the taste, the connection, the familiarity, the assurance of them being filled, at that moment, with whatever that Christian experience has been," to go back and engage her context.

As previously mentioned, participants who grew up in a predominantly Latino/a(s) church noted that their churches served as places to preserve their distinctive cultural roots. Some interviewees remember their church celebrating *el mes de la Latinidad* (Latino/a(s) month), with food and music from the different countries represented in their membership. Others talked about their appreciation for the music and worship style, allowing them to express their emotions freely. Bryan shared: "Puerto Ricans are passionate people. The expression toward God, through theology, or musicality, through worship is always passionate." Esteban, in his forties and currently a worship leader of a predominantly Anglo-American church in Chicago, shared how he felt worshiping in Spanish with a Puerto Rican flavor: "I love Hillsong and Elevation, but there's just something about the Spanish worship to me that I don't know what it is." Esteban considered that music had played an essential role in connecting him with the Puerto Rican culture. It was something learned at home and church. Early in his childhood, he was introduced to traditional music such as *Salsa* and *aguinaldos Navideños and* instruments that are parts of Puerto Rican folklore, such as the *cuatro maracas* and *güiros*. As an adult, he has played with some renowned Salsa artists such as Richie Ray and Bobby Cruz.

Familial, Cultural, and Personal Christian Orientations

In addition to Puerto Rican music, many participants mentioned that other Puerto Rican cultural elements were paintings, flags, or other Puerto Rican artifacts that their parents had at their houses. Sofía, in her twenties and finishing her undergraduate studies, shared that at the entrance of the house, her dad has a decoration that symbolizes the Puerto Rican mix of three cultures, Taínos, Spaniards, and Africans, along with a Christian flag. Joanna, in her thirties, fondly remembered her dad having a painting of a *jibarito* praying over his food.[2] She found a similar version of the painting as an adult and hung it at her house. She said it reminds her of humility and gratitude; it brings her peace. "I gravitate to it," Joanna concludes. Angel, also in his thirties, said that although his parents did not have many Puerto Rican symbols around the house, the cultural attraction and instruction he received during his upbringing were so persuasive that now, as a parent himself, he has several of Cajiga's paintings displayed around the house. Angel reported that he wants his daughters to grow up with a Puerto Rican cultural presence, to be proud of their Puerto Rican heritage, as he is of his, and see it as part of who they are.[3] Angel's intentionality in having Puerto Rican cultural symbols and artifacts in his house may indicate his reflexivity as a parent of third-generation Puerto Ricans. Congruent with the current scholarship on constant ethnic reexamination, Angel's story suggests how a parent's role and how they think about their children's cultural identities influence his ethno-racial self-understanding and sense of belonging.[4]

This section has analyzed the most common cultural features the interviewees shared about their upbringings. In summary, these maintained a close connection with family and relatives, surrounded themselves with a Latino/a(s) network, traveled to Puerto Rico, had the church as an extended family, traditional music, and other symbols and artifacts resembling the Puerto Rican culture. The following section will read more about some of these features connected with a religious understanding.

---

2. A *jibarito* is a Puerto Rican peasant. Merriam-Webster defined it as a "Puerto Rican small farmer, rural worker, or laborer especially of mountainous regions" ("Definition of JIBARO" https://www.merriam-webster.com/dictionary/jibaro).

3. Cajiga is a renowned Puerto Rican artist that paints Puerto Rican traditional scenes such as *jibarito* houses, *Flamboyán* trees, and *El Morro* fort.

4. Torres et al., *Understanding the Latinx Experience*.

Faithful Inheritances

CULTURAL EXPRESSIONS AND CHRISTIAN VALUES

When asked about their upbringing and any memory of a tradition kept at home that they perceived as connected with their Christian faith, almost every interviewee said *Las Navidades* (Christmas season celebrations). Participants generally showed more excitement—laughing and smiling—when recollecting stories of their childhood around the traditionally long Puerto Rican Christmas season than in any other part of the interview. Most participants also observed a nostalgic emotional tone. When Esteban described his family's Christmas traditions, he did it by sharing how he felt about them: "[I still get the] feeling of the times, of the music, the food, the family and the tree." Similarly, Victoria's recollection of *Las Navidades* was, "precious . . . Oh my gosh! Nothing compares." Esteban, Victoria, and many other participants expressed that *Las Navidades* was the most significant Puerto Rican celebration in their families because it encompasses many things: family gatherings, music, food, and their faith.

Most interviewees were acquainted with three religious events celebrated during *Las Navidades: Noche Buena, Navidad,* and *Los Tres Santos Reyes* (Christmas Eve, Christmas, and Three Kings Day). Some families emphasized *Navidad* exchanging presents and sharing meals that morning, while others preferred *Noche Buena* or *Los Tres Reyes*. Many attended church services, visited family, or had family visiting during those days. In her twenties and an advocate in higher education, Carol recalled that none of her friends at school knew about the visit of the wise men celebration (*Los Tres Santos Reyes*), but her family celebrated it. She still sends gifts to her nephews and nieces on Three Kings Day. Jessica, mother of four kids living in Indiana, does not send her children to school on Three Kings Day; they stay home to commemorate the magi's visit and celebrate as a family with gifts. Victoria's parents made their kids believe in Santa Claus and the Wisemen. She had fond memories of the latter because of its meaning and the traditions behind it: "And so we'd leave out the grass so that the camels of the Wisemen [could] come in [and eat]. My parents would like to scatter it [the grass] and make like a little pathway." According to these participants' stories and experiences, these three traditions are rooted in the Christian tradition yet culturally integrated.

Most participants shared that Puerto Rican Christmas celebrations during their upbringing were opportunities for connecting with family, friends, neighbors, and church members—also regarded as extended family. Angel's descriptive recollection of the Christmas celebration growing up was: "[T]hose were the days where everybody would come over the house . . . I don't remember one year . . . [where Christmas was] not celebrated at my house with everybody, not just family, people from church. We're talking everybody would come over." Likewise, Mildred, in her forties and a worship leader at a church in New York, relived her memories and emphasized the breadth and inclusiveness of the gatherings: "I remember one specific Christmas where we had literally like sixty people in our house and like the majority of them slept over . . . We had people everywhere . . . I remember like waking up the next day and just like being so happy because I had all my family in one place." Angel and Mildred also reflected that their respective family Christmas celebrations were not close family gatherings but events that brought people together; Advent was the background motive. Advent and family appeared to go hand-in-hand for these participants.

Las Navidades, as most participants recalled, was full of Puerto Rican cultural elements such as food, music, and *parrandas*—or *matutinos*, as called within Christian circles.[5] Sonia's story of her family's way of preparing Puerto Rican traditional dishes emphasizes the family bonding that occurred, particularly during the Christmas season:

> [E]very Christmas making the process [for *pasteles*] altogether. All the woman, you know, we're over there chopping up, boiling all the . . . vegetables that we need, all of that good stuff. And . . . that's a bonding moment for us. And that's how we prepare, you know, that's how we know, that's a sign that the Holidays are coming because we're getting together and making food.[6]

Likewise, Victoria also reflects on the bonding created through the Puerto Rican traditional food during *Las Navidades*, emphasizing sharing: "I think creating meals and sharing meals is something that is so much a big part of us and also specifically for my family." Sonia and Victoria preserve these cooking traditions and share traditional Puerto Rican food during Christmas with family, friends, and neighbors.

In connection with the traditional dishes, interviewees also mentioned that Las Navidades was also a time to celebrate the birth of Jesus with others

---

5. Puerto Rican *parrandas* or *matutinos* are events where a group of people surprise their family friends by visiting in the middle of the night and playing traditional music outside the house—usually with Nativity-related lyrics—until the family wakes up and allows the group inside. After spending some time there, the group rejoins and moves to another house.

6. *Pasteles* are a typical Puerto Rican Christmas season dish made from plantain and other root vegetables and stuffed with pork or chicken.

Faithful Inheritances

through music, *parrandas*—or *matutinos*. Andrés, in his thirties and a pastor in the Chicago area, detailed: "[*Los matutinos* are] the one thing we did do in between Christmas and New Year's, sometimes even New Year's. We would go after the service, and we would just go to people's houses with *güiros* and maracas and, you know, go crazy. And then eat a little bit and then go to the next house." Andrés recalls this experience as an expression of joy, happiness, and fellowship that only happened during *Las Navidades*. Angel also said: "So that [*matutinos*] I definitely remember, because I remember being in church buses at like one or two or three o'clock in the morning, right." Andrés and Angel observed that these *matutinos* mainly happened among the church members and were fellowship opportunities, strengthened relationships, and communal outspoken Christian celebration. Even participants not raised in Christian homes were acquainted with or participated in *parrandas* while visiting relatives in Puerto Rico.

Another salient cultural aspect that participants reported during this part of the interview that explored some Christian elements from their upbringing was hospitality. Hospitality constantly emerged in connection with the participant's recollection of growing up in a Puerto Rican household and their church experience. Victoria considered that among Puerto Ricans, hospitality is a common attribute that generates a sense of warmth among the recipients: "[W]armth has been something that so many people have commented on [when interacting with her church and family], and a lot of that comes with that feeling of wanting to be hospitable, wanting to share what we have, wanting life to be a joyful celebration."

Victoria sees hospitality as an inherent Puerto Rican attribute across generations, in and outside the island. She narrated that when she visited her family in Humacao, Puerto Rico, "everyone was so friendly." She could ask anyone on the street how to get to a specific place, and people would kindly help her. Victoria observed that the same is true of her Puerto Rican acquaintances from her local church.

Also sharing on hospitality, Ramón, who lives in the Chicago area and is in his forties, reported: "[it] seem[s] like when I was growing up, we always had people at the house, and we were always celebrating something." Ramón commented that his parents' household was a place where people continuously gravitated to because they were welcomed and treated. That is something he learned from them. Sonia reflected on how her hospitality was taught at home: "My mom taught me to say hello to everyone and to be polite and stuff like that." Sonia sees this formation to be more evident

Familial, Cultural, and Personal Christian Orientations

in the church: "When I go to my church or even when I go to the church in Puerto Rico . . . they [church members] will go up to people . . . welcome them, and they'll have conversations with them." As a Puerto Rican, Sonia believes that hospitality is something she finds different from other people in the United States. Jessica also reflected on how hospitality relates to her Puerto Rican culture:

> That's also something that has been very consistent hospitality, the orientation of hospitality and how it just flows from natural people, from Puerto Ricans to connect with people in the first few minutes of the conversation. They're just, you know, planning their next get-together and let's get coffee or, you know, drink something. You have something more? Come to our house.

Other participants alluded to their Christian values and beliefs connected with their Puerto Rican hospitable orientation. Gustavo, in his twenties and currently serving as a pastor in New Jersey, elicited a story synthesizing what other participants shared on the relationship between their culture and Christian values:

> I'll tell you my first experience going to the island when I went to my family's house to visit the *tíos* and the *primos*. I had never met [them] before. I went to the island for the first time when I was eighteen years old. So, most of it was new. These people I had never seen before. Yet they opened their doors for me, you know, they fed me. They [paused] they made sure that I had a bed to sleep on while I was there visiting every night. It was *viandas con bacalao* like this large feast just for me. And most of them are non-practicing Catholics, you know, they don't really go to church or, you know, go to mass or anything like that. Yet they were very hospitable to me. So, I see . . . I guess an intersection between making people feel at home and also my faith, I feel like it's kind of like a double inheritance, bringing that along with Christianity, because for me, that's what Christianity . . . that's a major tenet of Christianity, just integrating people into the family. So, yeah, I definitely see a connection there.

As Gustavo described, this "double inheritance" of hospitality is a value that many interviewees described through their stories. It is something that they have embraced for life as Christians and Puerto Ricans.

Some participants expressed that *pedir la bendición* (asking for blessing) from their parents is cultural and distinctive of the Christian tradition.

Faithful Inheritances

Some interviewees still practice this as a symbol of deference before God and honoring their folks.

In summary, participants considered *Las Navidades* a season when family and their Christian faith were coupled. Furthermore, they observed cultural traditions as natural vehicles of their Christian values. Lastly, participants appear to know how hospitality and deference to others are Christian values and cultural distinctives.

Along with the previous cultural expressions intersecting Christian beliefs and values, there is another set of shared experiences during the participants' upbringings: Christian values. As previously mentioned, not all the participants were raised in a Christian home; however, all expressed growing up in an environment with high regard for Christian values. In her fifties, Crystal described how her mother sent her and her siblings to church with their neighbors every Sunday morning. Crystal disclosed that her mom believed in God the church's work and that Christian education was necessary for raising good people. Other participants, such as Raquel and Carmen, stressed how important it was to the parents to acquire a Christian value system. Raquel, in her fifties, rendered: "I literally, you know, was born, and then as soon as my mom could take me to church, she did . . . to the church that we grew up in." Likewise, Carmen, in her twenties, reported: "So, I [grew up] in a very religious household, . . . Christianity was a huge part of our daily life and a huge part of my life as a young adult." Ramón said he had a particular pride in being Christian within the denomination where he grew up.

Church attendance was no small matter among participants. Many recall attending church multiple days a week and various services on Sundays. Angel commented that church attendance was almost a measure of holiness, commitment, and devotion to God. The more time spent at church, the more distant the person was perceived to be from the world. Axel, in her forties, disclosed: "Sunday mornings, we went to the Bible study and then, . . . we had a [second] service . . . [Later] at night, we had a [third] service, and . . . during the week, we had a couple of services here and there. Overall, we grew up very happy." Similarly, Carol recounted the regularity of church attendance and its influence on family life:

> Obviously, the church was a very big part of our life . . . We were not that family that only went to church on Christmas or whatever . . . [W]e definitely went every week, maybe sometimes more than once a week. And my cousins were the same. So my mom has

Familial, Cultural, and Personal Christian Orientations

a sister . . . [they] lived very close to each other. And so, it was the same, go to church every Sunday, talk about things in the house. It was about the church or about the Bible, or about God. I don't think we necessarily like sitting down as a family, like every night maybe to pray, or to do devotional, or anything like that. But it was always within the house kind of talking about that stuff. If you weren't feeling good [physically], or emotionally, or if something was going on, it's like, "Oh, let's pray about it. Let's talk about it." That kind of stuff.

According to Axel, Carol, and other participants, being constantly involved in local church life was central for their families. They all observed how Christian values and structure influenced their family rhythms, conversations, and schedules.

Christian values were also transferred at home. Many participants had a family member serving as a pastor, elder, evangelist, or church planter. Today, a pastor in the Chicago area, Bryan, shared: "My father was a minister . . . My mother . . . had she had the opportunity to go to seminary, she would have been a phenomenal theologian. [S]he taught me my theological foundation." Sonia, whose father is a pastor and church planter, narrates how religious instruction was transferred through generations: "[My grandmother] was very religious. And she instilled that [in my mom], you know, reading the Bible and knowing your Bible verses . . . knowing [and] reciting something different every day." Lastly, Esteban comments on how his parents imparted biblical instructions in the house: "I felt that they were really good about explaining things to me when they corrected me or when they prohibited me from doing certain things, such as the point that I didn't feel the need to rebel." According to Carmen, Bryan, Sonia, and Esteban, as important as attending church was for them growing up, their parents played an important role in transferring the Christian values and beliefs system they follow today.

James, who is preparing for ministry and is part of the leadership of a predominantly Anglo-American church in Wisconsin, shares his experience and observations on Christian education, comparing his Latino/a(s) church upbringing and his current context:

So, I think one thing I have noticed is that the aspect of community, doing faith within community, even the idea of discipleship, was something that I almost felt was heightened in my Puerto Rican context or my Latino context church. Because one thing about discipleship, I think, that's clear about the way Jesus did it, is that he

Faithful Inheritances

> is doing life with people. And I think that when I'm in the Latino context, I find myself more naturally just doing that than I would in another context. So . . . I don't think that's just because being in the Anglo context is foreign to me, but I do believe that it has to do with the way in which I have experienced Anglo-sort-of practice their faith . . . [in] more of an individualistic sense. Whereas like that comes easy in a Latino context, doing it in community. Like it's just because it's part of who we are as people.

James, the son of a Puerto Rican pastor of a small Latino/a(s) congregation, believes his culture and faith are "aligned." He elaborated on his thoughts, explaining how he is invited to teach and disciple men at his dad's church and how the experience is more convivial and accepting than in his local church. James observes that in his local church, teaching and discipleship have an individualistic, sometimes political stance that often creates tensions in relationships and disunity.

Javier works as an engineer and serves as an elder at his local church in Baltimore, where he sees a connection between his Christian faith and cultural family orientation.

> [F]amily is very important to us as Puerto Ricans, so family and being together and spending time has always been huge in my family. That's how my parents brought us up, and we have a pretty big family. When we all get together right now, brothers, sisters, and nieces, and nephews . . . we're almost forty people. When we have our gatherings, everybody tends to go. So, family is a big thing. So, translating that into Christianity, you know, your family is your number one ministry. And so, I think that adapts very well to Christianity and the fact that we are very family-centered and very focused on being there for each other. I think that's a perfect fit for what we expect as Christians for someone to do with their family and then further on with your family in Christ.

Javier and other participants refer to church members as family. His understanding of the cultural attributes of togetherness and community seems to permeate his understanding of the church as a family and a community. His experience, alongside that of James and Gustavo, appears to create a relationship between their Puerto Rican cultural values of community and family and the Christian values of unity and justice. In all the participants' stories, the sense of community seems linked to an enacted responsibility.

Summarizing, many participants disclosed that church attendance and Christian education were prioritized and valued by their parents. From

Familial, Cultural, and Personal Christian Orientations

attending as a family to sending the kids to the church with a neighbor, these families highly regarded Christian values. Sometimes, church attendance was accounted as evidence of deep commitment and consecration to God. Reportedly, Christian values and instruction were expected to be received at church through the pastor and leaders and at home through parents. As a result, conversations at home were commonly related to their Christian faith.

SALIENT CHRISTIAN BELIEFS

As participants reflected and recounted the stories of their upbringing, the interviews transitioned to the person's most significant Christian beliefs. This section reports the contributions that came in stories and reflexive thinking. The question behind the following responses concerned the participants' understanding of the essential Christian values. To facilitate the exploration, the findings were divided into four categories: (1) loving others, (2) justice, (3) salvation and proclamation, and (4) spiritual disciplines. The first three Christian beliefs were equally distributed between ELC and AAC participants. However, spiritual disciplines were exclusive to ELC. It is important to note that this does not imply that AAC participants do not practice spiritual disciplines. It only means that spiritual disciplines were absent in their responses.

Loving Others

One of the recurrent answers and comments on this question was the importance of valuing, caring, and loving others. Some participants shared how some family members influenced how they relate with others. Carol shares that her mother transferred the Christian values of humility, tolerance, love, and acceptance of others. She recalls her parents' house always open for everyone, including all the kids from the neighborhood. She collects her thoughts by saying: "I think that's something that was brought up a lot in our household in terms of Christianity and in terms of just being like good people."

Other participants, like Gustavo, stressed the importance of being understanding and loving others. Gustavo ponders his Christian formation at home: "I would say [I learned to be] friendly, easy to get along with and understanding." Ramón recalls how his dad was always willing to serve and help others in any way he could. He particularly remembers his dad taking people to the airport. Considering these things, Ramón asserts that his dad was "driven by compassion" for others. In these stories, the participants point out how Christian beliefs and values are transferred from their parents and seemingly intertwined with cultural distinctiveness.

"Christianity is caring for others," Wendy explains. Wendy, who lives in Boston, has worked in the same hospital for twenty-four years, and enjoys volunteering at church, says: "[B]eing a Christian, . . . You've got to be a humble person. You've got to care for others." Wendy is now in her fifties and has been a Christian for twenty years. During all these years as a follower of Christ, she has always looked for ways to show people they are valued and loved. She cares for others by holding monthly meetings at her house—even throughout the COVID-19 pandemic—for women victims of domestic violence. According to Wendy, loving others means that "everyone needs a space to open up . . . [having] someone to trust."

Many participants see caring for personal relationships as an enactment of Christian love. Similar to Wendy, Carol sees Christianity as considering loving others unconditionally. "So, I think for me it [Christianity] really is about the love. It's about that compassion—that humility. No one is better than anybody else, regardless of what you've done, what you've studied, or what your credentials are." Carol has faced ethnic and racial discrimination at work from her peers and superiors. Yet, she chooses to be "tolerant, empathetic and understanding" of their biases. Grace's experience is consistent with Carol's. Grace, who lives in El Paso and recently completed her undergraduate degree, shares that she also has experienced discrimination for being Puerto Rican. People have criticized her curly hair, accent, and skin color. For her, an essential Christian belief is to respond with love and give grace as Jesus did: "It is our duty to love one another." In both cases, participants respond with Christian love to their offenders.

In his sixties and as a lawyer in Florida, Julio also lived through racial tensions at T.C. High School in Virginia. He recalls attending the school the year after Herman Boone became the football team's coach that caught the attention of Hollywood in the movie *Remember the Titans* (2000). Julio states: "You know, whatever that issue is, you know, that person may have a difficult time forgiving. But I would say that forgiveness is key; be honest with yourself, serve, and love others." Julio believes forgiveness is vital to loving and caring for others and every relationship.

While Wendy's expression of love for others is enacted in caring for the wronged, Carol, Grace, and Julio's experiences focus on loving those

Familial, Cultural, and Personal Christian Orientations

who wronged them. Their Christian beliefs and values help them follow through, honoring God through their relationships.

"The Great Commandment" was often directly quoted or alluded to by the participants.[7] Yet the part that was stressed the most was loving your neighbors. Ramón puts it this way:

> [What] comes up to me is always relationship. And I think that's the biggest thing that the Bible teaches us, relationship is not about everything else. It's about relationships. Because when Jesus said the greatest commandment was [to] love God with all your heart, with all your soul, with your mind, that's a relationship, you know. And then the other part was love your neighbor, that's a relationship. So, when I look at the biggest, most important belief is always going to be a relationship. And then with the Puerto Rican culture, that's also very important, relationship . . . having trust.

Carmen also ponders on the human relational side of "the Great Commandment": "I think for me, the kind of, especially growing up in our culture . . . which is very divisive and very, very difficult to have disagreements and discord. But, you know, the tenet, the Christian tenet of love. Your calling as a Christian is to love Christ and love others, and to love them as I have loved you has been very important to me." Ramón and Carmen emphasize the cultural and practical aspects of the Great Commandment toward human relationships. Many of the examples and stories shared by the participants had to do with the hospitable orientation of their families.

Another way in which participants articulated their value, care, and love for others was through the relationship between the cultural and familial way to relate with others and their relationship with Jesus. Angel, a college admissions officer who attended a Pentecostal church during his upbringing and much of his young adult life, says: "I think what's most salient for me as a second-generation Puerto Rican Christian is probably the emphasis on relationships . . . We tend to be very family-oriented, and we tend to be very relational." According to Angel, the relational aspect of the Puerto Rican culture is transferred to the church's theological emphasis on having a relationship with Jesus. "There's an emphasis on the personal

---

7. The Great Commandment to which participants made reference is found in Mark 12:29–31: "The most important one," answered Jesus, "is this: 'Hear, O Israel: The Lord our God, the Lord is one. Love the Lord your God with all your heart and with all your soul and with all your mind and with all your strength.' The second is this: 'Love your neighbor as yourself.' There is no commandment greater than these" (NIV).

relationship with Jesus, right? The daily prayer. The daily meditation. You know, it's you know, Jesus is your homeboy."

Axel, a musician at his local church, also highlighted the prominence of the teaching about having a personal relationship with Jesus:

> So, you know that aspect of having a relationship with God surpasses everything else, and it comes on top of everything else . . . you grow spiritually. Yes? And that actually changes your heart from within. If you're talking about [Jesus as] your friend, for some people, that might look like, "Oh, my goodness, he's out of line." But he has a relationship. And because he has a relationship, you can also see the fruits of that relationship in his life.

Angel and Axel both believe in having a relationship with Jesus. Angel's contribution indicates that the cultural and familial orientation toward a relationship with others helps to process what it means to have a personal relationship with Jesus more naturally. Meanwhile, Axel points out how a relationship with Jesus influences the rest of the relationships. Both contributions highlight the prominence of relationships in practice and Christian teaching.

Justice

Other participants expressed how the cultural sense of community helped them relate to others in an increasing sense of justice. Such is the case of Gustavo, a pastor in New Jersey, who, after intentionally building a relationship with people coming from other Latin American countries, realized that marked differences existed between him as a Puerto Rican and them.

> Where I grew up, not everyone was Puerto Rican. Of course, we had a lot of friends that were from different parts of Latin America, and they were living among us. And I always felt like they were part of us. They were part of our community . . . [I felt] privileged in the sense that I didn't have to go through the struggle that my friends went through, not having not having proper documentation to get their driver's license or to apply for financial aid at school. So, this is something that I became passionate about just from youth growing up . . . something that I guess I felt as a burden. I look at the struggle of my Mexican American or Salvadoran American neighbors, and I can't help but see myself in it . . . The only difference that sets us apart, really, is the fact that Puerto Rican Puerto Rico is a colony from the United States. If we didn't have that status, I'd probably be going through the same struggle,

too . . . And when you grow up with that, you kind of, you know, develop a voice in speaking out against those things.

Gustavo shared more about his heart for justice for minorities. He seems to understand that his Puerto Rican culture and Christian faith have given him lenses and tools to observe, connect, sympathize, and act in favor of others.

Joanna's undergraduate major is history. She grew up in a household with infrequent expressions of Puerto Rican culture. However, during her college years, she started her process of ethnic research. This inquiry led her to work on a thesis paper on Lolita Lebrón, a Puerto Rican nationalist famously known for entering the United States House of Representatives on March 1, 1954, gun in hand, and shouting, "Viva Puerto Rico."[8] Since then, Joanna's interest has grown, not precisely on Lebrón's political leaning, but on the sense of justice, particularly the one originating from the gospel's message—giving voice to the socially and politically marginalized. Today, Joanna enacts the Christian value of justice through her job as a journalist.

> So, for me, a really important part of my job as a journalist is kind of the deep sense of optimism that I think I can only have from my faith. And journalism is really hard profession; you are often tasked with shining a light on some of the deepest inequities and problems in society. And for me to approach that work as a Christian is to say these problems are worthy of being talked about in a productive way, and they're worthy of being known. And we should tell those stories with empathy and with thoughtfulness . . .

This sense of Christian responsibility, standing out for others, was a repeated topic in the participants' stories. Grace notices comfort in knowing that she has an advocate in Jesus. That also gives her the courage to act in favor of others. "How Jesus is more comforting to me is knowing that I have a voice, that I have an advocate, that I have a healer [who] stands up for me. And I want to be like Jesus and stand up for others in that sense. But like, if I see someone being profiled like I'm at a gas station, and I see someone being profiled, I call it out," Grace explains.

In summary, the experiences and stories these participants shared indicate that justice is a Christian belief deeply valued and enacted by second-generation Puerto Ricans. Therefore, the next chapter will explore the sense of belonging.

---

8. Martin, "Lolita Lebrón."

Faithful Inheritances

Salvation and Proclamation

When asked about what they think was the most significant Christian belief and value observed within their Puerto Rican communities, participants also mentioned the Good News of salvation in Jesus Christ. Sonia, a psychology student in Houston, was recently in a sentimental relationship with someone from another belief system. In addition, she found herself away from home and interacting more with non-believer college students. Reflecting on these experiences, she concludes that no other Christian belief was challenged more than salvation by grace only through Jesus Christ. She is grateful that that was something deeply instilled at home.

Similarly, James recalls how central the doctrine of salvation has been for him since he was growing up in a predominantly Puerto Rican church:

> "[W]hen I think about Christianity, I often do think about it as a message of salvation and a message of hope for a dying and lost world. And like, our Christianity is not it's not only meant for us, it's meant for others, and we are to take part in that in that movement of making it known to others. You know, I think growing up, like, again, in a Latino church, that was that was really important.

Mildred also shared the importance of the message of salvation in Jesus as personal and relational: "And just that salvation, that salvation aspect is so key and so important . . . I would say that's central to how I interact with people." In most conversations, the Christian belief of salvation in Jesus Christ was often followed or connected with sharing the message.

Gustavo recalled a story from high school when he befriended people who eventually came to faith.

> I just had this odd ability of making them [people] feel comfortable, whether it was something that was intentional or not. I remember throughout my high school years where I didn't really have a passion for my faith or for ministry at all. I just wanted people to feel welcome. And so, I was able to do that. I have friends who were eventually baptized because I just talked to them and invited them to eat lunch with us [his family]. And those friendships grew into something deeper.

Gustavo grew up in a Latino/a(s) church in New Jersey, and he was acquainted with the Great Commission and sharing the Good News.[9] But,

---

9. Although there are various commissioning statements from Jesus in the Gospels, such as Mark 16:15–18, Luke 24:44–49, and John 20:21–23, when participants shared

according to Gustavo, that came out casually and naturally and not out of a strategy or urge. He considers that his family was instrumental in this.

Other participants also reflected not only on the role of the family but on the role of their Puerto Rican culture in the calling to share the Good News. An example of this is Jessica, an academic and ordained minister in her denomination, who reflected on the relationship she observes between her Puerto Rican culture and sharing the gospel:

> I'm very Puerto Rican, very Puerto Rican. I feel that God then planned, that he chose for me to be Puerto Rican on purpose and with a purpose, and that that is part of my theology of creation. And because of that, then God intends to use that to redeem the world in some form or fashion. And I don't really believe this about myself. I believe this for every culture. It's not exclusive to mine, but this is the culture that I've been given. And how I steward it, I do believe, is part of the broader, bigger narrative and the plan that God has for us.

Jessica continued sharing how the Puerto Rican culture allows her to broaden the understanding of the gospel to people with different upbringings, particularly Anglo-Americans. She shared how her "keen awareness" of being loved by God gave her the confidence to conduct herself with a self-understanding of high value and dignity. In her words: "I don't have an emptiness and a void . . . I'm not longing for love in anyone or any other place because the love of God consumes my heart." In Jessica's experience, understanding who she is as Puerto Rican through God's love made her complete and compelled her to live and share the gospel.

> I can only capture what my mind and my heart can conceive to think about the abundance of the love that I still have yet to experience and discover about God and about myself, the way God sees myself. Then I view that, and I say, how could I keep this to myself? How could I be so selfish and not want others to also have the awareness of how much God loves them.

---

about what is commonly known as "the Great Commission," they were referring to Matt 28:18–20: "Then Jesus came to them and said, 'All authority in heaven and on earth has been given to me. Therefore go and make disciples of all nations, baptizing them in the name of the Father and of the Son and of the Holy Spirit, and teaching them to obey everything I have commanded you. And surely I am with you always, to the very end of the age'" (NIV).

Faithful Inheritances

Spiritual Disciplines

ELC participants shared that a meaningful set of Christian beliefs and values is the spiritual discipline they practice as part of their daily lives. The disciplines mentioned more often were prayer and study.

When prompted to share some experience that could illustrate the most significant Christian value, Andrés replied that his mother and grandmother have been the most influential models of a prayer life. "I would wake up seeing them praying often," Andrés added. He considered their example formative in elevating prayer in his own life.

Another participant, Nelly, also alluded to the parenting transfer of the spiritual discipline of prayer to their kids. In her case, she teaches her children about the importance of prayer.

> I mean, I'm trying to think of something that I teach my kids because if it's important to me, that means I'm telling it, passing [it] to my children . . . And I think that one of the things I'm constantly saying to my kids is, 'pray about it.' It's important. Pray about it. And they're constantly praying, like: 'I was in the middle of a basketball game . . . [and] I was praying in my head,' or, 'Mom, I took a test, and I had to pray because I was having a hard time.' You know, I'm always saying your communication with God is important . . . He's important. And from that, that's just a value that we cannot be Christians and not speak to God and not have time with him.

In Nelly's story, prayer appears to have a prominent role in her life. Moreover, prayer seems to be highly regarded and practiced as a family, acknowledging and inviting God's presence to every joint endeavor.

On a similar note, Eric also shared how prayer is a priority in his life as a crucial part of his decision-making process:

> My spiritual life, prayer is important, you know. It's not something that I just do just to do. My decisions in my life my major decisions have all been through prayer. So, I won't you know, I didn't get married to my wife without a considerable amount of prayer. I didn't buy my home without considerable prayer. So all of my major life decisions are to be sought with God.

For Eric, prayer is an enacted Christian belief that seems connected to the pursuit of clarity, wisdom, and discernment given by God, particularly for decisions that carry a personal gravitas.

Another spiritual discipline often mentioned by many participants was the study of Scripture. Joanna considers that studying the Scriptures is a way of intimacy with God. "Actively engaged and continuing to try to work on my intimacy with the Lord and attempting to do it in a way that I think I most connect with the Lord, which is through quite formalized teaching. I think it was one of the questions, 'How do you feel most connected to the Lord?' And I think part of it is also that structured learning," Joanna added. She shared that the active and continuous seeking of God through the study of the Bible, as a personal discipline, makes her love for God grow. She also teaches this to her daughter so that she can practice structured study daily. She believes that her daughter will come to love God more by doing so.

Studying the Scriptures is vital for other participants to cope and engage with society as Christians. Carol sees the study of the Scriptures as a lens through which to observe and understand society. "Something that's going on societally that we can interpret through the lens of the Bible or through the lens of Jesus and other folks that are represented within the Bible . . . being able to come into a space like that is really enlightening and eye-opening," says Carol. Other participants also used the lens metaphor when discussing engaging with Scriptures through the discipline of study. Bryan remembers his mother's warning to this day: "The Bible is often studied through the lens of a white paradigm." He says to remain vigilant about what lenses he uses in his study.

Similarly, Jessica refers to her Puerto Rican cultural lenses while studying the Scriptures: "So when I read Scripture, I read it through a Latino lens. Now, I read it thinking about my own cultural experience versus the cultural experience of which the narrative was written and how that influences me. And so, I feel like I read the Bible through a Hispanic lens. And so, because I do that, then I preach differently, and I preach to different things." These three participants' stories and experiences highlight some practical aspects of the spiritual discipline of study: (1) to understand how to engage socially, and (2) to remain culturally relevant devotionally and ministerially.

SUMMARY AND CONCLUSION

This chapter has explored the findings concerning SGPRs' familial, cultural, and Christian orientations. Concerning their upbringings, participants highlight the strong bond with family and relatives, other Puerto Ricans, or Latino/a(s) networks, such as their local churches. Hospitality, including others, Christian education, and cultural customs, such as traditional dishes and *matutinos*, were all cultural expressions and Christian values

Faithful Inheritances

observed, learned, practiced, and valued within the community (i.e., family and church).

At this point, it is essential to note that participants attending ELC were overtly positive, describing their church upbringings. However, the conversations sustained gave no clear indication of why they eventually decided to branch out of the Spanish-speaking first-generation Latino/a(s) congregation, an experience often referred to as the "silent exodus."[10] Moreover, it fell outside the scope of this research. However, based on the interview dynamics, it could be suggested that the lack of negative experiences shared by this group could be driven by nostalgia, sharing selective memories, and involuntary empathy with the researcher, as Puerto Rican. These dynamics are typical in qualitative research methods.[11] Nevertheless, their insights add to understanding the topic and provide a nuanced approach to further research on the silent exodus.

Other discussions found in this chapter include the salient SGPRs' Christian beliefs. These include loving others, justice, salvation and proclamation, and spiritual disciplines. Although one would have expected more theological engagement about God, as it is with first-generation Latino/a(s), SGPRs emphasized their relationship with Jesus and their enactment of their faith.[12] Further research could be done on this theological area.

---

10. Conde-Frazier and Lee, "Intergenerational and Intercultural Issues."

11. Clandinin, "Narrative Inquiry"; Maxwell, *Qualitative Research Design*; Merriam and Tisdel, *Qualitative Research*; Freeman, *Modes of Thinking*.

12. Costas, *Christ Outside the Gates*; Ortíz, *Hispanic Challenge*; Martínez, *Walk with the People*.

5

Findings on Sense of Belonging

Place, Culture, and Church

THIS CHAPTER EXPLORES THE sense of belonging of SGPRs to their contexts. This section comprises the participants' contributions through the conversations, stories, and responses related to the second research question, which explored the Christian beliefs that influence the way(s) in which participants perceive their belonging in the United States. The findings are organized into belonging and place, belonging and culture, and belonging and church. In this chapter, distinctions between the two groups, AAC and ELC, are more significant than in the previous chapter. Only AAC participants reported a sense of estrangement and hindrances to the sense of belonging to their churches.

BELONGING AND PLACE

This part of the interview started by asking participants about their identification with the place where they live in the United States. The answers were grouped into four categories: (1) sense of mission, (2) cultural enclaves, (3) diversity, family, and friends, and (4) estrangement. As previously noted, the stories and reflections that comprise this last group, estrangement, were shared by AAC participants only.

Faithful Inheritances

A Sense of Mission

When participants share their identification with the place where they live, work, or study, they usually talk about having a sense of mission and purpose. Participants expressed their Christian faith in the function of self-identification with the places they operate. "I love living in Wisconsin, especially the area I'm in. It's nice. Very quiet. So, you know, God willing at some point, you know, we're always trying to outreach to the community . . . But, hopefully, at some point, he [God] uses me in particular . . . to be able to do something significant in that community," Axel shares. Andrés also has a similar perspective on the subject.

> I definitely feel like I belong for the most part . . . What I definitely like about being here . . . and especially now that I'm learning about different countries . . . , the different struggles in different countries. I realized there's so much opportunity here . . . So, here's just a practical example. I became a baseball coach a few years ago. Now I'm part of a board, but at our church, one, two, three, four, five people from the Waukegan Baseball League, just within the last two years, have given their life to Jesus . . . and that's just my interactions with them through coaching and then with my family members, the parents, you know. It's little by little God is opening doors. I live my life with that in mind; it is just the realness of eternity. Eternity is so real that I want to leverage all of my relationships to help impact someone's eternity. . . . That Christian belief [eternity] drives who I am now. [E]verything I do is with the lens of eternity.

Andrés believes that God allows him to connect with people to "expand his kingdom, to help populate heaven." He understands that every circle of influence is an opportunity to impact someone in Waukegan with Christianity. For him, building relationships and serving the community is a way to faithfully respond to God's calling.

Although Andrés emphasized the opportunities for sharing the gospel with others as part of his sense of belonging, he also nuanced his response by saying: "I feel like I do have equal opportunity. I know that's not true for all of my friends. I do have, as close to equal opportunity as possible, [although] I don't know if it's really 100 percent equal opportunity." This time, Andrés was alluding to job and study opportunities rather than evangelistic.

Other participants expressed a sense of belonging to the place they live through their involvement with the community's issues. James experienced first-hand the 2020 racial tension developments in Kenosha. For

Findings on Sense of Belonging

him, belonging to the place where he lives and attending church are connected to his response as a Christian to the social issues regarding racial reconciliation and injustice.

> I just feel like it's hard right now. I think I belong in Kenosha because people are sort of claiming this town as theirs . . . I live there too now. And I felt safe, and I felt like I was understanding what was going on. So, it's hard right now. My church as well, like, you know, its majority white. That's been a struggle. There's just people that are at different points in life, and they come from different perspectives. And you have to kind of wrestle with that and just kind of try to also bring understanding and try to bring another perspective as someone that's from a different culture and like that becomes hard. Do I not need to be here? I don't know. I don't know, maybe belonging is something that comes with time as well, and sometimes you kind of have to fight for where you're at and just kind of try to share the truth.

James suggests a responsibility to engage with racial issues and conversations as a Christian and Latino/a(s). During the conversation, he continued bringing up the racial tensions in and outside the church and how his commitment to stay and advocate was essential to his Christian faith, even when the circumstances were challenging.

Other participants articulated their sense of belonging out of a location awareness of social justice issues because it provides a space to respond as Christians. In Carmen's case, the history of civil rights and the opportunity to be part of a community that cares about justice mainly make her feel connected to Memphis.

> [Memphis] producing a lot of city leaders who still care really deeply about civil rights and injustices, I think has been really powerful to me. You know, Memphis is big enough to where there's always something to do and be a part of and, you know, be entertained by. But it's small enough to where if you want to make a difference and want to have a stake in the city, it's pretty easy for you to do so. And I've loved that . . . I think that is a huge connecter.

Carmen did not grow up surrounded by a solid Puerto Rican network. She moved to Memphis with her parents when she was still a child. However, today, as an adult, she feels connected to Memphis not because it is where she grew up but because of cultural diversity and social justice, elements she deeply values. Moreover, Carmen sees her place of residence and work as opportunities to shine the hope of the gospel on social inadequacies and injustices. "No matter what, there is always hope. There is always a second chapter. There is always the ultimate promise of God making the world right," she concluded.

Cultural Enclaves

Participants feel they belong to a particular physical location through Puerto Rican and Latino/a(s) cultural expressions. In other words, participants' identification with location hinges on how the places represent or provide a presence for their own culture. For example, Carol explains how she developed a sense of belonging at Boston as an undergrad student:

> I lived in Boston for the past eight years. And most of my identity there revolved around being a student and being a student leader at my campus because that's where I spent like, 95 percent of my time. But what I'm grateful for is that a school that I went to was very diverse. It was a majority-minority campus. So, there were a lot more students of color than there were white students. And so, I got to meet a lot of people. One of my best friends from my undergrad career is from Columbia. So, just like having that space and then also finding those moments of Puerto Ricanness in Boston. I remember going to a particular neighborhood in Boston called the South End that has historically been Puerto Rican. And so I remember going to that neighborhood. There's a Puerto Rican restaurant there that I frequented often. There's a Puerto Rican Day parade. And so we always, I always went to that weather with friends or my cousin or whomever it may be. And so there was a class (or book), I think, that focused on the history of Puerto Ricans in Boston . . . So definitely finding those moments of Puerto Ricanness within my time in Boston because it wasn't something that was happening every day like in Orlando.

Carol's story encompasses a movement from Orlando, a highly Latino/a(s) populated city, to Boston. Although she identified several elements that helped develop a sense of belonging to her new place, the finding of a Puerto Rican presence in Boston—expressed through various means—mainly influenced her identification with Boston during those years.

Another participant, Victoria, similarly reveals how the surrounding businesses and crowds resemble her Puerto Rican culture and other Latino/a(s) cultures, making her feel she belongs. She compares her experience of belonging to the place where she lives to the island of Puerto Rico:

Findings on Sense of Belonging

> Orlando, Florida, is a place that [I identify] with. So many Puerto Rican restaurants and Latin culture and so many Hispanics, especially Puerto Ricans—especially after the hurricane ravaged my island. And, I definitely feel I belong. I don't feel out of place. I don't feel I get strange looks. I have felt out of place going back to Puerto Rico because as I got a little older, we started visiting less and less . . .

In her last remarks, Victoria also suggests that cultural proximity, familiarity, and continuity make her feel connected to a place. "I love my island, but I never lived there. I didn't grow up there. There are inside jokes and terminologies and even just geography that I'm not familiar with," Victoria added. On a similar note, Sandy expressed how her love for the island of Puerto Rico differs from feeling she belongs to a place: "Yes, I do certify Boston is my home because I've been here most of my life. And, I do know Boston more than Puerto Rico . . . When I just go to visit Puerto Rico, I feel lost." Vitoria and Sandy's comments seem to establish a difference between loving the island of Puerto Rico and the feelings belonging to the places they currently inhabit.

Another participant who shared his experience of having cultural enclaves was Ishmael. As with Victoria, Ishmael lives in Orlando, Florida. A while ago, his brother moved to Wisconsin. When Ishmael visited him, he felt like an "outcast" in something as simple as going to the grocery store: "We're like going to the store, and we barely saw any Hispanic speaking person there . . . And like even when we went to the store, there wasn't a simple seasoning called *adobo* in the store." Ishmael laughs, sharing his story while acknowledging the role of ordinary cultural cuisine in his sense of belonging.

Diversity, Family, and Friends

In addition, many participants talked about the importance of having family and friends around them and how it influences their sense of belonging to the place they live, work, or study. For Gustavo, New Jersey feels like home because of the family and multicultural relationships built over time.

> Because most of my family lives here in New Jersey, like most of my cousins and my siblings are here. This is where I grew up. And though I at times have felt like I was on the receiving end of microaggressions or racism, I know that that's not the sum of its parts . . . New Jersey is a wonderful place because of all the

Faithful Inheritances

> different backgrounds and different cultures that come together and feeling embraced . . . It might just be that the cultural diversity here kind of lends to everyone understanding that they are outsiders, yet they treat each other as one of their own.

Gustavo's experience of belonging seems to be a relational experience with others journeying in similar circumstances (family and non-majority friends). In his story, he indicates that having these relationships helps him endure any micro-aggressions he could receive.

Raquel has lived in New York, Massachusetts, and Florida. She lived in three different places in New York, all culturally diverse, especially Latino/a(s), except for Upstate New York. "So, we always gravitate to find our culture wherever we went, and we found it. And, wherever we live, we never felt like our culture was in prison . . . we were surrounded by family." For Raquel, the experience of belonging seems to correlate to being surrounded by family and a multicultural environment. Moreover, she suggests that not having these could affect her Puerto Rican culture.

Sense of Estrangement

Not all participants felt they belonged to the place where they lived, worked, or studied. All the participants who expressed feeling disconnected or estranged currently attend AAC. This is the case of Bryan, who grew up surrounded by family and relatives and a robust Puerto Rican and Latino/a(s) community around him. However, he lives in a predominantly Anglo-American neighborhood in Illinois where his kids have made good friends, but not him. "So, that's great for them [his kids]. For me, no. To see a Latino in this community, it's not common. My wife is black. My wife is African American. There's no African American here. So, yeah, you know, that's why," Bryan explained. He added that he must drive a considerable distance to get Puerto Rican food and the same for his wife to get her hair done. In Bryan's story, the absence of friends, family, and a community with similar racial and cultural features accounts for his sense of disconnection and identification with the place he lives and works.

Like Bryan, Mildred lives in a predominantly Anglo-American community. Despite living in the exact location for many years, she and her husband have tried to make friends, but it has been challenging for them.

> We have new neighbors that just moved in—by the end of the summer—that live to our right. And then we have older neighbors that

> live on the other side, and they haven't always been the nicest to us. And it's not for lack of trying. But yeah . . . I mean, it's quiet. We live in a really quiet street. But I would say that most of our fellowship has been outside of where we live . . . I don't know if I would say that I feel at home in my neighborhood in the sense of like the deep, deep roots that kind of has been from my church family.

When Mildred refers to deep roots in her church family, she signifies her previous church, a predominantly Latino/a(s) congregation, not the current. Her story suggests a lower sense of belonging to a place without meaningful relationships.

Another salient aspect of estrangement that emerged in the conversations was the participants' awareness of the ethno-racial tensions created by their presence in specific settings. Grace expressed this by saying that the only place she felt she belonged was the short time she spent in New York City, not because of the cultural diversity, family, or friends, but because she "was invisible there."

> [W]hat brought me the most comfort is that I was invisible there. And for once in my life, not someone wasn't pointing out how different I looked or how different I was, asking me a question about my culture or life . . . No one asked me questions . . . No one points out anything. I have curly hair and white skin. I'm just walking across the street, and no one cares. No one cares.

Grace has experienced numerous ethno-racial assaults and micro-aggressions because of her physical attributes, accent, and cultural expressions. As a result, she does not feel she belongs anywhere. For her, belonging means "diversity and inclusion," which she realizes has been missing.

Grace and Mildred are not entirely alone in this sense of estrangement and do not have roots. Angel sometimes feels like a "wanderer." "I've been around the world, and I really I don't feel like I have roots anywhere . . . I'll always be Puerto Rican. As you know, Marc Anthony says it's in the blood," Angel continued. However, the most pressing issue preventing the development of a sense of belonging in the United States is dealing with social and racial biases and prejudices.

> I'm aware like; there's an awareness there that I'm not like most of the people around me. And, you know, I understand. I understand the biases. I understand the prejudices. I understand. I understand the implicit bias that people have about somebody who looks like me. You know, the current political climate . . . the current climate

> of the community and the country doesn't help. I understand that I'm a brown person, you know, who could be equated with being a black person. You know? So, yeah. So, when there's a cop behind me. Yeah, I get as nervous as a black person because I know that I'm a shade away.

Angel is mindful of how his skin tone influences his daily interactions with others, contributing to estrangement in the United States.

BELONGING AND CULTURE

After discussing the sense of belonging in the United States, the conversation advanced toward how the participants relate to American and Puerto Rican cultures. The findings reported in this section are grouped into two categories: (1) strategizing and negotiating and (2) biculturalism. AAC participants only shared the conclusions of the latter category.

Strategizing and Negotiating

Participants talked about strategizing and filtering their day-to-day interactions depending on their context. A good example to introduce this finding is Javier's engagement as an engineer in a predominantly Anglo-American environment, vis-à-vis his interaction with the men's group from church.

> I would say that at work, it's really more the American side of me. I guess you can call it my white side because, you know . . . I have to be very proper, and it's very technical. So you have to communicate with a certain level, I guess, certain verbiage and demonstrate to [the] colleagues that you know what you're talking about so that if decisions need to be made, your opinion is heard. So, at work . . . , I want to speak in proper sentences and with a certain degree of vocabulary that someone can understand and know that I know what I'm talking about. Whereas if, like the men of the church are going out to hang out somewhere at one of the guy's houses, it's just, I don't want to call it a 'free for all,' but . . . That's definitely a spot where I lean on my Puerto Rican heritage because . . . the [group] is almost half Puerto Rican and half Dominican. So, there's more Puerto Ricans there that I can draw off. And so, we definitely joke around a lot. And we love to, like, get on each other's case about stuff and just rag on each other like they say.

Javier's story contrasts the need to conduct himself with mindful caution at work to be heard and considered by his peers with the freedom to be more joyful and casual among his Latino/a(s) community from church. Moreover, he refers to the different ways he conducts himself as his "American side" or "white side" at work and "Puerto Rican heritage" among his Latino/a(s) friends. This alludes to the behavioral complexities of race, ethnicity, and cultures in different settings and the individual's self-understanding.

Javier is conscious of avoiding his gestures and mannerisms at work. "Puerto Ricans are very emotional. We like to exaggerate everything. We use our hands when we talk. We get loud . . . We have to make gestures when we talk," Javier continues, "because I'm just in a different atmosphere, I automatically know that I have to kind of act a different way."

Many participants shared similar stories about their conduct in a work environment where most were Anglo-American. As previously observed, Javier approaches his relationships and interactions differently at work or among friends. Carol switches between English and Spanish at work to create certain connections and dynamics in her favor. "It's the only way to survive," Carol explains, referencing her professional environment in the academy.

> Depending on whom I'm interacting with, I'll say my name in Spanish, or I'll say my name in English. If I'm interacting with students, I almost always say hello and introduce myself with my name in Spanish because I want students to know that they can come to me if they are Latino or not . . . [S]o that they see somebody and hear somebody's name that sounds like theirs. I think that for me is very important when I interact with students and which obviously throws my colleagues off; my colleagues are like, 'What the hell is going on here?' Because they're just so confused all the time. And I'm OK with that because I definitely use that to my advantage. And I think in terms of, you know when I am interacting with colleagues, in my professional work, I find those people that I trust many times, finding other Latino colleagues, even though they're not directly working in the same area I am. And so that's a space where I can be a little bit more comfortable, let my guard down a little bit more. But, when I am often interacting with Deans and Associate Deans, just by the nature of my job, who are all white dudes . . . So, I, you know, I'm always using, strategically, the words to engage with them . . . thinking about the ways that I'm addressing them, like Dr. so and so, or whatever it may be to stroke their ego and get the things that I need.

In Carol's story, she seems to strategize her interactions according to the audience, deferring to Anglo-American colleagues depending on their position and hierarchy within the institution. This behavior toward the majority culture at work seems to create a contrast with the "comfortable" space she finds among other Latino/a(s) peers.

In the same way, Gustavo, a pastor of a predominantly Anglo-American congregation, articulated something to this effect: "I feel like I'm being more of a burden if I'm overtly Latino [at church]. I don't necessarily feel like I'd be 100 percent welcomed. So, I am not as Puerto Rican as I can be in that space, but I don't know if I ever present myself as American 100 percent." Gustavo explains that he is keenly aware of the potential negative impact on his church members if he allows himself to make certain gestures or use certain words—commonly used among Puerto Ricans—from the pulpit while preaching. "Code-switching. That I often do, on a weekly basis, when I am at my church," said Gustavo.

Another powerful story of self-awareness, strategizing, and negotiation comes from Angel, but this time, adding the element of race. Angel considers that he negotiates at work, church, neighborhood, and the grocery store at different levels every day. At his university workplace, he and his boss are the only "people of color" in the academic advisor's office. Angel continued:

> Anyway, I navigate all those things every day, and you know how I do it? I don't think about how I do it. I just do it. You know, I'll go to Publix and, you know . . . my English is accent less. I don't have an accent, but I know that what people see is a brown person. Right? So I'm aware of that. I'm aware that, you know, I am brown person with a beard. There was a time when I would always get stopped at the airport because my beard was a little longer and, you know, being brown, and I don't quite look Hispanic necessarily.

Angel's remarks accentuate the element of race in how to relate to American mainstream culture and Puerto Rican culture. In particular, he emphasizes his awareness of skin color, physical features, and accent as a negotiation skill to conduct himself as a Puerto Rican in Anglo-American environments.

Like Angel, Sonia also shared how her work experience requires self-awareness of her ethnicity and race and corresponding modifications. Sonia utilizes two components to discern her behavior in any particular place. First, she considers the context where she is at, and second, the relationship with the person she is with at that place.

Findings on Sense of Belonging

> I found that I tend to mold myself to the situation and show parts of me that are more fitting to the context one needs me. Definitely, like an example is at work. I, other than the worship minister, who is African American, I'm the only other person of color. Everyone else is [Anglo] American. So, finding the fine line of still being—not being proud—but showing off my culture, as well as not making anybody uncomfortable. Because they don't understand what I'm talking about. They can't relate to what I'm experiencing.

Sonia's self-awareness of race and ethnicity seems to mediate how she conducts herself among the majority culture at work. Mainly, a whole expression of her Puerto Rican identity will not be well-received or accepted at her job. However, Sonia also commented that this differs among her close friends and trusted acquaintances. "[Among close friends] I find that I am more. I can let loose, and I can just be myself . . . I let my Puerto Rican influence show more because I know that they accept it, and I know that they understand it," Sonia concluded.

However, the strategizing and negotiating between cultures also occurs in individuals who are more assimilated to the American mainstream and struggle to connect and relate with their Puerto Rican culture. This is the case of Carmen, who, as previously noted, grew up in an assimilated household.

> I am in kind of a, maybe, in a different situation than some [other] Second-generation Puerto Ricans who are brought up with more of the culture and the language because I actually feel extremely comfortable in the American world. Or, when I go to Puerto Rico, I really struggle to know how to act and relate. And so, you know, I feel more foreign by far in Puerto Rico than I do in the States, which makes sense. But, I also struggle to know how to kind of authentically own my Puerto Rican identity, especially in my workplace, which is being a journalist, is very public-facing.

Carmen also shared that her Puerto Rican identity development is constantly being revised. She considers that not mastering the Spanish language is a "humongous barrier" that prevents her from creating a robust connection with the Puerto Rican culture yet does not deter her "owning of a Puerto Rican identity." When she attends work-related conferences or meetings, people have certain expectations from her contributions as a Puerto Rican, "but, I'm not very vocal [in those spaces]," Carmen acknowledges. Carmen also noted that she constantly reads the news from Puerto Rico to stay informed as a journalist and to relate more to the culture. In sum, this also appears to be her strategy of discovery and definition.

Faithful Inheritances

Biculturalism

The previous subsection observed several examples of strategizing and negotiating between cultures. This section will focus on participants who take a non-negotiating stance between cultures. The following stories belong exclusively to AAC participants.

Some participants expressed that they were bothered by having to decide between the American mainstream and the Puerto Rican identity at some point in their lives. Julio commented: "It's almost, at first I thought, well, do you have to choose? And then some people say, 'Hey, I'm going to be this, and I'm going to be part of this culture." [They] forget about the past." Julio's wife is African American. He explained his position through the lenses of his marriage: "I think it's been our Christianity, really, that has allowed us to not only stay together, but just kind of have no preference in terms of Puerto Rican and African American. You know? Just to be Christlike, really, and make that the goal." Julio, who has navigated multiple racial tensions over the years living in different States, seems to prefer staying away from personally choosing among cultures and places Christlikeness not only as the goal but as the answer to the cultural, racial, and ethnic tensions.

Julio describes himself as Puerto Rican, and so does Raquel. However, in Julio's case, Christlikeness supersedes culture; for Raquel, it supersedes character. In particular, Raquel points to her professional self and her character as distinctive of who she is as a Latino/a(s):

> At work, everybody knows I'm Hispanic . . . I'm a professional before I'm Hispanic or American . . . I think my character supersedes culture . . . I think I have a problem with people who adapt or act a certain way when they're around Hispanics or non-Hispanics. I see myself as the same. I don't adapt or change my behavior just because. At school, I'm a professional no matter what, so I don't adapt the way I act, whether I'm around Hispanics or non-Hispanics. I'm just pretty much the same.

Raquel sees no need to adapt, strategize, or negotiate across cultures. She believes in being just herself, a Hispanic, despite the context. Raquel works in a school, and in many instances, she advocates for other Latino/a(s) families that bring their children there. "I'm a huge advocate for Hispanics . . . I have a passion for my culture. I don't act differently around them . . ., I advocate more for them because that's who I am," Raquel added. With this, Raquel's story implies a personal orientation where choosing or negotiating cultures does not outweigh her integrity and morality.

Findings on Sense of Belonging

One last significant illustration shared by participants was their liminality, or biculturalism, as a strategy to cope with their surroundings. When asked how she related to the American mainstream and Puerto Rican cultures, Jessica articulated that she went through rethinking and broadening her understanding of being Puerto Rican and American to what she was taught. She believed that by accepting the North American sociocultural definitions of what it meant to be American and Puerto Rican, she was conceding a personal privilege. "I was extending the privilege to everybody else to strip me of this portion of my identity that they didn't have a right to," Jessica said. She resolved to redefine what Puerto Rican meant to her:

> I created a huge shift for me in being able to say with a greater depth I am Puerto Rican. This is how I identify and guess what Puerto Rican means. There's a 100 percent affiliation of heart, mind, and soul, just incredible, to Puerto Rico ... And then I have 100 percent of affiliation here in the mainland. And there's no reason why I have to negotiate those two. They are what they are.

Jessica seems to relate to both cultures as a Puerto Rican. She refuses to choose or move between being American and being Puerto Rican in her definition. Moreover, she indicates that the weight of ethnic ascription relies heavily on society when invested in the person.

In summary, the stories shared in this section discuss different ways Second-generation Puerto Ricans relate to the American mainstream and Puerto Rican culture. As observed, participants either strategize and negotiate their relationship with both cultures or assume a stance of redefinition without constantly modifying and adapting to their context.

BELONGING AND CHURCH

This last section explores the participants' responses concerning their sense of belonging to their church. The question(s) participants were asked at this point of the interview were: How do you identify with the church you attend? Do you feel you belong? What do you appreciate the most? What do you dislike the most? To facilitate the discussion, the responses were grouped into three categories: (1) participation, (2) church as family, and (3) hindrances to belonging. It is essential to note the distribution of the answers provided. Under the category of participation, ELC participants' contributions were higher than the AAC group. Although participants from both groups articulated a sense of belonging through participation at church, only a few AAC participants acknowledged participation at church to factor into their sense of belonging. Contributions made under the category of family-oriented community exclusively represent the answers and stories from ELC participants. Lastly, the category hindrance to the sense of belonging exclusively represents most AAC participants' answers and stories.

Participation

The contributions grouped under this subsection of participation concern opportunities for participants to connect with their local churches in some service capacity. Most interviewees reported and shared experiences participating in some ministry, activity, or event at their local churches that made them feel they belonged.

When asked about their sense of belonging to the church, Axel shared part of his journey with the last two churches he attended. Axel commented that it was difficult for him when he started attending church with his best friend. Soon after coming to church, he was invited to play the drums with the worship team, and after a while, he was asked to lead the worship team. According to Axel, this series of events solidified his faith and commitment to the church to the point that even after leaving it five years ago, he still calls it "my church." Axel left his church to join a church planting team aiming to serve second-generation Hispanics. Axel has been part of this church plant for five years, and he is grateful to be part of this church planting group and witness, in his own words, "growth in every area." Now discussing his current church, Axel reported: "I definitely belong [here]. And I know that God put me here for a reason. Now I'm a deacon. I'm leading a small group . . . I'm a member of the Board."

Nelly's story is like Axel's; shortly after starting to attend church, someone approached her and extended an invitation to serve. She received that invitation as an act of love. According to Nelly, this took her by surprise because things were different at her old church: "They [the new church] loved me right away, which I felt like, you usually get to know a person before you start, like, loving them. That's how I felt [my old] church was . . . careful about whom they loved and whom they didn't. But this [new] church was like, 'No, we love you now, and we want to use you.'" Nelly states that this invitation to serve felt like "real love for the first time." Since then, Nelly has been active and attending this church with her four kids and husband for over four years. Nelly and Axel's stories suggest a relationship between inclusion through service and a sense of belonging and commitment to the church.

Findings on Sense of Belonging

Another story that continued nuancing the subject of participation was rendered by a member of an AAC. Carmen feels she belongs to her church mainly because it recognizes gaps or broken things, and they need people to connect and serve to fill the gaps and fix what is broken.

> So, you're talking about a church that has room for participation, and . . . the church also has room for improvement. I think that . . . especially [in] American Christianity, there's this desire for a church to, like, be another product that you consume. Like you show up at church, and everything is set for you, and the programming is flawless, and the music sounds amazing. And your kid goes to the daycare. That's incredible! And you go home, and it was like a really wonderful experience. But . . . there's just not a lot of, you know, there's not a lot of relationship to that. And so what I like about downtown when I say it's messy is that, like on any given Sunday, something could go wrong.

The first half of Carmen's story stems from her college years when she attended megachurches that invested considerable resources in producing a high-end quality experience. She never felt she belonged to those churches, never participated, nor contributed in any way. However, her sense of belonging changed when she began attending her church, which she describes as small and relatively new—ten years old. "It's a smaller context," Carmen continues, "I know the pastors, and they know me . . . if something's going on in my life, I can go to them . . . [Also] our small community group that's been a huge source of relationship." These messy, small, and relational characteristics affect Carmen and influence her sense of belonging. Her story indicates that her sense of belonging to the church is correlated to an atmosphere where things are not flawless, and relationships are cultivated; therefore, participation and service are encouraged.

Other interviewees shared the relationship between church participation and their sense of belonging in familial terms. For example, when asked the same question about belonging to the church, Sofía replied, "I feel like I do," and immediately explained why by comparing her teammates at the communication ministry with a family. She narrated: "It's kind of like one of those family reunions every week, is how I feel about my church . . . You meet every week, and you can talk about whatever. And then you go home, and then you come back to the family reunion next week, and there's something new." Sofía also mentioned how friendly and approachable the communication team is and how everyone knows each other's names.

Likewise, Sonia considers volunteering and serving at church to make her feel part of a family. "I submerged myself into helping in volunteering so that I could feel like I have a place," Sonia commented. This season of COVID-19 has been hard for her sense of belonging because she was watching and not participating most of the time. Sonia explains: "Throughout those first few months [of the COVID-19 pandemic], I felt like, oh, well, I'm just I feel like I'm just watching, but I'm not participating in the church, in the church family." In Sofía and Sonia's experiences, participation seems to lead to a sense of family, creating a sense of belonging to the church.

Church as Family

The second category is the church as a family, and it covers the stories related to how participants sense they belong to their churches mainly because they perceive it as a family. Unlike the sense of belonging through participation, which could also carry a sense of family, this family-oriented category did not indicate service or ministerial contribution to the church. Again, it is essential to note that all the stories found in this group come from ELC participants only. No AAC participants commented on belonging to a church that felt like family to them. However, some AAC participants mentioned small housing groups from the church as places to build community.

When asked about their sense of belonging to the church, ELC participants underscored the significance of relationships, feeling part of a family, and a deep understanding of community usually derived from shared experiences. Joanna recounted what connected her with her church: "I met my husband there. I was baptized there. I was married there. I presented my daughter there, you know. I think I feel connected because a lot of them have known me since I was a kid." In addition, she needs to be at the same church where her wedding bridesmaids are. "I want my children to know [them]," she explains.

Likewise, Victoria reported how the relationships at her home church make her feel she belongs there. While studying abroad, Victoria's parents constantly shared how people asked about her and prayed for her. She also recounts how people sent her messages and prayers via Facebook. When Victoria returned and went back to her home church, the pastor announced from the platform, "We're so happy to have her back." Victoria

Findings on Sense of Belonging

recalls that people from church made a line after the service to say hi and greet her back. "There is nothing like my home church . . . So much love," she concludes.

Another mentioned aspect was feeling cared for and loved by a community of faith that feels like a family. Like Victoria, Javier also says he loves his church and feels comfortable there. However, he also shared a memorable experience where love was enacted toward his family. He recalls that the ultrasound revealed no heartbeat during the twelfth week of his wife's first pregnancy, and the baby had stopped growing. Javier narrates:

> That was a very tough blow for us. And the church just, kind of, spilled over with calls and cards and coming to visit us when the time was right. [The] pastor came to his wife; they were like one of the ones that immediately came . . . Everyone just came and supported us. Were there for us. Prayed over us. Gave us space when we kind of didn't want to see anyone but always let us know that they were there too. So, they were caring and understanding. There was a lot of empathy.

The experience of feeling loved is something he perceived since he started attending the church. "You feel very warm and loved like right from the get-go," Javier explains. He describes his community as very welcoming and sincere in their love, something that has made him and his wife "feel very comfortable . . . and be very active in the church."

Participants shared how church relationships influence their sense of belonging in these first three accounts. In Joanna's case, significant events such as weddings and enacted signs of affection and care in Victoria's and Javier's stories also have a role in developing belonging in an ELC.

Sometimes, ELC participants shared characteristics from their congregations that made them feel connected and belonging. Sandy accentuated that her church was a humble, loving community that knew how to care and serve others: "I have seen them, right now, in the pandemic, gone more than the extra mile getting food to the people, calling them: 'Do you need anything?'" Victoria commented on her church's warmth and sense of community: "I think that definitely has to do with the Puerto Rican warmth that we inject into it and the joy that we live with and that sense of community." Carol also reported: "I definitely feel very much at home. Very much like I belong. Very much like I'm accepted and welcomed no matter what." Juan and Nelly, two other participants, commented that local churches were characterized as non-judgmental and loving and forgiving,

Faithful Inheritances

respectively. Nelly expanded by sharing how her church received her and never shamed her because of her past mistakes. She used to live in shame because she was pregnant before getting married. Even years after being married and having a stable family, this was an unresolved issue until she came to her current church. "This church made me feel like you're free, you're loved, you're forgiven, and you don't have to keep revisiting your life's mistakes," Nelly reflected.

Hindrances to the Sense of Belonging

Most AAC participants did not feel they belonged, identified with, or were connected to their local congregations. Their stories and experiences cover a broad spectrum of social, cultural, and ethno-racial issues.

Several participants commented that the institution's structure and rigidity negatively affect their sense of belonging despite their church involvement. Bryan, a campus pastor of an affluent AAC, considers the ministry approach corporate-oriented and transactional. When asked about his sense of belonging to the church, Bryan answered: "No, I don't belong, but is the hand of God why I'm here." Bryan was hired to start an ethnic ministry and reach out to the Latino/a(s) population near the main campus. For three years, Bryan recounts having to convince the board members to stop looking at this new church plant regarding numbers, offerings, tithes, and more like a church representing a different socioeconomic demographic. Bryan disclosed:

> I'm part of a budget that's about twenty million dollars. So, they're used to writing a check for everything . . . We don't know how to do church. [I've had] difficulties doing real ministry, like one-on-one people ministry. How do you grow a church? How do you grow a church plant? How do you connect with the community? So, my main role has been, in the last three years, just educating them in that process. And, when you deal with different communities, you [must] have different expectations of the community. [That the] city that we're targeting is [one of the] largest Hispanic cities in Chicago, and it's mostly immigrants. And, for instance, the giving expectation [from the board] was for me to grow this community, to grow this church body so that the giving could be around fifteen to twenty thousand dollars a month . . . I just flat out told them, 'That's not going to happen ever. Unless you're talking about thirty years down the road.'

One thing to notice from Bryan's remarks is his emphasis on a different approach to ministry. His AAC has a wealthy and corporate approach to ministry incompatible with the Latino/a(s) demographic they are trying to reach. Bryan seems to be articulating a tension between his relational approach to ministry among Latino/(s) and a budget ministry orientation from his AAC, consequently affecting his sense of belonging.

Other participants brought up the ministry and organizational structure aspects shared by Bryan. According to Angel, his church has missed many ministry opportunities because of its slow decision-making process, especially when the matter at hand does not understand the Latino/a(s) community. "They [his church] care about the right stuff. But it's like they take so long to make a jump . . . [T]hey overthink things and . . . [it] keeps them from spreading the kingdom and from reaching people," Angel commented. Although Angel is active in his church as an elder and board member, he feels he could do more with his gifts and talents. Some time ago, Angel recounted an opportunity presented to start a Spanish-speaking church plant, something he called "a church within a church." He felt that this was the opportunity God was providing for him to lead that ministry startup. According to Angel, the church missed the opportunity to start this Latino/a(s) ministry because of uncertainty about another ethnicity and their expectations of figuring everything out their way. However, later, Angel also disclosed that he wonders if, in part, the church questioned his abilities to lead such efforts. Bryan and Angel, ministry to and from Latino/a(s) in their respective churches were limited by notions of doing ministry as AAC.

Another area where participants mentioned ministry differences that made them feel like they did not belong was worship services. Eric is part of the worship team of his church. He narrated how he feels uncomfortable raising his hands whenever he leads worship during the Sunday service at 10:00 AM because the audience is mainly Anglo-American. However, on the next service at noon: "That's when 150 percent [Puerto Rican heritage] comes out . . . , their culture is a little bit more low key." Also, Mildred shared the testimony of a gentleman who attended a service led by the Latino/a(s) worship team at a particular event: "I'm so happy that I came today. He said, you guys, there's such a presence of God and a presence of love and family. [Our church] needs this." Likewise, Bryan recalls when the Puerto Rican worship leader stopped the service and made an altar call. Bryan acknowledges that doing something like that would have been

Faithful Inheritances

impossible during mainly Anglo-American service. After a debriefing with his team—mostly Latino/a(s)—after the service, Bryan told them: "[W]e're not going to compromise our identity. We can't compromise our identity because God works through us visibly different."

These three accounts highlight some cultural differences in worship styles that SGPRs find in their AAC and how these influence their sense of belonging. In particular, engaging unreservedly and emotionally during the worship service and having the flexibility to step outside the plan are seemingly deeply valued cultural and ethnic identity attributes.

Another hindrance to belonging is ethnic and racial biases and stereotypes. Gustavo reflexively shared a story to explain how and why he still feels like an outsider at his church as an AAC pastor.

> I would say most of the time, I feel as an outsider . . . I think it is primarily based on just the different cultural backgrounds . . . , a different worldview, different values. So, it's hard to do ministry and feel like you belong there . . . The first instance I would say I felt like an outsider [was] my first weekend there as pastor. I invited my family to come. It was pretty much like an installment ceremony where they accepted me as their church pastor . . . I mentioned like maybe four or five times that I was from Puerto Rico. After the whole church service was over, my family was waiting in the area, and one of the church members, an older gentleman, Anglo American, approached my family and said: 'Welcome! I just want to let you guys know we have other Mexican families here, so you can always come and join us.' It kind of left a sour taste in my mouth.

This experience has marked Gustavo during all his ministry years as the church's lead pastor. Sometimes, he has blanked with an English term, and even though he knows it in Spanish, he would not say it, fearing how his church will perceive him: "I don't want to come off as too ghetto for them, just because I grew up in a place where they might think or call it ghetto or hood or whatever." Through this story, Gustavo indicates how a recipient of ethnic and cultural biases and stereotypes is negatively affected in the relationship with the church and the sense of community and belonging.

James reported another way his sense of belonging to his church was hindered. In 2020, James, alongside other people from church, primarily members of minoritized groups, participated in a forum about politics and race issues. During the debrief session, an Anglo-American gentleman from

Findings on Sense of Belonging

church turned very antagonistic, first about the forum and then against the forum participants. As the person walked away, James remembered:

> So, me and somether people of color that were after [the forum], we were kind of like, 'What the heck just happened?' . . . I'm like, I could be in a Latino church right now where everybody gets this . . . and I don't really have to struggle with convincing people about this stuff . . . And you begin to feel like, well, maybe I should think about doing something else or going somewhere [else].

Like James, Gustavo also shared how difficult it is for him and his church to agree on social justice issues. "It's just we're in two different worlds most of the time. So, I would feel more at home if we were able to come together and agree on, you know, the values that at least I see arising from Scripture, which encompasses justice and human rights and empathy."

Both James' and Gustavo's narratives seem to reveal how challenging certain preconceptions are within majority-culture churches, particularly those related to ethnicity and race. Presumably, this also highlights the inability to sustain a fruitful communication of mutual regard between majority-culture groups and minoritized groups within the church.

Some participants noted the need to educate the congregation regarding this communication issue. Grace believes every AAC "should have a diversity leader in general." Grace has felt disappointed by AAC pastors and leaders and concluded that they operated out of ethnic and cultural ignorance. "[Today], I try to see through the fluff of a lot like American Christianity that says, 'You belong here,'" Grace sustains. Grace presumes that the declaration is unauthentic without the intentionality of learning about the other.

Bryan sees the role of education as part of his ministry as a Latino/a(s) pastor within an AAC. He has dialogued with the AAC leadership on different occasions about how the Latino/a(s) expression of their Christian faith differs from theirs. "And it was a hard-fought battle until they started attending the services and started saying, 'Oh, they actually end on time. But it's good content,'" Bryan commented. Bryan and Grace highlight how education, experience, and involvement of the AAC could positively or negatively influence participants' sense of belonging.

Lastly, SGPRs attending AACs sense different kinds of community. Participants, like James, distinguished between their understanding of community as Puerto Ricans and Anglo-Americans. "I think that the idea of the Christian faith and community is one way that my culture and

Faithful Inheritances

faith do align. I do find it hard sometimes being in an Anglo-American church . . . the way that Christianity is perceived and oftentimes practiced it is very individualistic," James resolved.

In turn, Jessica explained that her time visiting Latino/a(s) churches gave her the endurance to return to her AAC. She intentionally set time to visit a Latino/a(s) church during her travels before or after her commitments with AACs. Jessica explains:

> I think that while I [am with] a Latino church . . . , it [gives] me the taste, the connection, the familiarity, the assurance of them [the Latino/a(s) community] being filled at that moment with whatever that Christian experience has been. And then when I engage or return to whatever setting may be that might be predominantly white, then I sort of have the energy.

Jessica alludes to life-giving and life-draining community experiences, being Latino/a(s) the former and Anglo-American the latter. She also suggests that in the Latino/a(s) church, there is a sense of community and ethnic assurance that serves as a place to recharge emotionally.

Sharing how she felt at her local AAC, Jessica is uncomfortable saying she belongs.

> I feel like I'm respected. I don't know that I would use the words belonging, but I know that I'm loved. And I know that I'm respected . . . But I do value intentionality, and I do value I can journey with you as a church if you are trying to make the right decisions that respond to my spiritual needs, even if you're not doing it . . . So, it's not necessarily a place that I feel I belong to. I don't feel like I don't belong to it either.

According to her account, belonging is different from feeling respected and loved. However, considering her previous comments, belonging seems to produce a state of well-being.

SUMMARY AND CONCLUSION

In summary, this chapter has explained the findings concerning belonging to a place, culture, and church. In the first sub-section, participants shared that some of the ways they identify with the place they live are through a sense of mission, cultural enclaves, diversity, family, and friends. On the other hand, AAC participants disclosed having a sense of estrangement

Findings on Sense of Belonging

from the places they live because of racial tensions, lack of meaningful relationships, and social prejudices.

Regarding this aspect of estrangement, one cannot overlook the overwhelming, unconstructive experiences of AAC participants. The reason they decide to stay in their AACs amid their negative experiences is unclear. However, based on their stories, five reasons were observed. First is their sense of mission and responsibility for the next generation of Latino/a(s). Second, they are paid staff of the church. Third, they have relatives or spouses who previously attended or prefer AAC. Fourth, their locations need more Latino/a(s) presence. Fifth, they are attached or inclined to a particular Christian tradition or theological stream. Nevertheless, this surprising aspect remains unclear and merits further research.

Another finding discussed in this chapter is SGPRs' understanding of having a robust sense of belonging to the American mainstream and Puerto Rican cultures. Findings were grouped into strategizing and negotiating and biculturalism. Some of the strategizing and negotiating included code-switching and modification of gestures and mannerisms. Regarding biculturalism, AAC participants opt toward integrating both cultures and avoiding choosing.

Finally, belonging and church encompasses participation, family-oriented community, and hindrances to belonging. This sub-section marked a broader difference between AAC and ELC participants. Some salient findings are that inclusion, participation, and contribution increase the sense of being loved and belonging to a family. On the other hand, if there is no active participation and the individual is positioned on the receiving end, the sense of belonging seems to be lower.

6

Findings on Understanding and Participation in Mission

THIS CHAPTER CONTAINS THE findings concerning the third research question on how participants understand their participation and co-laboring in the Great Commission. Participants were prompted to share their priorities as Christians, stories, and experiences that could illustrate these priorities, their understanding of and participation in God's kingdom, and their involvement at the local church. The findings described in this chapter follow the same order under three sections: priorities as Christians, understanding of mission, and participation at church.

PRIORITIES AS CHRISTIANS

This section is organized into two subsections: (1) Outward-bound Christian values and (2) Inward-bound Christian values. The former group contains Christian values with outreach and relational orientation. The latter includes the findings of those Christian values that are individually formative but not necessarily relationally or outreach-oriented.

Outward-bound Christian Values

When asked about their priorities as Christians concerning their understanding of their active role in the kingdom of God, participants from AAC and ELC shared how Christian beliefs influence their interactions with others. Carmen articulates, in the form of a reflexive question, that her priority as a Christian is to be a good neighbor, particularly to people whose culture

Findings on Understanding and Participation in Mission

and race are different from hers: "Am I being a good neighbor to people whose lives look different than mine, and am I humble enough to learn ways in which I am not the neighbor that I should be?" Carmen added that one way she is reminded to stay humble and learn is her surroundings: "Living in a majority black city, being raised in a majority white culture, definitely kind of a tenet of humility is very important to me. Am I learning? Am I growing?"

Similarly, Ramón shared that his focus as a Christian is to care and respect people for who they are, especially from different cultures. "[It's] recognizing that as we're bringing different cultures, different people, we got to recognize that it's not about changing them, it's about nurturing them." These participants share a personal awareness of the cultural differences that surround them and their responsibility as Christians to love, listen, understand, and care for them without any cultural imposition or expectation on their behalf. Their answers point to a high regard for including cultures, ethnicities, and races within the church.

Javier commented that one of his priorities is modeling a good Christian character to his colleagues. For him, it is crucial to build trust and be honest with his relationships at work, even when it means acknowledging a mistake. Javier understands that this is his way of enacting the golden rule and witnessing his faith at work. Likewise, Victoria understands that it is her responsibility as a Christian to nurture and care for her relationships. "It's been such a blessing, on a personal level, to connect with people. Sometimes, people just need someone to listen. In other instances, I've been able to talk about that dark period of my life," Vanessa shared. According to Vanessa, caring is also a proof of character and a way to let others see Christ in her.

Other participants disclosed that the Christian value of grace was central to their faith and to relate with others. Wendy considers that her priority is to humbly extend grace to others through service: "Grace and humbleness to the caring for others. You know? [I'm] always thinking of how could I help other people." Wendy also comments that grace is vital to the outreach work around her community. Another participant, Grace, shared that during the current season of her life—living near the Mexico border—she has been compelled to give grace to others: "I'm offering that grace to others . . . , especially in the Latino community where I am, where people are very heavy, very heavy guilt complex . . . I can only share that because . . . the grace [of] Christ was offered [to] me." Grace is convinced that grace is the bridge of communication that connects her with other Latino/a(s) suffering injustices, being away from family, and being overwhelmed. "That's what we [the church] ought to be doing," she added, noting that conventional ways of evangelism, practiced during her upbringing, are irrelevant to her current context.

Bryan also brought the Christian value of grace, which he considers foundational to his ministry toward other Latino/a(s) and how he relates with the AAC. "To any ethnic group, you have to show them love, love God. You have to demonstrate grace . . . , you have to be a peacemaker [between majority and minoritized cultures]," Bryan added, reflecting on his role and years as a pastor at his AAC. He also understands that God has placed him in a position to educate and influence his AAC, yet he still finds it draining. "It is exhausting. This is difficult. Especially when they [the AAC leadership] say things that are insulting . . . They say not such nice things, and then, great, you have to learn how to extend grace." In Grace's and Bryan's experiences, extending grace to others amid difficulties appears to be a priority. Participants enact their commitment to their faith despite their sense of belonging to their location, culture, and church.

Another group of participants disclosed love and service as their priority as Christians. Some participants articulated that their family was their first love and service recipient. Sofía and Angel commented that family was their first ministry. Andrés elaborated and shared his mission statement, including his commitment to his family: "To submit my all. So that God can use me to serve my family, my church, and my community." For Andrés, there is nothing more important than devoting his life to love and serving these three groups in that particular order. Another two participants, Angel and Gustavo, commented on their understanding of serving others. "You put others first . . . I'm comfortable enough with my identity and with who I am that I don't need to be the center of actually anything," Angel explains. In turn, Gustavo shared: "[My priority is] to live a life of service. Serving people without question, without reserve. Really, just pouring yourself out. Making sure that people are having a better experience because you are around." In the answers of these participants, loving others is a priority enacted as service and deference to others.

Raquel also embraces the dyad of love and service as her priority and what she expects her daughters to learn. It is about "loving others and serving others," she said. Raquel has had a long friendship with a single mother and her daughters for over a decade. Raquel narrates:

> I taught one of her girls when she was in second grade . . . Now she's nineteen, and she has a child of her own . . . This is how long it's been that I've been in this girl's life . . . My girls know . . . It's important that they see me, love, and serve also . . . I will call her and see [how] she [is]. We check up on each other . . . I've helped her fill out forms. I've translated for her. I've helped her daughter, who now is an adult, and as a kid.

In Raquel's story, loving and serving others are Christian values that inform her life and a bridge that crosses generations and creates solid relational bonds. "And so, they're a big part of who I am," Raquel concluded.

Lastly, participants also shared the Christian values of love and compassion for others as a priority in their lives. Axel opines that these two, love and compassion, are how he shares his Christianity with everybody regardless of their background, social status, or current state. "You know, Jesus came to this earth, and he hung out with prostitutes and tax collectors . . . and that's one thing he had, love and compassion for people . . . And then I think that's two big things that will help us reach people no matter where they're at." Axel constantly prays about this because he believes that is how Christians should become Jesus to others. Nelly commented that her natural impulse is impatience and uncaring with people, but God has softened her heart so she can love people even through their "messiness." "I feel like he's [God] put in my heart like a therapist's heart. Like we have to get to the root of the problem. You have to pray. You have to love them . . . love conquers all . . . I feel like being a Christian has helped me just deal with people behind the scenes," Nelly disclosed. One way in which she has observed how much she has grown in loving compassion is at her work. Nelly explains that she used to get upset with the clients because they always complained about religious or racial discrimination. Now, she listens with more empathy and compassion, something she attributes to God and the Christian values she has embraced.

Inward-bound Christian Beliefs and Values

Participants also commented on prioritizing Christian beliefs and values that are not necessarily oriented toward others but their relationship with God. Sofía shared that her faith in Jesus is a priority. After breaking out from an inter-faith sentimental relationship, Sofía felt almost swayed. "[Now] I'm always making it [faith in Jesus] stronger and making it feel personal, not just because I belong to a certain church or because I belong to a family.

Faithful Inheritances

Just making it my own . . . This is part of who I am," Sofía reflected. Sofía also observed that this process of strengthening her relationship with Jesus has an intellectual and experiential component. Both components help her carry out her Christian faith confidently among non-Christian acquaintances. As a result, Sofía declares: "I think just being unashamed in my beliefs and not shying away from speaking my truth . . . So, I think just reflecting my life and my actions on what my faith tells me to be like, and it's not letting myself be molded by the world."

Like Sofía, other participants also emphasize having a personal relationship with God. Javier says one of his priorities is to "maintain a good relationship with God." He explains that to do that, he must spend time in prayer, "seeking him." Eric also commented: "These are my priorities: 'to be grounded in his word and in prayer.'" Eric recounts that these spiritual disciplines were something he learned growing up at his father's church and still hold for his spiritual growth. In turn, James shares that having a relationship with God means being dedicated to living for him and being holy. "I want the Lord to increase," James concludes. Correspondingly, Nelly highlights the way she perceives Puerto Ricans' love and then makes a connection with her desire to have a relationship with Jesus:

> Puerto Ricans love hard . . . like [they are] dedicated and loyal . . . I feel like that's how I want to serve the Lord. Like, I want to be dedicated. I want to be loyal. I want to love Christ hard. You know what I'm saying? No matter what. No matter what I'm going through at the moment, I want to give my all. And, I love that about our people that we're all in, you know, all the time, everything.

The experiences of these participants heighten the importance of caring for the inner being through several spiritual disciplines. Although such practices focus on having a more substantial and growing personal relationship with God, they also seem to reveal practical life, such as in Sofía's and James' remarks.

UNDERSTANDING OF MISSION

This section recounts the findings relating to the participant's understanding of the mission. During this part of the interview, conversations circled the participants' understanding of mission and contribution to the kingdom of God as an expression of what is commonly known as the Great Commission.

Findings on Understanding and Participation in Mission

All participants understand the mission and contribution to the Great Commission more relationally, especially among their circles of influence, such as family, friends, co-workers, and communities, and less of an evangelistic endeavor or missions abroad. Sonia sustains that her church's response to the Great Commission is the evangelism explosion's five-finger rule. She believes this approach is faulty: "How do I get into that conversation? I'm not going to be like Jesus loves you . . . Like, they've heard that before . . . I'm not good at this." Sonia has shared her concern at her church yet has not seen change. Angel considers that the understanding of the Great Commission has changed. "It's not just limited to Saturday mornings and handing out tracks and knocking on doors . . . , is every opportunity that God created," Angel argues. Angel considers being on mission everywhere he goes. "To do mission is every time standing in line at the supermarket . . . , I can end up talking to somebody, and the conversation can lead to a conversation about Jesus," Nelly recalls that at her church, missionaries were regarded in high esteem and she perceived that everyone who wanted to obey the Great Commission had to go to Africa. Her understanding has changed over time:

> The Great Commission it's a calling on my life from Christ . . . I still feel very strongly about missions, like, God, whatever you want to send me, just send me . . . So yeah, I talk to my coworkers and my family members here and there, but I haven't talked to people next door. I haven't invited them for dinner and share Christ. And that's important. That's part of the Great Commission. The Great Commission is to talk to everyone everywhere you go.

Although participants value the expressions of mission—in the sense of sharing the gospel with a different culture abroad—and evangelism, their current understanding of participation in God's mission seems to lean toward a more personal and observable involvement.

Julio considers that his primary mission at this season of life is to reach his children with the message of Christ. "[I'm] sharing with them the importance of, you know, having an active life with Christ as the center of it," Julio discloses. Likewise, Carmen formerly understood the Great Commission only in missions abroad. Now she understands it in terms of reaching out to her friends without losing their friendship: "Something that I really loved about my life journey is that I've been in situations where I've had really strong friendships with non-Christians and have maintained those relationships over time." For these participants, obeying Jesus' command in Matthew 28:18–20 is more than executing evangelistic methods and doing missions outside the United States. Their expressions of mission entail family and friends.

Other participants also see their participation in the Great Commission as personal and relational. Raquel shares that she lives the Great Commission by acting and helping others. She observes: "I think there are more aspects to witnessing than presenting the gospel by talking to people . . . there's also witnessing through action." Other participants, such as Carol, believe that sometimes the Great Commission is wrongly interpreted and practiced by Christians, and as a result, "Christianity is shoved down your throat." She believes that listening, understanding, and relating with people are essential. She uses the iceberg illustration with her students to explain how much lies underneath the surface of each person, such as history, beliefs, and values. Carol understands that it is crucial to "have conversations and be in spaces with other people where they can talk about their Christian beliefs . . . , about how they grew up . . . , and I can talk about how I grew up and where are the commonalities . . . You have to get a little bit more vulnerable."

Ishmael, in turn, witnessed how a Christian co-worker tried to persuade a Muslim co-worker for a long time apologetically. Still, this approach only resulted in distancing and futile argumentation. Ishmael says he never sided with his Christian co-worker because he thought his friend was using an aggressive approach. Later, Ishmael narrates that the Muslim co-worker's father passed away, an opportunity to strengthen their relationship. Ishmael listened to his friend grieve his loss and then shared how his father has been an absent figure in his life. "I tried to relate to him and understand where he's coming from," Ishmael stated. Ishmael obeys Jesus' command in Matthew 28:18–20 by establishing a relationship with his Muslim friend. In Ishmael's remarks, similar to Carol's, authenticity and understanding seem to be underlying distinctives of their understanding of mission.

One last salient way participants define mission and contribute to the Great Commission is by establishing relationships with the community and serving its needs. Grace, who observes the needs of an immigrant community near the border, says: "I would like to be more involved in that realm [of non-profit and community service to immigrants] rather than how I was in ministry preaching and teaching." As a pastor, Andrés mobilizes his church to connect with schools, community organizations, and other government agencies to influence them "under the banner of Jesus Christ." He continues by saying that his vision of participating in the Great Commission is "to multiply the church in as many avenues as [they] can." In Joanna's case, her profession provides her opportunities to connect and serve people from the community with the hope of the gospel. Joanna narrates:

> So, I also realize somewhere that seeing people in the image of God is huge in my profession because they're typically parents who are not perfect . . . None of us are, but those are the ones who really kind of struggle . . . One of the things I usually tell my clients is, especially those who have drug addictions . . . , I say, 'You matter.' I remember saying this to this one client . . . in the middle of a trial as she was going to lose her parental rights. And I just look at her, and I'm like, 'You know, you matter. Like, you got to get yourself out of this. Like you matter for you. You matter for your child.' . . . And she just looked at me and said, 'Nobody has ever told me that I matter.' . . . So I make it my point now to start that way because I felt so blessed that the Lord was able to use me to tell her that.

Although Joanna has never been on a short mission trip, she is committed to giving money to mission events abroad so others can go. Joanna's experience, along with Grace and Andrés', reveals an understanding of participation in the Great Commission through working with the community in different ways.

PARTICIPATION IN CHURCH

Participants shared their opportunities for participation and ministry engagement at their local churches in the last part of the interview. Like the previously discussed priorities, the most prominent areas of participation are grouped into (1) serving the church community (inward orientation) and (2) being commissioned to serve others (outward orientation). In addition to these two, the third category consists of AAC participants' observations and stories of disappointments with participation and expectations from the church. AAC and ELC participants' contributions are balanced in serving the church community category. However, only ELC participants mention being actively involved in church ministries with an outreach scope.

Serving the Church Community

Participants shared, in diverse ways, how their churches provide opportunities for them to serve the body of Christ. Bryan and Gustavo are both

Faithful Inheritances

pastors in AACs. James has been called to be part of a leadership training program at his church. He has served at the young adult ministry through training, organized services, led worship, and participated in a men's discipleship group. James, a seminary student, is grateful for this learning opportunity and considers it aligned with his calling and giftings. Another participant, Javier, shared that he serves as an elder, musician, and treasurer at his church. When asked about participation at church, Joanna replies that God has gifted her with "a supernatural gift of hospitality," and the church is a venue to use it. She narrates: "So, my thing was anybody [that] came to the church, I felt like I'd be the first one there. 'Hey, how are you? Nice to meet you. So good to have you here.'" In hindsight, Joanna clarified that she had observed that hospitality gift from her mom. In turn, Ishmael is a youth leader at his church and is willing to serve in any capacity: "So I'm focused on youth, but I'm also wherever they need me."

Victoria shares that she was called to serve as a worship leader at her church, which is not offered to everyone. Music is something she is very passionate about; therefore, she sees this opportunity as a privilege and a formative process. "I've learned so many life lessons from being a [worship] leader in that sense, and God has humbled me in a lot of ways, beautiful ways through that process," Victoria reflects. Similarly, Sonia considers herself blessed to be part of the worship team. She understands that God has provided an outlet to put her faith into action through music. Sonia speculates using her musical talents is a way of spreading the Good News, especially because she is not good with words: "So, I feel like everyone has their own way of spreading their [faith in Jesus] throughout the world . . . And not all of us are the same."

Other participants, such as Sofía, are active members of the communication team at their local church, in charge of media, sound, lights, and projections. Sofía comments: "They needed people in communications, so I started doing communication." Before serving in communications, Sonia served in children's ministry, but she had to decide between them. Eventually, she settled on communications because, as she puts it: "I'm good with technology." Ramón is also passionate about his role in communications. "I'm a visual storyteller," Ramón says. He sees this ministry as an opportunity to help people connect with the church.

Participants also described their involvement in discipleship and teaching at their local congregations. Mildred comments that she is starting discipleship with some women who recently attended church. Mildred

Findings on Understanding and Participation in Mission

acknowledges that discipling others "is a heavy responsibility" because it is about helping people "know who they are in God so that they can then be a light to other people," she concludes. Gustavo comments that as a pastor of an AAC, one of his goals is to disciple people and help them grow spiritually rather than numerically.

> My faith organization heavily emphasizes numeric growth, and I don't know if my church is at that point where we can just focus on that . . . I'm really more concerned about the spiritual health of my church, the Christian maturity. There's a saying, you know, healthy mothers give birth to healthy babies. And so, I really want my church to be at a healthy place where we can start doing that, fulfilling the Great Commission, because I'd hate to, you know, bring newcomers into the church where they might not feel welcomed or loved and taken care of.

Gustavo connects the spiritual health of a Christian community with the inclusion and reception of others into that community. He considers this to be at the center of his ministry.

Serving in Ministries with an Outreach Scope

Only ELC participants mentioned actively serving in ministries from their churches with an outreach scope. For example, Wendy leads a women's ministry at her house under the umbrella and commissioning of her pastor and church. According to Wendy, it is safe for women to be vulnerable and share their stories. Elaborating on the ministry scope, Wendy shares:

> I'm a leader for the women's [ministry] . . . Women go through a lot, and we're quiet people. We don't tell what's going on. We don't like to open up and tell everybody what's going on in our lives. So . . . and they won't say anything unless you give them that trust . . . [Y]ou have women that come to church and [are] quiet. And I think having a group of discussions that will help women open up and trust you can help. We have had women with domestic violence that, [and you'll never know] unless you come and meet.

Wendy believes these spaces and ministries are essential because people attend church without sharing their hardships. She acknowledges that it is not because people do not care but because relationships and trust take time. Wendy feels privileged to be serving these women for more than a decade.

According to Javier, despite having several roles at his church, he enjoys making outreach connections. "I'm one of those people that like to go out [and] connect with people . . . I like to go out to businesses that take the time to hear you out and network with them . . . definitely been a strength of mine," Javier recounts. Javier has brought people from the community to the church as part of this ministry. "I like to be part of this web, [this] networking, leading [people to] church," Javier discloses.

Obstacles for Participation

Some AAC participants share how their churches miss opportunities to create spaces of participation. Jessica compares her previous experiences with predominantly Latino/a(s) churches with her current AAC. Referring to one particular Latino/a(s) church in Florida, she says: "The church clearly understood itself as a sending agency and also viewed the need for missions organizations . . . that it was then necessary to have mission organizations because the church was failing to do its kind of work." Jessica observes that her current AAC lacks this kind of initiative and is stagnant in mobilizing all its people into a mission.

Moreover, Jessica reflects that the AAC still does mission with a colonial approach. According to Jessica, this creates severe problems for Latino/a(s) or other non-majority culture groups in their midst. "I thought they [AAC] were superior, and I suffered from the intellectual colonialization of thinking that they were the better race, and they were the better people and that they had access to an American dream that I would not have access to," Jessica explains. According to Jessica, this perception of the AAC prevented her from participating in church and appropriating the mission. She finished her thoughts by arguing that the church, in general, must remain vigilant to the way it relates with others and do mission: "[We must be] sure that we don't get caught up in the same cycle that was so damaging to our faith and what we have believed, and that robbed us of our identity."

Bryan also commented on the relational dynamics between the AAC and Latino/a(s) in which the latter is not perceived as having the credentials to participate. He states: "[Latino/a(s)] have to understand that we have a voice, we have something to say. And the conversations and evangelical Christianity have only been binary. It has been black and white. There's a third voice, us. There's a fourth voice, Asians." From his own experience, Bryan reflects that even though the times have changed and the United States is growing increasingly diverse, the participants at the AAC are the same. He shares that the AAC values specific credentials, such as finances, studies, and heritage, and that without those, it is difficult to find a way to participate. "Not that credentials define who we are as people, but the credentials give you a bigger audience," Bryan concludes.

In addition to Jessica and Bryan, other participants share similar thoughts and experiences with the AAC. For example, Phoebe describes an unpleasant experience she had a few years ago working as a Children's Director at an AAC. "I felt like they were trying to check a box. They wanted to be multicultural. They wanted to be progressive. 'Let's hire a young Latina,' but then they said, 'Oh, she has a mind,'" Phoebe narrates. According to Phoebe, the church was unprepared to have a strong Latino/a(s) leader. As a result, she often struggled to hear or accept her ideas among the church staff. As a result, she does not work at that church anymore. On a similar note, James comments that he feels tired of the racial tensions at his AAC. When he thinks about the future, he envisions serving in a church where people can be one community that helps each other, grow as equals, and fulfill the Great Commission without racial tensions. "I want to pastor a church of people who are, you know, we're here together, and we're doing life together as one people . . . Just so much a part of how I grew up and what I saw in my father's church," James concludes.

SUMMARY AND CONCLUSION

In summary, this chapter presents the participants' priorities as Christians, their understanding of participation in the mission, and their experiences serving at their local congregations. Some of the most salient Christian beliefs and values relate to Christian character, loving and serving others, and personal relationships with God.

Participating in the kingdom of God and contributing to the Great Commission was nuanced among participants as something personal and quotidian. This includes social justice, discipleship, and relational witnessing.

Finally, AAC and ELC SGPRs have different ways and opportunities to participate in their churches. Participants from both groups described being active in ministries that serve their churches, while only ELC participants shared being active in outreach ministries. In addition, AAC participants shared some of the obstacles to their participation.

7

Discussions of Findings, Missional Implications, and Conclusion

THIS RESEARCH EXAMINES HOW Christian beliefs influence second-generation Puerto Ricans' (SGPRs) ethnic self-understanding and sense of belonging in the continental United States. The introductory chapter argued that Latino/a(s) Ethnic Identity Models (LEIMs) could not answer the following questions: How and to what extent do Puerto Ricans' Christian-oriented beliefs influence their self-understanding? What does belonging mean for Puerto Ricans? How is the ethnoreligious identity of SGPRs constructed and maintained amid a predominant Anglo-American Congregation (AAC) vis-à-vis English-speaking Latino/a(s) congregation (ELC)? Three research questions, one per chapter, probed the previous LEIMs observations. Chapter 4 looked at how SGPRs understand the relationship between their Christian beliefs and their Puerto Rican self-identification. Chapter 5 disclosed the findings concerning their sense of belonging concerning place, culture, and church. Lastly, chapter 6 unpacked participants' understanding and participation in the mission.

This chapter responds to the three research questions that guided this study in interaction with the growing knowledge of LEIMs, discusses its missiological implications, and concludes by suggesting ideas for future research. It explores the concept of faithful inheritances as it relates to the ethnic and religious identities of second-generation Puerto Ricans (SGPRs). These inheritances passed down through generations encompass Christian beliefs and cultural traditions that shape their sense of self and belonging. As we delve into the findings, we will see how SGPRs navigate these dual

Discussions of Findings, Missional Implications, and Conclusion

inheritances within Anglo-American Congregations (AAC) and English-speaking Latino/a(s) Congregations (ELC) and how these inherited values influence their participation in church and community life.

PRIMARY CHRISTIAN BELIEFS AND VALUES INFLUENCING THE CONSTRUCTION AND MAINTENANCE OF SGPRS ETHNIC IDENTITY

As previously stated, over the last forty years, the social sciences have produced six significant LEIMs: (1) the Mexican-American to Chicanismo Model, (2) the Chicano Ethnicity Model, (3) the Multidimensional Model, (4) the Bicultural Orientation Model, (5) the Racial Identity Orientation Model, and (6) the Lifespan Model of Latinx Ethnic Identity Development.[1] Despite the differences between these LEIMs in process and content orientations, variables, and definitions, the most salient concepts found in these LEIMs are race and ethnicity and self-awareness and well-being.

This section discusses the significant Christian values influencing SGPRs' ethnic identity construction and maintenance. The discussion is held with those mentioned earlier salient LEIMs concepts and the LMLEID from Torres, Hernández, and Martinez.[2] The discussion is organized in two parts: (1) Christian beliefs and ethnic self-identification, (2) Christian beliefs and sense of belonging. These subsections also elaborate on the differences between SGPRs attending AAC and ELC.

Christian Beliefs and Ethnic Self-identification

CHRISTIAN AND CULTURAL COMUNIDAD

Not all SGPRs grow up surrounded by a robust Puerto Rican or Latino/a(s) network. Instead, the circumstances and contexts vary from one family to another. For example, some SGPRs, such as Carmen, may grow up in American assimilated households with few expressions of the Puerto Rican culture and almost a non-existing Latino/a(s) network around them. In

---

1. Arce, "Reconsideration of Chicano Culture"; Keefe and Padilla, *Chicano Ethnicity*; Felix-Ortíz et al., "Multidimensional Measure"; Torres and Phelps, "Hispanic American Acculturation"; Ferdman and Gallegos, "Racial Identity Development" and Ferdman and Gallegos, "Latina and Latino Ethnoracial"; Torres et al., *Understanding the Latinx Experience*.

2. Torres et al., *Understanding the Latinx Experience*.

Faithful Inheritances

comparison, others mature surrounded by multiple expressions of Puerto Rican traditions, customs, and symbols.

Similarly, in Julio and Crystal's cases, not all SGPRs grow up in a family that attends a Protestant church. However, despite the presence or absence of a Puerto Rican network, the expressions of Puerto Rican culture, and the family commitment to a Protestant church, all SGPRs report the presence of Christian beliefs and values in their families. This suggests that the presence, to any scale, of the Puerto Rican culture in an SGPR household encompasses a series of Christian beliefs and values, whether recognized as such or not.

Conventionally, the influence of Christianity in Puerto Rican culture concurs with scholarly work.[3] SGPRs casual sayings during the conversations, such as *Gracias a Dios* (Thank God); mentions of *pedir la bendición* (ask for blessing) to their folks; memories of Puerto Rican artifacts intertwined with Christian elements (such as in Sofía and Joanna's stories of having the Puerto Rican flag and *jibarito's* paintings respectively); and preserving the celebration of *Noche Buena, Navidad*, and *Los Tres Santos Reyes* (such as in Jessica, Carol, and Victoria's stories). According to these participants' stories and experiences, the family emphasis and commitment to these traditions are rooted in the Christian tradition yet culturally integrated.

In the same way, SGPRs who grew up attending protestant churches talk about the intersection of Puerto Rican culture and how they lived their Christianity. For instance, Puerto Rican folklore instruments and music were employed at the worship services (as in Bryan and Esteban's experiences). Equally important are the *matutinos* during the Christmas season (as in Angel and Andrés' recollections), merging faith and culture, more precisely, the proclamation of the gospel and folklore.

As a result, the practice and observation of these intersecting expressions between culture and Christian beliefs merge, ultimately pointing to *comunidad* as the converging element and referential framework for SGPR ethnic identity. *Comunidad* seems to mediate and sustain all the previous ethnoreligious expressions, *matutinos, la bendición*, and *las Navidades*. The absence of *comunidad* would mean the absence of the critical cultural transferring entity. SGPRs stories and experiences suggest a two-fold definition of *comunidad*: (1) as a group of people with—or invited to share—the same interests, and (2) a way of life. For SGPRs, *comunidad* is something that

---

3. Aponte, *¡Santo! Varieties of Latino/a Spirituality*; de la Torre, *Hispanic American Religious Cultures.*

Discussions of Findings, Missional Implications, and Conclusion

they do, join, invite others into, create, are part of, enjoy, and live daily. It provides meaning for relating with others and their surroundings through a tightening relationship of cultural heritage and Christian beliefs in tangible and intangible ways.

SGPRs understanding of *comunidad* resembles De La Torre's definition. De La Torre explains that *comunidad* for Latino/a(s) is not equivalent to the English term community; instead, it is a religious sharing with a historical and theological foundation.[4] Furthermore, de La Torre states that at the grassroots of *comunidad* are charity, solidarity, and accompaniment that bring together spiritual and cultural expressions.[5] To this definition, Martínez adds Christian hope as a unifier that creates a sense of community.[6] Both authors focus on the tangible and intangible components of *comunidad*: A group of people and a set of beliefs, as well as cultural expression and theological understanding.

Complementary to these tangible and intangible components, SGPRs think of *comunidad* as family, church, and neighbors and observe their cultural and Christian expressions, bringing them together. For example, for SGPRs, *las Navidades* are more than a festivity; they are an opportunity to see family and friends, eat traditional dishes, or exchange gifts. This is evident in Angel and Mildred's narratives of large gatherings around the Advent motive in their houses. Sonia and Victoria's remarks about preserving the tradition of cooking and sharing Puerto Rican traditional dishes during Christmas with family, friends, and neighbors. As well as Andrés' observation of *comunidad* and proclamation through *matutinos*. Arguably, SGPRs consider *Las Navidades* the most significant Puerto Rican celebration in their families because it enfolds family gatherings, music, food, and Christian faith. More importantly, it is a time to create deeper *comunidad* and strengthen relational bonds among family, relatives, friends, church members, and neighbors.

It is important to note that hospitality is how *comunidad* is perceived by SGPRs. Cultural and Christian values of hospitality and others in the family abounded in the participants' stories and were associated with the *comunidad*. For example, Javier talks about his church's family and how hospitable they are. In the same way, this is observed through Victoria, Sonia, and Ramón's stories commenting on the relational warmth leanings

---

4. De la Torre, *Hispanic American Religious Cultures*, 142–47.
5. De la Torre, *Hispanic American Religious Cultures*, 142–43.
6. Martínez, *Walk with the People*.

and the hospitable and inviting character of their families and churches toward the surrounding community and neighbors. These participants shared they observed hospitality while traveling to Puerto Rico and during their upbringings in the United States, feeling welcomed and making others feel the same. Likewise, Gustavo reflects that hospitality is a Christian tenet and, at the same time, cultural, making it a double inheritance.

These stories stand out as examples of the intricate relationship between culture and Christian values. Moreover, they characterize SGPRs' understanding of *comunidad* as a cultural and Christian heritage they received and embraced, which mediates how they relate with others and their surroundings. Family, church attendees, friends, neighbors, cultural celebrations, hospitality, solidarity, empathy, and charity are tangible and intangible manifestations of *comunidad*.

This study suggests that because *comunidad* has a cultural and Christian meaning for SGPRs, it becomes a fundamental factor influencing their ethnic orientation and self-understanding. As previously discussed, LEIMs scholarship disputes either an ethnic development process (focusing on the self-understanding of how their ethnic and racial identity informs their decisions) or an ethnic status orientation (focusing on behaviors and attitudes). However, these SGPRs' stories and experiences suggest that both approaches could coexist and that Christian values may inform them.

For instance, considering content-oriented models, SGPRs' behaviors and attitudes toward *comunidad* are set as an initial orientation during their upbringings, which later will be internalized by the maturing individual. SGPRs are seemingly born into a sense of *comunidad* that enacts hospitality, setting a referential framework of attitudes and behaviors. Likewise, using the premise of process-oriented models, *comunidad* is externally defined by the family and surrounding network during the individual's upbringing, inaugurating the initial stage of ethnic identity development. SGPRs stories suggest that after traversing the multiple stages of ethnic development, individuals have internalized *comunidad* as part of their ethnic identity.

Therefore, both content-oriented and process-oriented models play an essential role in discerning SGPRs' ethnic identity distinctives. As we have observed with *comunidad,* it provides an early ethnoreligious orientation and a referential framework for life-long ethnic identity development. Therefore, new integrative perspectives of these models should be further explored.

Discussions of Findings, Missional Implications, and Conclusion

CHRISTIAN VALUES AND MEANING-MAKING

Equally important, another salient finding that merits discussion in this section is Christian values and meaning-making. Scholarship on LEIMs, notably the Lifespan Model of Latinx Ethnic Identity Development (LM-LEID), perceives meaning-making as a necessary process of self-awareness that generates belonging and strategies to make sense of the world. It is a process through which the individual gathers new ideas and behaviors and decides what to retain and leave as part of their racial and ethnic identity.[7] As discussed in previous chapters, Christian beliefs have been absent from this meaning-making discussion, particularly LEIMs. However, this study suggests that in the case of SGPRs, the meaning-making process conducive to racial and ethnic self-understanding and how to relate with the world seems to be filtered through Christian beliefs and values.

The four categories of enacted Christian beliefs this study identified are two associated with the racial and ethnic meaning-making process: (1) loving others and (2) justice. These suggest a compound meaning-making of cultural and Christian values stemming from SGPRs' upbringings and personal experiences.

According to the LMLEID, dissonance or disruptive events like racism or environmental change led to personal ethnic identity exploration and continuous meaning-making.[8] Some of these dissonant events were observed in stories such as Julio and Jessica facing racism and observing KKK manifestations at a very young age, respectively, and in Angel's awareness of his skin color while at the supermarket. Also, in Gustavo's experiences of micro-aggressions, in Grace's feelings of being profiled because of her curly hair and skin color, and in Carol and Phoebe's stories of facing discrimination at work for being Latinas. Some dissonances happened during the formative early years, while others later in life—nevertheless, both precipitate SGPRs to a meaning-making process founded on Christian beliefs.

When participants discuss Christian values aimed at loving others, they often connect with dissonance stories. For example, Carol processed her discrimination experience at work, concluding that she should love unconditionally and be tolerant and empathetic as a Christian. Grace understands that she must respond with love and Grace despite the profiling. Wendy started a women's ministry at her house, observing the pain inflicted by domestic violence. Julio embraces forgiveness amidst racist aggressions,

7. Torres et al., *Understanding the Latinx Experience*.
8. Torres et al., *Understanding the Latinx Experience*.

and Jessica finds respite care at the Latino/a(s) church to go back to her context and love people who wronged her. These stories focus on loving those who have wronged them. Moreover, they reveal how Christian beliefs and values help them cope and honor God through their relationships.

In addition to loving others, justice is another salient enacted Christian belief. Like loving others, justice stories relate to a continuous meaning-making process. Gustavo, Joanna, and Grace observe the social discrepancies and marginalization of minoritized groups in their midst and feel the urge to advocate with empathy. For SGPRs, this sense of responsibility stems from cultural formation and Christian beliefs. Specifically, this sense of responsibility can be seen in Gustavo's burden for other Latino/a(s) who struggle with documentation and poor working conditions and in Joanna's sense of justice that derives from the gospel and influences her work as a journalist. Also, this sense of responsibility can be observed in Grace's understanding of having an advocate in Jesus and wanting to emulate him where she lives, near the Mexico border.

Samuel Escobar states that the Christian belief in justice is one of the challenges the church in the United States must face, considering the increasing migration trend.[9] Escobar states that Christians must have a prophetic voice of justice and equality enacted as education, social assistance, and discipleship toward immigrants.[10] Additionally, Efraín Agosto asserts that Latino/a(s) prophetic voice of justice comes into being by the Scriptures with a sense of justice and a reclaiming of culture.[11] As observed in Gustavo's, Joanna's, and Grace's examples, the enactment of justice by SGPRs resembles that prophetic stance that originates from the Bible and a personal conviction of the gospel message toward other minoritized groups. Subsequently, it evidences a meaning-making process of who they are as SGPRs about others.

In all instances, and to summarize, SGPRs seem to understand that their Puerto Rican culture and Christian faith have given them lenses and tools for a continuous meaning-making process that empowers them to observe, connect, sympathize, and act in favor of others to strengthen their racial and ethnic self-understanding. In principle, this is congruent with the LMLEID meaning-making process that entails new ideas and behaviors to make sense of the world and retain or drop them as they positively

9. Escobar, "Migration."
10. Escobar, "Migration."
11. Agosto, "Reading the Word," 160.

Discussions of Findings, Missional Implications, and Conclusion

or negatively affect their racial and ethnic identity. However, as observed in this section, this study suggests that SGPRs committed to their Puerto Ricanness utilize their Christian beliefs and values to process new ideas and behaviors about their racial and ethnic identity and engage with them in their surroundings.

Furthermore, this study affirms the relationship other LEIM scholars have observed between positive self-esteem, a sense of well-being, and a committed racial and ethnic self-understanding.[12] However, it also adds to the body of knowledge by arguing that this positive self-esteem and well-being result from a committed racial and ethnic identity and the Christian beliefs and values influencing it. As it has been shown, SGPRs' experiences of dissonance and looping to meaning-making might create a decline in self-esteem and well-being. Still, their Christian beliefs and values help them reconfigure, reorient, and overcome. In short, there is seemingly a close relationship between SGPR's Christian values and their meaning-making process influencing ethnic self-understanding, behaviors, and attitudes.

Christian Beliefs and Sense of Belonging

After considering how Christian beliefs influence SGPRs' racial and ethnic self-understanding, this section discusses the sense of belonging. As stated in the introduction of this research, the social sciences have made significant contributions through LEIMs in understanding how Latino/a(s) develop their sense of membership and belonging in the continental United States. Yet, it has overlooked the influence of Christian beliefs on the sense of belonging. This section discusses SGPRs' sense of belonging to the American and Puerto Rican cultures and how their Christian beliefs and values influence them. The discussion includes the differences between AAC and ELC and SGPRs' meaning-making process.

GEOGRAPHICAL BELONGING

A place to start this discussion is considering the preponderance SGPRs give to the message of salvation in Jesus. As we have observed in chapter 5, sharing the gospel, the proclamation, and spreading of the Good News of Jesus has been present in SGPRs' upbringing. This could be observed in

---

12. Arce, "Reconsideration of Chicano Culture"; Bernal and Knight, *Ethnic Identity*; Knight et al., "Social Cognitive Model"; Keefe and Padilla, *Chicano Ethnicity*; Torres et al., *Understanding the Latinx Experience*.

Faithful Inheritances

James' remarks when he says, "making [Christ] known to others . . . in a Latino church, that was really important." Similarly, Gustavo recalls being so acquainted with the Great Commission that inviting and sharing his Christian faith was natural. The emphasis on salvation in and through Jesus, at church and home, has significantly influenced how SGPRs perceive their Christian beliefs, making it one of Christianity's central tenets.

These formative experiences during their upbringing naturally influenced how SGPRs perceive and conduct themselves in their contexts. As a result, they seem to be mindful of their God-given responsibility in their relationships. This can be seen in Mildred's comments on how the Christian belief of salvation in Jesus is central to how she relates with people daily and Jessica's understanding of the purpose and calling as a Puerto Rican to participate in God's redemptive plans among her relationships in the States and abroad. In sum, SGPRs' understandings of salvation and their role in sharing it suggest a correlation with their ethnic self-understanding and sense of belonging to their context in the continental United States.

Consequently, SGPRs perceive they belong to their surroundings in the continental United States through their Christian faith, specifically, a mission conviction. SGPRs understand that God has a purpose for them in their environment and conduct themselves out of a sense of mission. In turn, this sense of mission influences their sense of belonging in the United States. Some examples of this are Axel's expectations of God's use to impact his community. This sense of mission could also be observed through Andrés' remarks of Waukegan being a field to "expand God's kingdom" and through James and Carmen's feelings of connectedness to their cities through a sense of responsibility to engage with racial and social justice issues Christians. From these examples, it is apparent that SGPRs allude to having a sense of calling from God to their locations, a conviction and commitment to reach out with the gospel to those they regularly engage and make life with. This sense of calling translates into an increasing sense of belonging to their locations.

Another way SGPRs belong to the places they live, work, and study is through cultural enclaves and meaningful social relationships. This means that SGPRs will feel identified with their location depending on the surrounding places representing their culture and the social relationships they sustain. This can be observed in Carol's and Victoria's experiences in Boston and Orlando, respectively, and finding a sense of belonging to their locations by becoming acquainted with Puerto Rican restaurants and the

Discussions of Findings, Missional Implications, and Conclusion

city's Puerto Rican history and representation. Likewise, Ishmael's feelings of dislocation in Wisconsin are caused by his inability to find a specific Puerto Rican seasoning. Through these stories, participants shared how their sense of belonging to a location relates to the places that provide access to and validate certain areas of their culture. From culinary cultural expressions to a university class to a Puerto Rican or Latino/a(s) restaurant, participants looked for enclaves that validate their culture to identify with their location in the United States.

In tandem with cultural enclaves, social relationships also play an essential role in belonging. This is observed through Gustavo's and Raquel's remarks of belonging because they had family there, and the location was culturally diverse enough to invite them to build a relationship. In Raquel's words: "We always gravitate to find our culture wherever we went, and we found it." These relationships include family members or friends at work, neighborhood, school, and church.

In the same way, SGPRs' feelings of estrangement validate those elements that produce belonging to a place. This could be seen in Bryan's and Mildred's feelings of estrangement because they are minorities in his neighborhood and have difficulty building significant relationships. Similarly, in Grace's case, feeling invisible because she had no one who accepted nor validated her race and authentically cared for her. These examples of estrangement affirm that the absence of meaningful social networks that acknowledge and affirm SGPRs' ethnic and racial identity negatively influences their well-being and sense of belonging to their location.

Through these experiences, some influencing factors in belonging to a place are a conviction of a God-given mission to reach out to others with the message of Jesus Christ and the cultural acceptance and affirmation found in the locality and through meaningful social relationships. In addition, SGPRs tend to have a stronger sense of belonging in places with cultural, ethnic, and racial diversity. Lastly, these examples also suggest a correlation between belonging to a place and well-being.

As noted in chapter 2, LEIMs scholarship sustains that a person's self-understanding and sense of belonging relates to a particular group as part of the larger society. But, equally important, it was also noted that LEIMs do not account for religion's influence on self-understanding and belonging. In other words, LEIMs focus on belonging to the what, not necessarily the where and how. The discussion sustained in this subsection complexifies this understanding. It suggests a broader relationship between people's

Faithful Inheritances

self-understanding and sense of belonging, not only to a group (the what) but also to a place (the where), both mediated by their Christian beliefs (the how). More succinctly, there are nuances to the sense of belonging, of which Christian beliefs and place are a part.

For instance, López Santiago's spatial analysis of *The Memoirs of Bernardo Vega* suggests that belonging corresponds to the combination of city, friendship, and meaning.[13] These three elements, in turn, correspond to the where, what, and how, respectively. Similarly, for SGPRs, belonging to their location in the United States (the where) encompasses other elements, such as a sense of mission derived from their Christian beliefs (the how) and the cultural acceptance and affirmation found in the locality and through meaning social relationships (the what). The result of these elements combined, as exemplified in *The Memoirs of Bernardo Vega*, is a deep sense of belonging, which López Santiago defines as place-making and community.[14]

Cultural Belonging

Another salient aspect of belonging is how SGPRs relate to American and Puerto Rican cultures. Participants were not asked to define what they understood by American mainstream culture; this was left open to observe their understanding through their stories. It is essential to note that when SGPRs refer to the American mainstream culture, they do so mainly in racial terms. Javier, for example, talks about his "white side," referring to the way he engages with the American majority culture at work. Angel and Sonia shared how their experiences at the supermarket or work require ethnic and racial self-awareness, primarily because Anglo-Americans predominantly comprise those settings. Finally, through Carol's and Gustavo's code-switching, they understand how the Spanish language has been racialized in their workplace and church environments.

SGPRs learn to strategize and negotiate between both cultures depending on their context. For example, in a predominantly Anglo-American environment, most SGPRs refrain from being overly enthusiastic, gesturing with their hands while talking, or using Spanish because it could distract some people around them. This could be observed in Gustavo's struggles at church, trying not to use any Spanish terms and controlling his gestures to ensure no one is offended. In the same way, Carol assesses her audience

---

13. López Santiago, "Geography of Bernardo Vega's Memoirs."
14. López Santiago, "Geography of Bernardo Vega's Memoirs," 161–74.

Discussions of Findings, Missional Implications, and Conclusion

before introducing herself, saying her name in Spanish or English. Also, Angel's continuous awareness as a "brown person with a beard" is shopping at Publix. These SGPR stories reveal how strategizing and negotiating take shape through self-awareness and self-restrictions, creating certain boundaries for their ethnic and racial expressions.

A second way SGPRs relate to the American mainstream is to defer to it. When SGPRs are mindful of their ethnic and racial differences in a predominantly Anglo-American context, they tend to strategize deferring to the American mainstream. An example is when Carol shares about interacting with colleagues at work; she uses particular vocabulary to engage with them. Similarly, Javier says he uses specific vocabulary to earn the regard of his Anglo-American peers. On the other hand, when in a predominantly Puerto Rican or Latino/a(s) environment, SGPRs allow their ethnic and racial expressions to show. Carol refers to this filtering as a strategy to connect with other Latino/a(s), while Javier has space to express his Puerto Rican heritage.

It is important to note that this process of strategizing and negotiating also occurs when SGPRs interact with predominantly Puerto Rican or Latino/a(s) contexts. For example, Carmen feels lost among other Puerto Ricans and Latino/a(s) because of her limited Spanish proficiency. Therefore, her strategy is to retract from potential settings where people may expect something from her because she is Puerto Rican.

Considering how SGPR strategizes and negotiates between cultures, it can be argued that it is a continuous belonging endeavor. SGPRs understand themselves as Puerto Ricans (ethnically) and Americans (citizenship), yet their sense of belonging to these cultures requires choosing one over the other depending on their setting. For SGPRs, one culture will always be virtually contested, making the sense of belonging uncertain. This state is what scholars disclose as in-betweenness or liminality.[15]

However, not all the strategizing and negotiation involves choosing or filtering ethnic and racial expressions. Some SGPRs have decided to stop modifying or adapting their behavior and have embraced both cultures. Both Julio and Raquel aim at Christlikeness to overcome the ethnic and racial tensions of choosing one culture or the other. Jessica considers herself affiliated in heart, mind, and soul to her Puerto Rican and American identities. She

---

15. Crespo, *Being Latino in Christ*; Conde-Frazier and Lee, "Intergenerational and Intercultural Issues"; Martínez, Juan Francisco, "Historical Reflections."

believes God has given her both cultures; therefore, she does not have to choose between them, nor will she allow others to choose for her.

Again, the stance acquired by these SGPRs finds its roots in Christian beliefs and resonates with Crespo's argument on wholeness in Latino/a(s) ethnic and racial identity through God.[16] As discussed in chapter 2, Crespo believes that a robust ethnic affirmation stems from obedience to Jesus' commandment of loving others as yourself.[17] Similarly, embracing and affirming both cultures also honors Christ's commandment. It provides them with a defined and stable sense of belonging in which they can be free to be from two cultures in any context or setting without neglecting or contesting one another. Further research is needed to investigate the emergence of a hybrid culture rather than biculturalism.

The LMLEID suggests a bicultural-informed Latino identity recourse to a Latino or Anglo orientation as a coping strategy.[18] However, this study suggests that bicultural individuals draw and strategize from Latino/a(s) and Anglo-American cultural elements. Still, some also find no need to negotiate between cultures because their Christian faith helps them cope with the social complexities. Moreover, the individual is released from the self-filtering caused by dissonant events, and their Christian beliefs take their place.

SGPRs inherit a rich tapestry of faith and cultural practices from their ancestors. This inheritance is not merely a static set of traditions but a living, dynamic force that shapes their identity and interactions within their congregations. For many SGPRs, their Christian faith is deeply intertwined with their cultural heritage, creating a unique blend that informs their worldview and sense of belonging. This dual inheritance often requires SGPRs to engage in a continuous process of negotiation and adaptation, balancing the expectations of their ethnic community with those of their faith community.

The dual identities of SGPRs in AAC and ELC present unique challenges and opportunities. In AAC contexts, SGPRs often navigate their ethnic identity by adopting a more assimilated approach, sometimes feeling pressured to minimize their cultural distinctiveness to fit in. Conversely, in ELC settings, there is a more robust affirmation of their Latino/a(s) heritage, where cultural practices and language are celebrated and integrated into worship.

---

16. Crespo, *Being Latino in Christ*.
17. Crespo, *Being Latino in Christ*, 92.
18. Torres et al., *Understanding the Latinx Experience*.

Discussions of Findings, Missional Implications, and Conclusion

This duality influences their participation in church activities, with SGPRs in AACs potentially experiencing a form of cultural dissonance that affects their engagement. At the same time, those in ELCs find a sense of solidarity and support that enhances their involvement. Understanding these dynamics is crucial for church leaders aiming to create inclusive environments that respect and affirm the ethnic and religious identities of SGPRs.

In summary, this subsection discussed the relationship between Christian beliefs and belonging to a location and its relation to SGPRs' ethnic and racial identity. SGPRs have a more profound sense of belonging to their location when they are convinced of a God-given mission and are surrounded by ethnic and race-affirming social relationships. Lastly, this section also suggests that bicultural negotiation strategies vary in the sense of belonging and highlights Christian beliefs as a significant influencer on coping strategies. As a result, we may conclude that a more comprehensive understanding of ethnic and racial identity construction and maintenance should also consider the individual's religious beliefs and formation, geographical awareness, and social relationships.

MISSIOLOGICAL EXAMINATION OF FINDINGS AND IMPLICATIONS

After discussing and analyzing the relationships between Christian beliefs and ethnic self-understanding and sense of belonging, this section delves into the missiological discussions and implications of the study. The discussion is divided into two subsections: (1) how SGPRs understand and participate in the Great Commission and (2) the church's role in the sense of belonging. Significant differences between AAC and ELC are discussed within each subsection.

Understanding and Participation in Mission

SGPRs understand the Great Commission as an act of obedience that all Christians are called to through their gifts, talents, and circles of influence. For them, it is more of a personal responsibility and obedience than a corporate one. Also, as discussed in chapter 6, for SGPRs personally, it is less of an evangelistic endeavor or missions abroad and more of a way of life amid their circles of influence. This can be observed in Nelly's comments on a personal calling from Christ to share his message with co-workers, family, and neighbors with whom she constantly relates. It is the same with Angel,

Faithful Inheritances

who sees his participation in the Great Commission as a conversation about Jesus in the supermarket. Also, Julio's awareness is to reach out to his children and family. These SGPRs' experiences and conversations suggest that they still value the Great Commission as cross-cultural missions abroad and evangelism, yet they own it as a way of life. It has moved from being exclusively a calling to some who have evangelist giftings to a personal endeavor that can be embraced and normalized out of their giftings.

Also, SGPRs understand their participation in the Great Commission as intentionally and authentically developing conversations, relationships, and friendships with non-Christians and people with other religious beliefs. An example of this is Raquel's commitment to her non-Christian friends and interest in their inner lives so that they can move one step closer to God. It is the same with Carol and Ishmael, who have had opportunities to establish inter-faith dialogues based on authenticity and understanding. These examples suggest that SGPRs see value in connecting respectfully with those with a different worldview and valuing the relationship over the differences.

Furthermore, SGPRs' stories suggest that their hospitable and relational cultural formation has equipped them to sustain inter-faith engagements through friendship. All the interviewees with inter-faith dialogues could nurture meaningful conversations through genuine friendship (i.e., Ishmael establishing a relationship with his Muslim friend). The experiences SGPRs have with other faiths come naturally through their social networks outside the church. They do not necessarily try to connect with people from different faiths to gain them for Christ or evangelize them. They are aware of their witnessing responsibility, but they see it as an organic consequence of their Christian lifestyle (i.e., Carol's remarks of Christianity being shoved down the throat and Carol's take on witnessing through action). SGPRs seem to draw from their ethnic and racial formation and Christian values to participate in the Great Commission with authentic inclusion and understanding of the other's differences.

This understanding of obeying Jesus' command in Matthew 28:18–20 aligns with Elizondo's *mestizo* theology, which states second-generation Latino/a(s) are rightly equipped for intercultural encounters because of their liminal ethnic and racial identity.[19] As discussed in chapter 2, Elizondo sustains that Jesus himself traversed an alienating experience of ethnicity and place of origin from dominant groups when he made Galilee his home

19. Elizondo, "Jesus the Galilean Jew."

Discussions of Findings, Missional Implications, and Conclusion

and eventually launched ground to his ministry.[20] Considering Elizondo's Galilean paradigm, SGPRs are strategically positioned as Jesus' followers mediate, reach, and reconcile from the in-betweenness yet access circles others cannot.

Lastly, SGPRs understand their participation in the Great Commission as serving others in their vicinity. This is either through connecting with school boards and community organizations (i.e., Andrés' church's vision) or finding opportunities to help them at their workplace (i.e., Joanna's anecdote of sharing the hope of the gospel to ex-drug addicts). SGPRs consider serving the community as a response to the Great Commission. Service does not need to be overtly evangelistic but driven by their convictions of a transformative gospel that can permeate multiple societal layers. This community investment is something that Chen and Jeung have also observed while researching Latino/a(s) immigrant Christian communities.[21] They contend that "faith, religion, and ethnic identity come together . . . peoples informed by their faith articulate their identities by engaging their social locations within the larger society."[22] In Andrés' terms, the church should be multiplied in as many places as possible.

In short, SGPR's understanding and participation in the Great Commission do not follow the conventional definition from their upbringings of missions abroad, door-to-door evangelism, and handing out tracts. Instead, participation in the Great Commission is relational and quotidian. It is expressed in reaching out to co-workers, family, and friends conversely and with genuine value.

The Role of the Local Church in the Sense of Belonging

Belonging Through Participation

Early in this chapter, it was argued that SGPRs have a higher sense of belonging to their location through a conviction of calling from God to engage and serve in their communities. The local church is the primary means to do so. Therefore, the church plays a vital role in SGPRs' sense of belonging by providing and facilitating opportunities to participate and serve. As we will observe, SGPRs' sense of belonging to the church is correlated with their sense of belonging to their geographical location.

---

20. Elizondo, "Jesus the Galilean Jew."
21. Chen and Jeung, *Sustaining Faith Traditions*.
22. Chen and Jeung, *Sustaining Faith Traditions*, 95.

Faithful Inheritances

When SGPRs have opportunities to serve in some ministry, activity, or event at their local churches, they feel they belong to the local church. This suggests a direct relationship between inclusion through service and a sense of belonging and commitment to the community of faith and their geographical location. This can be observed in Axel's and Nelly's experiences of feeling included and sensing God's love and purpose when they were approached by church staff and asked to join a ministry in their local church. Also, Carmen's remarks of never feeling she belonged to a church during her college years because of her lack of participation and involvement. This changed in her current local church, where she feels needed and invited to participate.

SGPRs attending AAC and ELC reported participating at their local churches by serving the church community in different capacities, such as in pastoral and leadership roles (i.e., Bryan, Gustavo, James, and Carmen), greeters, and hospitality (i.e., Joanna and Axel), worship team (i.e., Victoria and Sonia), media and communication team (Sofía and Ramón), and teaching and discipleship (i.e., Mildred, Nelly, Ishmael, and Andrés). Through these ministries and serving teams, SGPRs can create relational bonds that strengthen their sense of belonging to their geographical locations.

Obstacles to Belonging and Participation

Although SGPRs attending AAC and ELC reported participation at church, only ELC attendees reported having opportunities to serve in church ministries designed to reach others outside the church. No SGPR attending AAC reported being involved in outreach ministry. Some examples of these ministries are Wendy's ministry for women who have suffered domestic violence and Javier's involvement in the local community. This finding contrasts with the sense of mission concerning the gospel proclamation that SGPRs have since they have to their locations. Therefore, it can be argued that AAC does not provide nor facilitate a structure allowing SGPRs to respond to their sense of mission outside the church actively.

The complete understanding of why AAC limits from SGPRs agency is potential material for further research. Nevertheless, SGPRs attending AAC shared some of the obstacles they have faced in participation: (1) warring preconceptions and race issues, (2) a rigid approach to ministry, and (3) a different sense of *comunidad*. This first obstacle can be observed in Jessica's and Bryan's statements that participation in AAC, particularly in outward-oriented ministries, is racialized. In Jessica's words, her appropriation of

Discussions of Findings, Missional Implications, and Conclusion

participation in the mission was suppressed by an "intellectual colonialization of thinking that they [AAC] were the better race." In turn, Bryan states that Latino/a(s) are perceived as not having the credentials, education, or experience to participate. In Rodriguez's terms, they are "outsiders in the churches of the dominant group."[23] Their remarks allude to Escobar's observations and challenges regarding the history of social and cultural issues affecting the relationship of the AAC with Latino/a(s) and the who and how to do mission.[24]

The second obstacle to participation in AAC is that SGPRs perceive it as a rigid ministry approach. Bryan and Angel shared that they have differences with the AAC leadership in the way they do evangelism and outreach among Latino/a(s). Bryan argued toward a relational approach, while his AAC used a corporate evangelism approach, meaning that the latter expected a particular relationship between monetary investment and growth. Angel, in turn, complained about his AAC missing opportunities because of their uncertainty on how to relate with Latino/a(s) and expect to have everything figured out.

The third obstacle to participation is a different perception of the community. As suggested, SGPRs conceive *comunidad* as a cultural and Christian heritage they received and embraced, which mediates the way they relate with others and their surroundings. It is a source of meaning that binds and affirms their cultural heritage and Christian beliefs. SGPRs attending AAC struggle to find *comunidad* in their churches due to a lack of understanding and affirmation of their ethnic and racial identity. Therefore, it affects their participation, commitment, and sense of belonging. Jessica explains the difference in doing *comunidad* in either life-giving (Latino/a(s) congregations) or life-draining (AAC). It can also be seen in James' statement that faith and community align within the Puerto Rican culture but not in the AAC, where the community is individualistic. This does not mean that AACs have a non-biblical grasp of faith and community but that their cultural understanding presumably depends on how ministry and mission are conducted.

These obstacles indicate a lack of ethnic and racial sensitivity within these AACs. As a result, SGPRs experience estrangement from the church community and their surroundings. Furthermore, it can also be argued that SGPRs attending AAC could be perceived as recipients but rarely as

23. Rodríguez, "Becoming All Things," 211.
24. Escobar, "Migration."

Faithful Inheritances

mission agents. Manuel Ortiz foresaw and warned about this issue, saying that second-generation Latino/a(s) are looking for an affirmation and a place to express their ethnic and racial identity.[25] That tensions or perceptions of superiority and inferiority will only act to the detriment of the church's growth and the spreading of the gospel.[26]

It must be clarified that this does not mean that the church is the only place where SGPRs find agency. We have observed that SGPRs demonstrate agency and a sense of mission in their workplaces, neighborhoods, and schools. Yet, they do so out of a personal conviction and sense of responsibility as Christians, not because they are commissioned and supported by their local churches.

Belonging through Comunidad

These obstacles contrast with the experience of SGPRs attending ELC, who describe their church communities like family. However, ELC is not necessarily a place where culture and traditions are preserved, such as in first-generation Latino/a(s) churches.[27] The sense of having a church family is indeed something transferred and preserved by SGPRs. However, as discussed in chapter 5, this sense of belonging to a church family does not indicate service or ministerial contribution. Instead, it is relational and theological—which are attributes of *comunidad*.

ELCs provide SGPRs with a relational network that touches multiple aspects and seasons of a life lived together. This is observed in Joanna recounting significant life events at church, such as her baptism, marriage, and baby presentation. Another example was Victoria's sense of support and encouragement through calls, messages, and prayers while studying abroad. These gestures make her feel loved and known, just as family does. Like Victoria, Javier expressed feeling the loving care of his church during a rough season when his wife had a miscarriage. During that time, he described this community as empathetic and understanding, giving them presence and space when needed. From a vantage point, it is the antithesis of James' view of the AAC individualistic community. These examples reveal that the sense of belonging SGPRs derive within their ELCs is directly related to journeying together, which serves as a binding agent of *comunidad*.

---

25. Ortíz, *Hispanic Challenge*.
26. Ortíz, *Hispanic Challenge*, 82–87, 115.
27. Calvillo and Bailey, "Latino Religious Affiliation."

Discussions of Findings, Missional Implications, and Conclusion

As observed in chapter 5, some of the most salient distinctives of these ELCs are humility, love, hospitality, and forgiveness. SGPRs are registered as recipients and agents of these at any given point as part of their ELCs. A common denominator of these attributes is that they are all Christian values that cannot be self-consumed; they must be given to others. Therefore, they demand a relationship and a community. In other words, humility, love, hospitality, and forgiveness are intrinsic distinctives of the SGPR concept of *comunidad*.

These Christian beliefs add to Martínez's observations of faith and hope as the two salient Christian beliefs in the Latino/a(s) cultures.[28] It is unclear if Martínez's observations apply to first-generation Latino/a(s) in particular or all Latino/a(s) in general. Nevertheless, the differences still stand, mainly that faith and hope are Christian beliefs placed in God, while humility, love, hospitality, and forgiveness are vested in others. Yet, what they all have in common is that they all create a unifying sense of *comunidad*.

In summary, this section of missiological discussions and implications suggests that SGPRs attending AAC and ELC experience a strong sense of belonging to their churches and surrounding environments through inclusion, participation, and service in the church. The concept of faithful inheritances is particularly relevant when considering the missiological implications of this study. SGPRs bring with them a legacy of faith that is deeply rooted in their cultural history. This legacy influences their missional perception and engagement. In ELCs, this inheritance often manifests in a solid commitment to community and cultural preservation, which fuels their participation in church activities and outreach programs. In AACs, SGPRs may advocate for greater cultural sensitivity and inclusivity, drawing on their inherited values to bridge cultural gaps and foster a more inclusive community.

Conversely, SGPRs attending AAC perceive alienation and estrangement from their church community and the surrounding environment when their ethnic and racial identity is not affirmed or validated at their local church. Meanwhile, SGPRs attending ELC disclose a deep sense of belonging to their churches through *comunidad* and family. Moreover, the relationships SGPRs sustain at their ELCs provide a space where their ethnic and racial identity is uncontested, and life is lived together in *comunidad*.

---

28. Martínez, *Walk with the People*.

Faithful Inheritances

CONCLUSION

In summary, the findings underscore the significance of faithful inheritances in shaping the identities and lives of SGPRs. These inheritances are not static but are dynamically engaged with and adapted by SGPRs as they navigate their dual identities within AAC and ELC contexts. Future research should continue to explore how these inheritances evolve and influence new generations. By recognizing and honoring these faithful inheritances, church leaders can create more inclusive and supportive environments that celebrate their congregants' rich cultural and religious heritage.

This section will conclude the study by summarizing the key findings related to its scope and questions. It will also explain the study's value and contribution to the current literature and propose opportunities for further research.

Contributions to Current Literature

This research investigated how Christian beliefs influence SGPRs' ethnic self-understanding and sense of belonging. It was based on qualitative research, including twenty-seven participants attending Protestant AAC and ELC in the United States. The interviews were semi-structured, constantly prompting stories analyzed through three coding cycles designed for narrative scrutiny. The results suggest that Christian beliefs are present in SGPRs' upbringings through various cultural elements and traditions, providing a referential meaning-making framework to understand their ethnic and racial identity concerning others and their surroundings.

First, this research adds to the current literature to better understand the relationship between the Christian faith and ethnic and racial identity formation. During SGPRs' upbringings, Christian beliefs and values such as *comunidad*, hospitality, showing love and empathy to others, respect for parents, high regard for Christian education, and prayer were instilled at home and reinforced at church. In addition, cultural and traditional celebrations, such as *Las Navidades*, were opportunities for *comunidad* and proclaiming the gospel message. Consequently, SGPRs grew up connecting cultural elements with their Christian faith in an ethnoreligious formation. As adults, SGPRs enact these Christian beliefs and values daily, using them to make sense of their world.

The second contribution of this study is that SGPRs' cultural and Christian understanding of *comunidad* permeates the sense of belonging

Discussions of Findings, Missional Implications, and Conclusion

to their places of residence, workplace, school, and society. SGPRs relate and identify with their surroundings through a sense of mission and responsibility to reach others with the gospel message, cultural enclaves, and an affirming diverse *comunidad* of friends and family. Because SGPRs notion of *comunidad* is composed of cultural and theological elements, the local church tends to perform an adhesive or non-adhesive role in their sense of belonging. SGPRs attending AAC who reported a lack of participation, ethnoracial understanding, and *comunidad* at church also reported estrangement from their surroundings. In contrast, SGPRs attending ELC who stated high levels of participation, ethnoracial affirmation, and *comunidad* also described having a strong sense of belonging to their churches and locations.

These contributions add to the social sciences LEIM literature suggesting that Christian beliefs and values are part of SGPRs' continuous meaning-making process when dissonance is produced, and ethnic and racial identity is contested. The authority of Christian beliefs in constructing and maintaining ethnic and racial identity is manifested in SGPRs' relationship with others and their geographical location. This indicates a more rounded sense of belonging to people, places, and religious beliefs. This becomes even more meaningful considering that SGPRs sense of *comunidad* presumably permeates all LMLEID stages and remains pivotal to their continuous meaning-making.

Mission Studies Contributions

One missiological contribution of this research concerns how the gospel paves its way through the intricacies of Puerto Rican culture. For example, Christian and non-Christian Puerto Ricans greatly appreciate hospitality and religious celebrations—*Las Navidades*. These cultural markers represent potential mission enclaves. Moreover, since Puerto Ricans generally accept and practice these cultural markers, they represent a seed of the gospel waiting to be cultivated from a young age to adulthood and across generations.

Another contribution to mission studies is SGPRs' understanding and participation in the Great Commission as personal and relational, which is to be practiced daily yet influenced by their ecclesial context. SGPRs draw from their Christian values and cultural formation to interact with people around them despite their religious beliefs and cultures. However, they do so out of a personal conviction and response to Jesus' command, not necessarily because their churches commission, support, or encourage them.

Faithful Inheritances

AACs should be more intentional in encouraging and giving agency to SGPRs to engage in ministries that serve in and outside the church. This will help them feel more connected to their faith community and location.

A third missiological contribution is understanding how SGPRs perceive their sense of belonging, and ethnic self-understanding has practical and theological applications to the church and its ministries through *comunidad*. *Comunidad* emerged as the tangible and intangible element where SGPRs expressions between culture and Christian beliefs converge. It is both a goal and a mean, as it is a group of people and a set of beliefs. Moreover, it is a way to relate with others and witness others. *Comunidad* provides a sense of belonging, affirming and validating ethnic and racial identity. It is rooted in a theological understanding of a Christian community that shares Christian beliefs and values, such as hospitality and justice, and the complexities of a journey together. In short, despite their ethnic and racial composition, Christian faith communities should pay attention to the cultural and theological roots of *comunidad* if they want to serve faithfully, empower, and commission SGPRs in their midst.

Lastly, the findings from this study offer practical missiological implications for church leaders seeking to create more inclusive environments. For AACs, it is essential to recognize and celebrate the cultural diversity within their congregations. This can be achieved through incorporating Latino/a(s) cultural elements into worship services, providing opportunities for cultural exchange, and offering support groups for SGPRs to share their experiences. For ELCs, maintaining and enhancing cultural traditions while integrating elements of the broader community can strengthen the sense of belonging and participation. Training programs for church leaders on cultural competence and sensitivity can further enhance these efforts, ensuring that all congregants feel valued and included. By taking these steps, churches can better support the dual identities of SGPRs, fostering environments where their faithful inheritances are honored and nurtured.

Further Research

While this study has provided valuable insights into the experiences of second-generation Puerto Ricans (SGPRs), it is crucial to recognize the broader context of second-generation Latino/a(s) and the need for nuanced research based on their specific countries of origin. Each Latino/a(s) group, whether Mexican, Dominican, Salvadoran, or others, brings unique cultural, historical, and sociopolitical contexts that influence their religious

Discussions of Findings, Missional Implications, and Conclusion

and ethnic identities. Although some aspects of second-generation experiences are transferable across different Latino/a(s) communities, such as the challenges of navigating dual identities and cultural dissonance, the distinct heritage of each group can lead to different dynamics and outcomes.

For instance, the historical relationship between Puerto Rico and the United States shapes the identity and sense of belonging of Puerto Ricans in a unique way, different from the experiences of Mexicans or Central Americans. Research into these nuances can uncover specific factors influencing ethnic self-understanding, sense of belonging, and religious engagement. To capture these differences accurately, future studies must disaggregate data and focus on individual national groups within the Latino diaspora.

Moreover, this study did not delve into the potential theological nuances of the different SGPRs Protestant Christian traditions. For example, some traditions may emphasize discipleship, others on social justice, and others on evangelism. Therefore, the findings obtained through this study are broad and general. Further research could benefit from exploring specific Christian traditions influencing ethnoreligious formation. Understanding how these different theological emphases shape the identities and community involvement of SGPRs can provide deeper insights and more tailored support.

Additionally, this study suggests that the Latino/a(s) Ethnic Identity Models (LEIM) scholarship should creatively integrate various academic disciplines, such as theology and geography, to expand its understanding of a possible emergence of spatial hybrid cultures rather than bicultural ones. This interdisciplinary approach can uncover how physical spaces and geographical contexts influence the cultural and religious practices of second-generation Latino/a(s). Exploring these spatial hybrid cultures can offer new perspectives on how second-generation Latino/a(s) communities adapt and evolve in diverse environments.

Understanding these nuances can help develop targeted interventions and support systems within congregations and broader community settings. Church leaders and policymakers can benefit from this nuanced understanding by creating more inclusive environments that honor their congregants' specific cultural and historical backgrounds. This approach enhances the sense of belonging for second-generation Latino/a(s) and enriches the cultural fabric of the faith communities they are part of.

In summary, future research should delve deeper into the unique experiences of second-generation Latino/a(s) from various countries of

Faithful Inheritances

origin, acknowledging the transferable aspects and the distinct elements that shape their identities. Doing so can foster a more comprehensive and inclusive understanding of the Latino/a(s) experience in the United States.

Appendix A

Letter of Informed Consent

Dear participant,

MY NAME IS YAMIL Acevedo and I am a Ph.D. Candidate at Trinity International University in Deerfield, Illinois, U.S.A. Thank you for your willingness to participate in this research designed to explore the influence of Christian beliefs in the ethnic self-understanding and sense of belonging of second-generation Puerto Ricans. I will ask some questions to lead a conversation on this topic with the aim of hearing your personal experiences and stories. Your thoughts and insights will help me learn how second-generation Puerto Ricans process and give meaning to their life experiences, relationships, and environment.

All the information that you provide will be held in strict confidence. Your name will not be reported, nor connected, with your experiences. All participants will be identified by number Please know that your participation in this research is entirely voluntary and you are free to withdraw at any time during this study.

The interview may last up to ninety minutes. With your consent the interview will be recorded on my phone, digital audio recorder, or in my computer (in the case of video). These recordings will be transcribed after the interview for data analysis purposes. Audio and video files will be deleted at the end of the research process. Also with your permission, I will take notes during the interview to keep track of my personal thoughts, feelings, impressions, ideas, and questions.

Thank you once again for your participation in this research.
Kind regards,
Yamil Acevedo

Appendix A

By signing this consent form, I acknowledge that I have read and understand the above information, and have had the opportunity to ask questions. I voluntarily agree to participate in this study under the conditions described.

_____   _____
Print Name and Signature   Date

Appendix B

Interview Protocol and Guidelines

THIS SECTION PROVIDES A tentative plan for personal interviews. The aim of these guidelines is to make sure that the interview stories stay on topic and respond to the RQs in a way in which rich data could be retrieved. The researcher acknowledges that the participants' stories may relate to more than one of the RQs. Therefore, when the conversation allows it, the researcher will inquire further on these stories to reveal the presence of Christian beliefs, the ethnic self-understanding, and belonging. Depending on the circumstances and emerging themes, order, fluidity, adaptations, omissions, and revisions to these guidelines may be expected; consequently, not all questions will be asked.

Three main research questions guide this investigation. First, how do second-generation Puerto Ricans understand the relationship between their Christian beliefs and their ethnic self-identification? Interview questions one to three will cover this research question. Secondly, how do Christian beliefs influence the way(s) in which second-generation Puerto Ricans relate with the continental United States context? Interview questions four to seven will address this second research question. Finally, how do second-generation Puerto Ricans understand their participation in the mission of God? Interview questions eight to ten will explore this last research question. The researcher will ask the participants to consider each of the following questions in light of their personal experience, and provide an answer along with a personal story that illustrates best their answer.

The interview opening has a brief introduction explaining the methodology that will be used to facilitate the conversation. At the end of the interview the researcher will once again thank the participants for their help and time devoted to the interview. Then the researcher will ask them

Appendix B

if there is anything else they would like to add, and provide them with the researcher's email address in the event of future concerns, questions, or additional information.

PERSONAL INFORMATION

1. Name
2. Email
3. Age
4. Gender
5. Marital status
6. Place of birth
7. Place of residence
8. Educational background
9. Professional occupation
10. Do you identify yourself as a practicing Christian within the Protestant traditions?
11. Religious affiliation
12. Congregation ethnic composition: (1) predominant Anglo American, (2) predominant Latino/a(s) English-speaking, or (3) other.

PERSONAL INTERVIEW GUIDELINES

Thank you for your willingness to participate in this research. During this interview one of my main goals is that I would like to get to know you better. To facilitate this conversation, I will ask you to consider each question in light of your personal experience, and as you answer, share a personal story that illustrates your answer. I want you to feel comfortable in sharing, as specifically as you can, not only your stories, but also your perceptions, feelings, ideas, motives, inspirations, and ultimately anything that will help in the understanding of who you are as a Puerto Rican and a Christian.

1. Let us start this conversation talking about your upbringings as a second-generation Puerto Rican. Share with me the story of your upbringings as you answer the following questions:

Interview Protocol and Guidelines

- 1.1. What was it like growing up as a second-generation Puerto Rican in the United States? (Note: Prompt for story.)
- 1.2. What were some Puerto Rican traditions that were transferred to you at home? Christian beliefs? (Note: Prompt for story.)

2. I would like to hear your stories on being second-generation Puerto Rican and Christian. Consider the following questions:

    - 2.1. How would you describe yourself as a Christian? Ethnically? Any stories that could represent your answers? (Note: Prompt for stories.)
    - 2.2. What relationships do you observe between your Puerto Rican ethnic identity and Christianity? (Note: Prompt for story.)

3. I would like you to consider this question: As a second-generation Puerto Rican, what Christian beliefs are significant to you? Why?

    - 3.1. Could you think and share any personal story that could illustrate this best? (For example, it could be a story of achievement, adversity, or even a meaningful decision made.)

4. Let us move now into stories that illustrate how is it for you, as a second-generation Puerto Rican, to living in the United States. We will follow the same format we have used so far, questions and stories. Take your time to consider the following questions:

    - 4.1. As a second-generation Puerto Rican, how do you identify with the place you live in the United States? Do you feel that you belong? What do you appreciate the most? What do you dislike?
    - 4.2. Now, could you think of a story that could represent your answers? (Note: Prompt for story.)

5. On a similar note, how do you identify with the church you attend? Do you feel that you belong? What do you appreciate the most? What do you dislike?

    - 5.1. Now, could you think of a story that represent your answers? (Note: Prompt for story.)

6. Now, in terms of cultures, as a second-generation Puerto Rican, how do you relate to the American mainstream culture and the Puerto Rican Culture? (Note: Prompt for story.)

Appendix B

7. Before we move to the last part of this interview, I would like to know, what is(are) the Christian belief(s) that describes best your life in the United States? Why? (Note: Prompt for story.)

    7.1. Now, could you think of a story that represent your answer?

8. In this last part of the interview I would like your to share some stories about your life as a Christian. Please, consider the following questions:

    8.1. What are your priorities as a Christian, and, why? (Note: Prompt for story.)

9. Share with me a story that illustrates your understanding and participation in what is commonly known as, the Great Commission.

10. What is your participation at church? How are you connected to your church? (Note: Prompt for stories.)

Thank you, so much, for your time and willingness to participate in this interview. Is there anything else you would like to add? Are there any questions? Please, take note of my email address in the event of any future concern, question, or additional information.

Appendix C

List of Participants[1]

ID	Interview date	Pseudonym	Gender	Age group	Congreg.	Christian Tradition / Theological Stream	State of Residence	Standard Occupation Class*
1	9/10/2020	Grace	F	18–25	Anglo American	Nondenom. Evangelical	TX	Student
2	9/14/2020	James	M	26–30	Anglo American	Nondenom. Evangelical	WI	Educational Instruction and Library
3	9/16/2020	Angel	F	46–50	Anglo American	Mainline Reformed	FL	Management
4	9/17/2020	Gustavo	M	26–30	Anglo American	Evangelical	NJ	Personal Care and Service
5	9/19/2020	Raquel	F	41–45	Anglo American	Mainline Reformed	FL	Educational Instruction and Library
6	9/24/2020	Julio	M	56–up	Anglo American	Reformed	FL	Legal
7	9/24/2020	Andrés	M		Latino/a	Pentecostal	IL	Personal Care and Service
8	10/5/2020	Sonia	F	18–25	Anglo American	Nondenom. Evangelcal	TX	Student

1. Standard Occupational Classifications as of 2018 U.S. Bureau of Labor Statistics (https://www.bls.gov/soc/2018/major_groups.htm#21-000). Student and Unemployed classifications were ascribed by the researcher.

Appendix C

ID	Interview date	Pseudonym	Gender	Age group	Congreg.	Christian Tradition / Theological Stream	State of Residence	Standard Occupation Class*
9	10/8/2020	Victoria	F	26–30	Latino/a	Mainline Evangelical	FL	Student
10	10/16/2020	Carmen	F	26–30	Anglo American	Mainline Evangelical	TN	Arts, Design, Entertain., Sports, Media
11	10/21/2020	Sandy	F	50–55	Latino/a	Nondenom. Evangelical	MA	Unemployed
12	10/22/2020	Carol	F	26–30	Latino/a	Mainline Reformed	MA	Legal
13	10/22/2020	Javier	M	41–45	Latino/a	Evangelical	MA	Architecture and Engineering
14	10/29/2020	Ramon	M	41–45	Anglo American	Nondenom. Evangelical	IL	Business and Financial Operations
15	10/29/2020	Phoebe	F	31–35	Anglo American	Mainline Reformed	VA	Arts, Design, Entertain., Sports, Media
16	10/29/2020	Juan	M	26–30	Latino/a	Pentecostal	IL	Business and Financial Operations
17	11/4/2020	Jessica	F	51–55	Anglo American	Evangelical	IN	Educational Instruction and Library
18	11/7/2020	Axel	M	36–40	Latino/a	Pentecostal	WI	Installation, Maintenance, and Repair
19	11/7/2020	Bryan	M	51–55	Anglo American	Nondenom. Evangelical	IL	Personal Care and Service
20	11/10/2020	Ishmael	M	18–25	Latino/a	Evangelical	FL	Student
21	11/10/2020	Eric	M	36–40	Anglo American	Nondenom. Evangelical	IL	Personal Care and Service
22	11/11/2020	Joanna	F	36–40	Latino/a	Evangelical	NJ	Legal

List of Participants

ID	Interview date	Pseudonym	Gender	Age group	Congreg.	Christian Tradition / Theological Stream	State of Residence	Standard Occupation Class*
23	11/11/2020	Crystal	F	51–55	Latino/a	Evangelical	NY	Office and Admin. Support
24	11/11/2020	Sofia	F	18–25	Latino/a	Evangelical	NY	Student
25	11/12/2020	Mildred	F	36–40	Anglo American	Nondenom. Evangelical	IL	Office and Admin. Support
26	11/13/2020	Nelly	F	36–40	Latino/a	Nondenom. Evangelical	NY	Business and Financial Operations
27	11/24/2020	Wendy	F	51–55	Latino/a	Pentecostal	MA	Office and Admin. Support

Appendix D

Chronology of Content-Oriented Latino/a(s) Ethnic Identity Models

THIS SECTION SURVEYS FIVE salient content-oriented Latino/a(s) Ethnic Identity Models chronologically. These five models are predecessors of the Lifespan Model of Latinx Ethnic Identity Development (LMLEID), discussed thoroughly in Chapter 2. Together, these comprised the developing scholarship of forty years on the subject. As mentioned in previous chapters, content-oriented models focus on behaviors and attitudes of the individual towards the in-group. On the other hand, process-oriented models, such as LMLEID, concentrate on the self-understanding of how ethnic identity informs decisions. The LMLEID will not be discussed in this section.

ARCE'S MEXICAN AMERICAN TO CHICANISMO MODEL—1981

The first model to consider is Mexican American to Chicanismo, created by Carlos H. Arce.[1] In this model, Arce argues that Chicanismo as an identity is complex and best understood through various complementing concepts. He proposes that the influences of culture, group consciousness, and personal explorations frame the identity formation of this group.[2] More specifically, Arce's model explores the movement of Mexican Americans to Chicanismo through a series of interconnected processes.

Arce maintains that the terms Mexican American and Chicano are sometimes used in social literature and media interchangeably despite their

---

1. Arce, "Reconsideration of Chicano Culture."
2. Arce, "Reconsideration of Chicano Culture," 187.

Chronology of Content-Oriented Latino/a(s) Ethnic Identity Models

significant differences.[3] Arce sees the Chicano identity as an ethnic and racial term created by government policies and laws.[4] On the other hand, Mexican American is perceived as a Mexican family with Anglo traditions and values.[5] Both terms imply a common Mexican background, but social and self-awareness differences provide the foundation for Arce's model.

These definitions have changed over the years. Twenty years after Arce's model was published, Lillian Comas-Díaz sustained that Mexican Americans have Mexican descent but possess American citizenship.[6] On their part, Chicanos create an identity to separate themselves from Anglo cultural assimilation, asserts Comas-Diaz.[7] Despite its origins, multiple names have emerged as ethnic identifiers, confirming the complex and changing reality of ascription and self-ascription that minoritized groups navigate over time.

Starting with cultural influence, Arce states that the acculturation theory has inadequately explained the Mexican-American movement from non-assimilation to assimilation.[8] Although he does not elaborate on the distinction between acculturation and assimilation, Arce believes that acculturation theory is too rigid. It presupposes American identity as a goal and leaves little space for an alternate form of exploration and discovery of the original culture.[9] Arce suggests that Chicanos may also inquire about their cultural origins to find pride and meaning.[10] This search is characterized by heritage pride through the following sequence: (1) questioning the legitimacy of the dominant group over the minoritized, (2) shifting the locus of responsibility from the in-group to the out-group in terms of stereotypes and oppressive conceptions, and (3) changing the meanings of stereotypes, committing to a positive self-concept within the in-group.[11]

This process implies a self-aware movement from a Mexican-American stage to a Chicano stage rather than to a complete Anglo assimilation.[12]

---

3. Arce, "Reconsideration of Chicano Culture," 177.
4. Arce, "Reconsideration of Chicano Culture," 180.
5. Arce, "Reconsideration of Chicano Culture" 183.
6. Comas-Diaz, "Hispanics, Latinos, or Americanos," 118.
7. Comas-Diaz, "Hispanics, Latinos, or Americanos," 118.
8. Arce, "Reconsideration of Chicano Culture," 178–79.
9. Arce, "Reconsideration of Chicano Culture," 182.
10. Arce, "Reconsideration of Chicano Culture," 184.
11. Arce, "Reconsideration of Chicano Culture," 184.
12. Arce, "Reconsideration of Chicano Culture," 185.

Appendix D

However, it is not completely clear if the search for ethnic identity comes as a reaction to forces of assimilation or as one's own choice.

A second factor influencing the formation of the Chicano identity is group consciousness. Identity self-awareness is heightened by a season of group exploration in which Mexican history is explored for political awareness while Mexican values and behaviors are explored for cultural awareness.[13] The historical and current relationships (e.g., acceptance, rejection) between the majority culture and Mexican culture will provide a particular orientation to the individual's quest.

Lastly, the Chicano ethnic identity development is incomplete without understanding the personal movement from self-hatred to well-being.[14] The author notes that the social identification of the individual with the group provides higher self-esteem and well-being.[15] Although this movement from self-hatred to well-being is directly connected to group identification, understanding one's ethnic identity is a personal decision.[16] While Arce did not develop a clear argument concerning the source of the individual self-hatred, he seems to correlate well-being and ethnic identity, implying the opposite occurs through assimilation.

In summary, this conceptual model proposes that cultural, social, and personal explorations influence the development of Chicano identity. It assumes a complex process that only integrates some sources of influence in its entirety and gives no clarity on sequencing, orientation, and definitions. The model lacks a robust methodology and leans more on the conceptual than the empirical, raising sustainability questions. Although dated, it is regarded as one of the first academic efforts to address Latino/a(s) ethnic identity.

KEEFE AND PADILLA'S CHICANO ETHNICITY MODEL—1987

Six years after Arce published his model, Susan E. Keefe and Amado E. Padilla introduced the concepts of cultural awareness and ethnic loyalty as two primary factors that shape the ethnic identity of people of Mexican descent in the United States.[17] As opposed to Arce, their research included 370 individuals from various geographical areas and social statuses, and

13. Arce, "Reconsideration of Chicano Culture," 185.
14. Arce, "Reconsideration of Chicano Culture," 182.
15. Arce, "Reconsideration of Chicano Culture," 182.
16. Arce, "Reconsideration of Chicano Culture," 182–83.
17. Arce, "Reconsideration of Chicano Culture"; Keefe and Padilla, *Chicano Ethnicity*.

Chronology of Content-Oriented Latino/a(s) Ethnic Identity Models

their goal was to present a framework to understand Mexican-American ethnicity socially.[18] In their work, Keefe and Padilla assessed five cultural spheres that they concluded were most indicative of cultural change: 1) language familiarity and usage, 2) cultural heritage, 3) ethnic pride, 4) ethnic interaction, and 5) ethnic distance and perceived discrimination.[19] The model consisted of a scale for Mexican Americans on which the opposite poles are a strong Mexican orientation and a robust American orientation.

The first variable, cultural awareness, identifies those who have a profound comprehension of the traditions of both cultures.[20] This orientation revealed that family experiences define individual preferences and self-identification.[21] For this group, the English language and other Anglo-American mainstream characteristics (e.g., heritage, traditions, celebrations, and values) have little importance.[22] The authors, therefore, imply that knowledge and understanding are the primary drivers of cultural awareness to the extent to which it has been transferred by authoritative sources in the individual's upbringing.

The second variable is ethnic loyalty. This variable identifies adherence to a particular orientation, either cultural or ethnic.[23] This orientation depends on individual interpretation, including attitudes and feelings, towards the group—i.e., self-concept.[24] Keefe and Padilla sustain that this variable defines those groups in which the third and fourth generations only speak English, know very little about their cultural heritage, yet continue to find pride in it.[25] Ethnic loyalty and cultural awareness are seemingly informed choices but in different levels of sympathy and commitment.

With these two variables, Keefe and Padilla developed an identity orientation matrix that relates ethnic identity and acculturation.[26] First, they created a scale ranging from type one, which is unacculturated, self-identified Mexicans with low empathy for the Anglo-American mainstream influence, to type five, which identifies little with the Mexican culture and

---

18. Keefe and Padilla, *Chicano Ethnicity*, 23.
19. Keefe and Padilla, *Chicano Ethnicity*, 46.
20. Keefe and Padilla, *Chicano Ethnicity*, 46.
21. Keefe and Padilla, *Chicano Ethnicity*, 48.
22. Keefe and Padilla, *Chicano Ethnicity*, 53.
23. Keefe and Padilla, *Chicano Ethnicity*, 46.
24. Keefe and Padilla, *Chicano Ethnicity*, 48.
25. Keefe and Padilla, *Chicano Ethnicity*, 52.
26. Keefe and Padilla, *Chicano Ethnicity*, 55.

Appendix D

more with the Anglo-American.[27] Next, the authors introduce the type three individual in the middle, bicultural. According to the researchers, this middle orientation accounts for the highest number of individuals on the scale.[28] Finally, type two is characterized by moderate ethnic awareness yet no acculturation, and type four scores low on both variables.[29]

Thus, Keefe and Padilla's model suggests a progression of acculturation across generations based on cultural awareness and ethnic loyalty. One of the most salient findings of the study is the commitment to the ethnic group from the first to fourth generations—this is what the authors called "ethnic social orientation."[30] Over time, ethnic loyalty decreases from first to second generation but remains almost constant until the fifth generation. In contrast, cultural awareness declines consistently from one generation to another.[31] The authors identify kin and familial bonds as the main influences for this ethnic commitment across generations.[32] However, it should be noted that Keefe and Padilla make no specific mention of religious practices, beliefs, and values as part of this heritage and cultural awareness transfer, nor of the potential changes of orientation during one's lifetime.

FELIX-ORTIZ, NEWCOMB AND MYERS' MULTIDIMENSIONAL MODEL—1994

The third model in this chronology is the Multidimensional Model. In this study, María Felix-Ortiz, Michael D. Newcomb, and Hector Myers present a multidimensional measure of cultural identity that includes language, attitudes (or values), behaviors, and familiarity with the Anglo-American and the Latino/a(s) cultures.[33] This became the first model to include values and attitudes in its metrics, and its central assessment is defining bicultural and monocultural orientations.[34] Borrowing from the acculturation theory, this model categorizes Latino/a(s) orientations as 1) Latino-identified individuals, 2) high-level bicultural individuals, 3) American-identified individuals,

27. Keefe and Padilla, *Chicano Ethnicity*, 55.
28. Keefe and Padilla, *Chicano Ethnicity*, 55.
29. Keefe and Padilla, *Chicano Ethnicity*, 55.
30. Keefe and Padilla, *Chicano Ethnicity*, 52.
31. Keefe and Padilla, *Chicano Ethnicity*, 52–53.
32. Keefe and Padilla, *Chicano Ethnicity*, 144–45.
33. Felix-Ortiz et al., "Multidimensional Measure," 110.
34. Felix-Ortiz et al., "Multidimensional Measure," 102.

Chronology of Content-Oriented Latino/a(s) Ethnic Identity Models

and 4) low-level bicultural individuals.[35] Compared to its predecessors, this model presents a significant complexity in understanding ethnic identity development, incorporating more areas of self-understanding and leaving behind a binary approach.

The findings of this study suggest that these four orientations differed in language use and preference, behavior, and cultural familiarity but demonstrated no difference in the variables concerning values.[36] Regarding language preferences, the Latino-identified felt more comfortable with Spanish than English, while high-level bicultural individuals were the most flexible with language use.[37] Conversely, American-identified individuals and low-bicultural individuals were more uncomfortable using Spanish.[38] This resonates with the research of Helen Rose Ebaugh and Janet Saltzman Chafetz, who contend that preserving the Spanish language is a crucial connection to ethnic heritage, traditions, and identity that otherwise would be lost.[39] The authors conclude that the degree of commitment to the Spanish language seems to correlate to the level of mainstream cultural adherence.

Concerning behaviors, the researchers noticed a difference in political activism. Latino-identified and high-level bicultural individuals were significantly more politically active than the American-identified group.[40] However, the reasons for this difference await further exploration. The authors did not develop a strong case for this variable other than an implied potential relation to increased civic duty due to cultural awareness. To this end, Candelo et al. and Ecklund et al. argue that when individuals find their ethnic identity is affirmed, their civic participation increases.[41] However, bicultural orientations were not considered in either of the studies.

In the last layer of the assessment, cultural familiarity and social affiliations, Latino-identified individuals and high-level bicultural individuals preferred interacting within Latino/a(s) homogeneous circles than with Anglo Americans.[42] This sphere of familiarity also identified that

---

35. Felix-Ortiz et al., "Multidimensional Measure," 111.
36. Felix-Ortiz et al., "Multidimensional Measure," 111.
37. Felix-Ortiz et al., "Multidimensional Measure," 110–11.
38. Felix-Ortiz et al., "Multidimensional Measure," 110.
39. Ebaugh and Chafetz, "Dilemmas of Language," 432.
40. Felix-Ortiz et al., "A Multidimensional Measure," 110–11.
41. Candelo et al., "Identity and Social Exclusion"; Ecklund et al., "Motivating Civic Engagement."
42. Felix-Ortiz et al., "Multidimensional Measure," 110.

Appendix D

low-level bicultural individuals felt uncomfortable with either culture.[43] However, certain ambiguity is perceived in the term homogeneous circles since Latino/a(s) groups are generally composed of people from different Latin American countries. Thus, familiarity should be understood within a particular cultural expression rather than general.

Felix-Ortiz, Newcomb, and Myers claim that one of the most significant contributions of their study is that the multidimensional approach provides a more reliable identification of cultural identity.[44] For example, although other models rely on Spanish-language usage to discern the level of acculturation, an individual could be wrongly grouped if they have lost Spanish fluency while maintaining a Latino/a(s) commitment. In addition, by including a scale of behaviors and cultural familiarity beyond language, the authors sustain that the study provides additional context-specific behavior that could help cultural identity assessment.[45]

The multidimensional model added a series of critical variables and values to understanding Latino/a(s) ethnic identity construction and maintenance. However, although the model claims the accuracy of Latino/a(s) commitment independent of Spanish-language proficiency, it does not clarify nor expand on cultural behaviors. When two cultures come into contact, discerning how one influences the other and how many particular behaviors could be attributed to one or the other becomes more challenging. Furthermore, as noted in Chapter 2, one could be committed to a specific ethnic identity without exhibiting a particular set of behaviors.[46]

An essential limitation of this study must be noted when assessing its value. The authors reported 130 participants, most Mexican, college-aged, and second-generation.[47] The authors acknowledged that the findings should be neutral because participants were all from one United States West Coast college, and over 68 percent were females.[48]

---

43. Felix-Ortiz et al., "Multidimensional Measure," 113.
44. Felix-Ortiz et al., "Multidimensional Measure," 114.
45. Felix-Ortiz et al., "Multidimensional Measure," 112.
46. Phinney and Ong, "Conceptualization and Measurement."
47. Felix-Ortiz et al., "Multidimensional Measure," 113.
48. Felix-Ortiz et al., "Multidimensional Measure," 113.

TORRES AND PHELPS BICULTURAL ORIENTATION MODEL—1997, 1999

The fourth model to consider is the Bicultural Orientation model. In 1997, Vasti Torres and Rosemary E. Phelps introduced the Bicultural Orientation Model (BOM); two years later, it was validated by Torres through further empirical research.[49] The BOM considers the relationship between acculturation and ethnic identity and assumes that as one aspect increases, the other decreases.[50] Therefore, the BOM has four quadrants with two intersecting lines: acculturation (a horizontal line with left-end low and right-end high) and ethnic identity (a vertical line with top-end high and bottom-end low). This creates a matrix with the following orientations: Hispanic orientation (top-left), bicultural Orientation (top-right), Anglo Orientation (bottom-right), and Marginal Orientation (bottom-left).

Like Keefe and Padilla, Torres and Phelps looked at the relationship between acculturation and ethnic identity, but they worked within a bicultural framework.[51] They aimed to determine if Hispanic (from European Spaniard descent) college students could fit within a bicultural framework in which they could be competent in both cultures while maintaining a sense of identification with their culture of origin.[52] The first study surveyed forty self-identified Hispanic students from a southeastern college.[53] The second study included 372 second-generation Hispanic students from different Georgia, Florida, and Texas colleges.[54]

The BOM suggests that it is possible to distinguish between students with high levels of Hispanic ethnic pride and those who chose an Anglo-American orientation.[55] Although the model validates a bicultural orientation, the researchers also noted that some students fell into the marginal quadrant, which, in principle, describes an individual who does not feel comfortable within either culture.[56] The authors call this an unexpected

---

49. Torres, "Validation of a Bicultural."
50. Torres, "Validation of a Bicultural," 287.
51. Keefe and Padilla, *Chicano Ethnicity*; Torres and Phelps, "Hispanic American Acculturation," 58.
52. Torres and Phelps, "Hispanic American Acculturation," 59.
53. Torres and Phelps, "Hispanic American Acculturation," 59.
54. Torres, "Validation of a Bicultural," 289.
55. Torres, "Validation of a Bicultural," 289.
56. Torres, "Validation of a Bicultural," 294.

Appendix D

finding that requires further investigation because no model or theory accounts for such an orientation or stage.[57]

The BOM leaves uncertain significance because of the inability to provide a coherent understanding of all its quadrants. The marginal quadrant could point to a necessary revision in the methodology implemented, questions raised, and even the research method used. However, it served as an initial exploration for Vasti Torres, who in 2019 developed the LMLEID alongside Ebelia Hernández and Sylvia Martínez.[58]

FERDMAN AND GALLEGOS' RACIAL IDENTITY ORIENTATION MODEL—2001, 2012

The last two models in this chronology come from Bernardo Ferdman and Plácida Gallegos. In 2001, these authors introduced a nuanced Latino/a(s) racial identity model. Their proposal was not the first to consider race as an identity marker. Previously, William E. Cross suggested a Nigrescense identity model for African Americans and Jean Kim for Asian Americans.[59] Race and ethnicity are closely related and sometimes intertwined in these models.

Ferdman and Gallegos state that although ethnicity and culture are of primary importance, race is still very significant for Latino/a(s).[60] They suggest that acceptance to the group requires a set of ethnic or cultural identifiers, not claims of ancestry.[61] Nevertheless, Latino/a(s) culture values race and ancestry as part of their heritage, *mestizaje*, seeing unity and fluidity in diversity and challenging the categories established by Anglo-American dominant culture.[62][63]

Ferdman and Gallegos argue that Latino/a(s) reaction to racial categories varies from denial and shame to pride and acceptance.[64] This suggests that postures toward categorization could not be anticipated or generalized. Instead, these will vary from one individual's understanding to another. Latino/a(s) receive indications of boundaries and belonging at an early

57. Torres, "Validation of a Bicultural," 294.
58. Vasti Torres, personal phone call, February 13, 2019.
59. Cross, "Negro-to-Black Conversion"; Kim, "Processes of Asian American."
60. Ferdman and Gallegos, "Racial Identity Development," 44.
61. Ferdman and Gallegos, "Racial Identity Development," 44.
62. *Mestizaje* is a group made up of many cultures and ancestors (Ferdman and Gallegos, "Racial Identity Development," 45).
63. Ferdman and Gallegos, "Racial Identity Development," 44–47.
64. Ferdman and Gallegos, "Racial Identity Development," 45.

Chronology of Content-Oriented Latino/a(s) Ethnic Identity Models

age from parents and later through contact with different groups unlike themselves.[65] These indications encompass ethnicity, culture, and race and inform conduct within different social circles.

Considering these realities, Ferdman and Gallegos suggest a racial identity model with myriad orientations that respond to the realities Latino/a(s) face in the United States. The factors used by the authors to define a Latino/a individual's orientation towards their identity are 1) the "lens" toward identity, 2) the personal self-identification preference, 3) perception of the group from the outside, 4) how "Whites" are seen from the inside, and 5) how race is perceived.[66]

The model also frames each of these categories into six different orientations. First, Latino-integrated refers to the individual capable of processing and coping comprehensively with the Latino/a identity.[67] Second, a Latino-identified individual sustains a broad Latino/a(s) identity and keeps in high esteem certain places and historical markers relevant to the culture.[68] The third orientation is the identified subgroup, which describes the individual who gives preference to their group, either ethnically or by country of origin.[69] Fourth, Latino/a as "Other" points to the uninformed individual in terms of history and background concerning their group; these individuals cannot discern differences from other subgroups.[70] The fifth orientation is undifferentiated, which refers to individuals unwilling to compare and accept society's dominant norms.[71] Lastly, the sixth orientation, White-identified, describes Latino/a(s) who self-identify as White and perceive themselves as superior to people with different skin pigmentation.[72]

In 2012, Ferdman and Gallegos published an updated version of their racial orientation model. In this later version, the authors engage with coping strategies that Latino/a(s) might use, their environmental values, and the challenges of a particular orientation.[73], the model was expanded

---

65. Ferdman and Gallegos, "Racial Identity Development," 46.
66. Ferdman and Gallegos, "Racial Identity Development," 49–50.
67. Ferdman and Gallegos, "Racial Identity Development," 50.
68. Ferdman and Gallegos, "Racial Identity Development," 51.
69. Ferdman and Gallegos, "Racial Identity Development," 52.
70. Ferdman and Gallegos, "Racial Identity Development," 52.
71. Ferdman and Gallegos, "Racial Identity Development," 53.
72. Ferdman and Gallegos, "Racial Identity Development," 53.
73. Ferdman and Gallegos, "Latina and Latino Ethnoracial," 66.

Appendix D

to account for potential behavior under certain circumstances for each worldview or orientation.[74] These new variables are 1) *key* challenges, 2) adaptive for, 3) behavioral, and 4) limitations. The proposal with these elements is that even when the individual is free to choose, their decisions are strongly influenced by family, organizations, and other social structures.[75]

Ferdman and Gallegos explain that ethnic identity is not static, even as this model suggests a particular location and perspective for some Latino/a(s).[76] Individuals could change orientations by changing context and environment or experiencing dramatic socio-political events.[77] Moreover, this model affirms the individual's adaptability and problem-solving creativity.[78] Lastly, they conclude that racial orientations are closely linked to a place or social location; therefore, identifying salient identity aspects and tracing their relationship has limited value.[79]

Although Ferdman and Gallegos' model provides a nuanced approach to ethnic identity models by identifying its close relationship to race, behaviors, and contexts, one of its hindrances is the methodology. The authors only base their research on professional experiences, observations, and practice. Such limitations represent a concern in terms of application. A more robust and explicit methodology that clarifies participant's selection, generation (i.e., second, first), social status, demographics, gender, and religious participation would have provided more understanding of its use and application.

Ferdman and Gallegos's proposal stands out from all the previous Latino/a identity models because it considers a framework of intersectionalities and multiple dimensions to understand the Latino/a(s) ethnic identity.[80] In particular, this model provides a new layer of understating ethnic identity construction and maintenance considering the increasingly racialized American society. This points to the fact that minoritized groups also process their identity beyond behavior, language, or traditions. For example, skin pigmentation and physical attributes also become crucial factors of ethnic identity formation.

74. Ferdman and Gallegos, "Latina and Latino Ethnoracial," 66.
75. Ferdman and Gallegos, "Latina and Latino Ethnoracial," 64–65.
76. Ferdman and Gallegos, "Latina and Latino Ethnoracial," 66.
77. Ferdman and Gallegos, "Latina and Latino Ethnoracial," 55.
78. Ferdman and Gallegos, "Latina and Latino Ethnoracial," 66.
79. Ferdman and Gallegos, "Latina and Latino Ethnoracial," 73.
80. Ferdman and Gallegos, "Latina and Latino Ethnoracial."

Bibliography

Acevedo, Yamil. "The Immigrant—גֵּר(Ger)—in the Old Testament and the Formation of the People of God's Identity." *Anabaptist Witness: A Global Anabaptist and Mennonite Dialogue on Key Issues Facing the Church in Mission* 6 (2019) 55–74.

Agosto, Efraín. "Reading the Word in America: US Latino/a Religious Communities and Their Scriptures." In *Misreading America: Scriptures and Difference*, edited by Vincent L. Wimbush et al., 117–64. New York: Oxford University Press, 2013.

Alegría, Ricardo E. "La Fiesta de Santiago Apóstol (St. James the Apostle) in Loíza." *Journal of American Folklore* 69 (1956) 123–34.

Aponte, Edwin David. *¡Santo! Varieties of Latino/a Spirituality*. Maryknoll, NY: Orbis, 2012.

Araujo Dawson, Beverly, and Laura Quiros. "The Effects of Racial Socialization on the Racial and Ethnic Identity Development of Latinas." *Journal of Latina/o Psychology* 2 (2014) 200–213..

Arce, Carlos H. "A Reconsideration of Chicano Culture and Identity." *Daedalus* 110 (1981) 177–91.

Ashforth, Blake E., and Fred Mael. "Social Identity Theory and the Organization." *Academy of Management Review* 14 (1989) 20–39.

Banton, Michael. "The Vertical and Horizontal Dimensions of the Word Race." *Ethnicities* 10 (2010) 127–40.

———. *What Do We Know about Race and Ethnicity?* New York: Berghan, 2018.

Barreto, Amílcar Antonio. "Speaking English in Puerto Rico: The Impact of Affluence, Education and Return Migration." *Centro Journal* 12 (2000) 5–17.

Barth, Fredrik. *Ethnic Groups and Boundaries: The Social Organization of Culture Difference*. Long Grove, IL: Waveland, 1998.

Belmonte-Stephens, Armida, and Gregg Jao. "Nurturing the Next Generation." *Common Ground Journal: Perspectives on the Church in the 21st Century* 12 (2015) 75–82.

Bernal, Martha E., and George P. Knight, eds. *Ethnic Identity: Formation and Transmission among Hispanics and Other Minorities*. Albany, NY: State University of New York Press, 1993.

Berry, John W. "Ethnic Identity in Plural Societies." In *Ethnic Identity: Formation and Transmission Among Hispanics and Other Minorities*, edited by Martha E. Bernal and George P. Knight, 271–96. Albany, NY: State University of New York Press, 1993.

Berry, John W., et al. "Assessment of Acculturation." In *Field Methods in Cross-Cultural Research*, edited by Walter J. Lonner and John W. Berry. Cross-Cultural and Methodology Series, 291–348. Beverly Hills, CA: SAGE, 1986.

Bibliography

Bronfenbrenner, Urie. *The Ecology of Human Development: Experiments by Nature and Design*. Cambridge, MA: Harvard University Press, 1979.

Brubaker, Rogers. "Ethnicity, Race, and Nationalism." *Annual Review of Sociology* 35 (2009) 21–42.

Calvillo, Jonathan E., and Stanley R. Bailey. "Latino Religious Affiliation and Ethnic Identity." *Journal for the Scientific Study of Religion* 54 (2015) 57–78.

Camacho Escobar, Joanna Marie. "Aquí Se Habla Español: Cultural Identity and Language in Post-World War II Puerto Rico." PhD diss., University of Texas, 2017.

Candelo, Natalia, et al. "Identity and Social Exclusion: An Experiment with Hispanic Immigrants in the US." *Experimental Economics* (2011) 1–21. http://link.springer.com/article/10.1007/s10683-16-9492-91.

Chafetz, Janet Saltzman, and Helen Rose Ebaugh. *Religion and the New Immigrants: Continuities and Adaptations in Immigrant Congregations*. Walnut Creek, CA: AltaMira, 2000.

"Changing Faiths: Latinos and the Transformation of American Religion." Pew Research Center's *Hispanic Trends Project* (April 25, 2007). http://www.pewhispanic.org/2007/04/25/changing-faiths-latinos-and-the-transformation-of-american-religion.

Chavez, Alicia Fedelina, et al. "Learning to Value the" Other": A Framework of Individual Diversity Development." *Journal of College Student Development* 44 (2003) 453–69.

Chen, Carolyn, and Russell Jeung. *Sustaining Faith Traditions: Race, Ethnicity, and Religion among the Latino and Asian American Second Generation*. New York: New York University Press, 2012.

Cheng, Min, and Steven L. Berman. "Globalization and Identity Development: A Chinese Perspective." *New Directions for Child and Adolescent Development* 2012 (138) 103–21.

Christerson, Brad, et al. *Growing Up in America: The Power of Race in the Lives of Teens*. Stanford, CA: Stanford University Press, 2010.

Clandinin, D. Jean. "Narrative Inquiry: A Methodology for Studying Lived Experience." *Research Studies in Music Education* 27 (2006) 44–54.

Clandinin, D. Jean, et al. "Negotiating Narrative Inquiries: Living in a Tension-Filled Midst." *The Journal of Educational Research* 103 (2009) 81–90.

Cokley, Kevin O. "Racial (Ized) Identity, Ethnic Identity, and Afrocentric Values: Conceptual and Methodological Challenges in Understanding African American Identity." *Journal of Counseling Psychology* 52 (2005) 517–26.

Comas-Diaz, Lillian. "Hispanics, Latinos, or Americanos: The Evolution of Identity." *Cultural Diversity and Ethnic Minority Psychology* 7 (2001) 115–20.

Conde-Frazier, Elizabeth, and Andrew Y. Lee. "Intergenerational and Intercultural Issues." *Common Ground Journal: Perspectives on the Church in the 21st Century* 12 (2015) 67–74.

Conzen, Kathleen Neils, and David A. Gerber. "The Invention of Ethnicity: A Perspective from the U.S.A." *Journal of American Ethnic History* 12 (1992) 3.

Cornell, Stephen, and Douglas Hartmann. *Ethnicity and Race: Making Identities in a Changing World*. 2nd ed. Thousand Oaks, CA: Pine Forge, 2006.

Costas, Orlando. *Christ Outside the Gates: Mission Beyond Christendom*. Eugene, OR: Wipf & Stock, 1982.

Côté, James E., and Charles Levine. "A Critical Examination of the Ego Identity Status Paradigm." *Developmental Review* 8 (1988) 147–84.

Bibliography

Crespo, Orlando. *Being Latino in Christ*. Downers Grove, IL: InterVarsity, 2003.

Cross, William E., Jr. "The Negro-to-Black Conversion Experience." *Black World* 20 (1971) 13–27.

Cruz, Jose. *Identity and Power: Puerto Rican Politics and the Challenge of Ethnicity*. Philadelphia: Temple University Press, 2010.

Daniel, Justin. "Migration and the Reconstruction of Identity: The Puerto Rican Example." In *Politics of Identity*, edited by Hudson F. Réno, 3–23. Palgrave. Macmillan: Springer, 2000.

Deaux, Kay. "Surveying the Landscape of Immigration: Social Psychological Perspectives." *Journal of Community and Applied Psychology* 10 (2000) 421–31.

de la Torre, Miguel A. *Hispanic American Religious Cultures*, Volume 1. Santa Barbara, CA: ABC-CLIO, 2009.

de Río-González, Ana María del. "To Latinx or Not to Latinx: A Question of Gender Inclusivity Versus Gender Neutrality." *American Journal of Public Health* 111 (2021) 1018–21.

Denton, Rachel Ann. "Hablo Español, You Know? Language and Identity in the Puerto Rican Diaspora." Thesis, University of Tennessee, 2014. https://trace.tennessee.edu/cgi/viewcontent.cgi?article=4152&context=utk_gradthes.

Díaz-Stevens, Ana María, and Anthony M. Stevens-Arroyo. *Recognizing the Latino Resurgence in U.S. Religion: The Emmaus Paradigm*. New York: Routledge, 2018.

Domínguez-Rosado, Brenda. *The Unlinking of Language and Puerto Rican Identity: New Trends in Sight*. Newcastle upon Tyne, UK: Cambridge Scholars, 2015.

Duany, Jorge. *The Puerto Rican Nation on the Move: Identities on the Island and in the United States*. Chapel Hill, NC: University of North Carolina Press, 2002.

Ebaugh, Helen Rose, and Janet Saltzman Chafetz. "Dilemmas of Language in Immigrant Congregations: The Tie That Binds or the Tower of Babel?" *Review of Religious Research* 41 (2000) 432–52.

Ecklund, Elaine H., et al. "Motivating Civic Engagement: In-Group versus Out-Group Service Orientations among Mexican Americans in Religious and Nonreligious Organizations." *Sociology or Religion* 74 (2013) 370–91.

Elizondo, Virgilio. "Jesus the Galilean Jew in Mestizo Theology." *Theological Studies* 70 (2009) 262–80.

Erikson, Erik H. *Identity and the Life Cycle*. New York: W.W. Nortony, 1994.

———. *Identity: Youth and Crisis*. New York: W. W. Norton, 1994.

Escobar, Samuel. "Migration: Avenue and Challenge to Mission." *Missiology* 31 (2003)17–28. https://login.ezproxy.tiu.edu/login?URL=http://search.ebscohost.com/login.aspx?direct=true&db=rfh&AN=ATLA0001382754&site=ehost-live&scope=site.

Farley, Reynolds, and Richard Alba. "The New Second Generation in the United States." *International Migration Review* 36 (2002) 669–701.

Felix-Ortiz, Maria, et al. "A Multidimensional Measure of Cultural Identity for Latino and Latina Adolescents." *Hispanic Journal of Behavioral Sciences* 16 (1994) 99–115.

Ferdman, Bernardo M., and Placida I. Gallegos. "Latina and Latino Ethnoracial Identity Orientations: A Dynamic and Developmental Perspective." In *New Perspectives on Racial Identity Development: Integrating Emerging Frameworks*, edited by C.L. Wijeyesinghe and B. W. Jackson III. New York: New York University Press, 2012.

———. "Racial Identity Development and Latinos in the United States." In *New Perspectives on Racial Identity Development: A Theoretical and Practical Anthology*, edited by C. L. Wijeyesinghe and B. W. Jackson III. New York: New York University Press, 2001.

Bibliography

Flores, Juan. *Divided Borders: Essays on Puerto Rican Identities.* Houston, TX: Arte Público, 1993.

Flores-González, Nilda. *Citizens but Not Americans: Race and Belonging Among Latino Millennials.* New York: New York University Press, 2017.

Flores-Hughes, Grace. "The Origin of the Term 'Hispanic.'" *Harvard Journal of Hispanic Policy* 18 (2006) 81–84.

Foley, Michael W., and Dean R. Hoge. *Religion and the New Immigrants: How Faith Communities Form Our Newest Citizens.* Oxford: Oxford University Press, 2007.

Freeman, Melissa. *Modes of Thinking for Qualitative Data Analysis.* New York: Routledge, 2017.

French, Sabine Elizabeth, et al. "The Development of Ethnic Identity during Adolescence." *Developmental Psychology* 42 (2006) 1–10.

Geertz, Clifford. *The Interpretation of Cultures.* New York: Basic, 1973.

Giles, Howard, et al. "Social Identity in Puerto Rico." *International Journal of Psychology* 14 (1979) 185–201.

Glazer, Nathan, and Daniel Patrick Moynihan. *Beyond the Melting Pot: The Negroes, Puerto Ricans, Jews, Italians, and Irish of New York City.* Cambridge, MA: MIT Press, 1970.

Gold, Rosalind, and Angela Manso. "The Hispanic Origin and Race Questions in Census 2020: Making the Best of Missed Opportunities and a Flawed Approach." https://hagasecontar.org/wp-content/uploads/2019/12/The-Hispanic-Origin-and-Race-Questions-in-Census-2020-Final.pdf.

Gómez, Laura E. *Manifest Destinies: The Making of the Mexican American Race.* New York: New York University Press, 2007.

Gonzalez-Barrera, Ana. "The Ways Hispanics Describe Their Identity Vary across Immigrant Generations." Pew Research Center (September 24, 2020). https://www.pewresearch.org/fact-tank/2020/09/24/the-ways-hispanics-describe-their-identity-vary-across-immigrant-generations.

Grosfoguel, Ramón. "Race and Ethnicity or Racialized Ethnicities? Identities within Global Coloniality." *Ethnicities* 4 (2004) 315–36.

Harris, Max. *Carnival and Other Christian Festivals: Folk Theology and Folk Performance.* Austin, TX: University of Texas Press, 2003.

———. "Masking the Site: The Fiestas de Santiago Apóstol in Loíza, Puerto Rico." *Journal of American Folklore* 114 (2001) 358–69.

Helms, Janet A. "Some Better Practices for Measuring Racial and Ethnic Identity Constructs." *Journal of Counseling Psychology* 54 (2007) 235–46.

Hogg, Michael A., et al. "A Tale of Two Theories: A Critical Comparison of Identity Theory with Social Identity Theory." *Social Psychology Quarterly* 58 (1995) 255–69.

Hughes, Diane. "Correlates of African American and Latino Parents' Messages to Children about Ethnicity and Race: A Comparative Study of Racial Socialization." *American Journal of Community Psychology* 31 (2003) 15–33.

Jenkins, Richard. *Rethinking Ethnicity: Arguments and Explorations.* Second Edition. Thousand Oaks, CA: SAGE, 2008.

Jiménez, Tomás R. "Affiliative Ethnic Identity: A More Elastic Link between Ethnic Ancestry and Culture." *Ethnic and Racial Studies* 33 (2010) 1756–75.

Keefe, Susan E., and Amado M. Padilla. *Chicano Ethnicity.* Albuquerque: University of New Mexico Press, 1987.

Bibliography

Kim, Jean. "Processes of Asian American Identity Development: A Study of Japanese American Women's Perceptions of Their Struggle to Achieve Positive Identities as Americans of Asian Ancestry." PhD diss., University of Massachusetts, 1981. https://scholarworks.umass.edu/cgi/viewcontent.cgi?article=4686&context=dissertations_1.

Knight, George P., et al. "A Social Cognitive Model of the Development of Ethnic Identity and Ethnically Based Behaviors." In *Ethnic Identity: Formation and Transmission among Hispanics and Other Minorities*, edited by Martha E. Bernal and George P. Knight, 214–34. Albany, NY: State University of New York Press, 1993.

Krogstad, Jens Manuel, et al. "Key Facts about U.S. Latinos for National Hispanic Heritage Month." Pew Research Center (September 22, 2023). https://www.pewresearch.org/short-reads/2023/09/22/key-facts-about-us-latinos-for-national-hispanic-heritage-month.

———. "Key Findings about Puerto Rico." Pew Research Center (March 29, 2017). https://www.pewresearch.org/fact-tank/2017/03/29/key-findings-about-puerto-rico.

Landale, Nancy S., and Ralph Salvatore Oropesa. "White, Black, or Puerto Rican? Racial Self-Identification among Mainland and Island Puerto Ricans." *Social Forces* 81 (2002) 231–54.

Leeman, Jennifer. "Racializing Language: A History of Linguistic Ideologies in the U.S. Census." *Journal of Language and Politics* 3 (2004) 507–34.

Lluch, Jaime Gerardo. "Unpacking Political Identity: Race, Ethnicity, and Nationhood in a Federal Political System." *Ethnopolitic*, 18 (2018) 1–23.

———. "Unpacking Political Identity: Race, Ethnicity, and Nationhood in a Federal Political System." *Ethnopolitics* 18 (2019) 178–200.

López, Irene. "'But You Don't Look Puerto Rican': The Moderating Effect of Ethnic Identity on the Relation between Skin Color and Self-Esteem among Puerto Rican Women." *Cultural Diversity and Ethnic Minority Psychology* 14 (2008) 102–8.

López, Mark Hugo, et al. "Who Is Hispanic?" Pew Research Center (September 23, 2021). https://www.pewresearch.org/fact-tank/2021/09/23/who-is-hispanic.

———. "Latinos Now More Negative about Their Place in America." Pew Research Center's *Hispanic Trends Project* (October 25, 2018). https://www.pewresearch.org/hispanic/2018/10/25/latinos-have-become-more-pessimistic-about-their-place-in-america.

López Santiago, Angel "Monxo." "The Geography of Bernardo Vega's Memoirs." *Centro Journal* 30 (2018) 152–77.

Marcia, James E. "The Ego Identity Status Approach to Ego Identity." In *Ego Identity: A Handbook for Psychosocial Research*, edited by James E. Marcia et al., 3–21. New York: Springer New York, 1993.

———. "Identity and Psychological Development in Adulthood." *Identity: An International Journal of Theory and Research* 2 (2009) 7–28.

Martí, Gerardo. "The Diversity-Affirming Latino: Ethnic Options and the Ethnic Transcendent Expression of American Latino Religious Identity." In *Sustaining Faith Traditions: Race, Ethnicity, and Religion among the Latino and Asian American Second Generation*, edited by Carolyn Chen and Russell Jeung, 25–45. New York: New York University Press, 2012.

Martin, Douglas. "Lolita Lebrón, Puerto Rican Nationalist, Dies at 90." *The New York Times* (August 3, 2010) sec. A. https://www.nytimes.com/2010/08/03/us/03lebron.html.

Bibliography

Martínez, Juan Francisco. "Historical Reflections on the 'In-Betweenness' of Latino Protestantism." *Common Ground Journal* 12 (2015) 26–30.

———. *Walk with the People: Latino Ministry in the United States*. Nashville: Abingdon, 2008.

Maxwell, Joseph A. *Qualitative Research Design: An Interactive Approach*. 3rd ed. Applied Social Research Methods Series 41. Thousand Oaks, CA: SAGE, 2013.

Meeus, Wim. "The Study of Adolescent Identity Formation 2000–2010: A Review of Longitudinal Research." *Journal on Research on Adolescence* 21 (2011) 75–94.

Merriam, Sharan B., and Elizabeth J. Tisdell. *Qualitative Research: A Guide to Design and Implementation*. 4th ed. San Francisco, CA: Jossey-Bass, 2016.

Mochkofsky, Graciela. "Who Are You Calling Latinx?" *The New Yorker*. https://www.newyorker.com/news/daily-comment/who-are-you-calling-latinx.

Moore, Marguerite. "Puerto Rican and Proud: The Varying Understandings of Puerto Rican Identity among Island-Born and Mainland Puerto Rican Students at Syracuse University." Capstone, Syracuse University, 2009.

Morales, Ed. *Living in Spanglish: The Search for Latino Identity in America*. New York: LA Weekly Books for St. Martin's Press, 2002.

Nelson, Lise, and Nancy Hiemstra. "Latino Immigrants and the Renegotiation of Place and Belonging in Small Town America." *Social and Cultural Geography* 9 (2008) 319–42.

Nieves-Squires, Sarah. "Cultural Identity and Bilingualism the Puerto Rican Reality." *Journal of Pedagogy, Pluralism, and Practice* 1 (1998) 42.

Noe-Bustamante, Luis, et al. "Facts on Latinos of Puerto Rican Origin in the United States." Pew Research Center's *Hispanic Trends Project*. https://www.pewresearch.org/hispanic/fact-sheet/u-s-hispanics-facts-on-puerto-rican-origin-latinos.

———. "Latinx Used by Just 3% of U.S. Hispanics. About One-in-Four Have Heard of It." Pew Research Center's *Hispanic Trends Project* (August 11, 2020). https://www.pewresearch.org/hispanic/2020/08/11/about-one-in-four-u-s-hispanics-have-heard-of-latinx-but-just-3-use-it.

Ocampo, Katherine A., et al. "Gender, Race, and Ethnicity: The Sequencing of Social Constancies." In *Ethnic Identity: Formation and Transmission Among Hispanics and Other Minorities*, edited by Martha E. Bernal and George A. Knight, 11–30. Albany, NY: State University of New York Press, 1993.

Ontai-Grzebik, Lenna L., and Marcela Raffaelli. "Individual and Social Influences on Ethnic Identity among Latino Young Adults." *Journal of Adolescent Research* 19 (2004) 559–75.

Orsi, Robert A., and Richard Alba. "Passages in Piety: Generational Transitions and the Social and Religious Incorporation of Italian Americans." In *Immigration and Religion in America: Comparative and Historical Perspectives*, 32–55. New York: New York University Press, 2009.

Ortíz, Manuel. *The Hispanic Challenge: Opportunities Confronting the Church*. Downers Grove, IL: InterVarsity, 1993.

Peña, Milagros, and Carlos I. Hernández. "Second Generation Latin@: Faith Institutions and Identity Formations." In *Sustaining Faith Traditions: Race, Ethnicity, and Religion among the Latino and Asian American Second Generation*, edited by Carolyn Chen and Russell Jeung, 93–112. New York: New York University Press, 2012.

Pessar, Patricia R. *A Visa for a Dream: Dominicans in the United States*. Boston: Allyn and Bacon, 1995.

Bibliography

Pew Research Center. "2002 National Survey of Latinos: Generational Differences." March 19, 2004. https://www.pewresearch.org/race-and-ethnicity/2004/03/19/generational-differences.

Phinney, Jean S. "Ethic Identity and Acculturation." In *Acculturation: Advances in Theory, Measurement, and Applied Research*, edited by Kevin M. Chun et al., 63–81. Washington, DC: American Psychological Association, 2003.

———. "Ethnic Identity in Adolescents and Adults: Review of Research." *Psychological Bulletin* 108 (1990) 499–514.

———. "A Three-Stage Model of Ethnic Identity Development in Adolescence." In *Ethnic Identity: Formation and Transmission among Hispanics and Other Minorities*, edited by Martha E. Bernal and George P. Knight, 61–79. Albany, NY: State University of New York Press, 1993.

———. "When We Talk about American Ethnic Groups, What Do We Mean?" *American Psychologist* 51 (1996) 918–27.

Phinney, Jean S., and Anthony D. Ong. "Conceptualization and Measurement of Ethnic Identity: Current Status and Future Directions." *Journal of Counseling Psychology, Conceptual and Methodological Issues in the Study of Race and Ethnicity* 54 (2007) 271–81.

Phinney, Jean S., and Victor Chavira. "Ethnic Identity and Self-Esteem: An Exploratory Longitudinal Study." *Journal of Adolescence* 15 (1992) 271–81.

Portes, Alejandro, and Rubén G. Rumbaut. *Legacies: The Story of the Immigrant Second Generation*. Berkeley, CA: University of California Press, 2001.

Quintana, Stephen M., and Nicholas C. Scull. "Latino Ethnic Identity." In *The Handbook of U.S. Latino Psychology: Developmental and Community-Based Perspectives*, edited by Francisco A Villarruel, et al., 83–97. Thousand Oaks, CA: SAGE, 2009.

Redfield, Robert, et al. "Memorandum for the Study of Acculturation." *American Anthropologist* 38 (1936) 149–52.

"Revisions to the Standards for the Classification of Federal Data on Race and Ethnicity." Executive Office of the President, Office of Management and Budget. https://www.whitehouse.gov/wp-content/uploads/2017/11/Revisions-to-the-Standards-for-the-Classification-of-Federal-Data-on-Race-and-Ethnicity-October30-1997.pdf.

Rodríguez, Daniel A. "Becoming All Things to All Latinos: Case Studies in Contextualization from the Barrio." *Stone-Campbell Journal* 11 (2008) 199–211.

Roehling, Patricia V., et al. "The Immigration Debate and Its Relationship to the Ethnic Identity Development and Well-Being of Latino and White Youth." *Hispanic Journal of Behavioral Sciences* 32 (2010) 292–308.

Rogler, Lloyd H., et al. "Intergenerational Change in Ethnic Identity in the Puerto Rican Family." *International Migration Review* 14 (1980) 193–214.

Romanucci-Ross, et al. *Ethnic Identity: Problems and Prospects of the Twenty-First Century*. 4th ed. Lanham, MD: AltaMira, 2006.

Rúa, Mérida M. *A Grounded Identidad: Making New Lives in Chicago's Puerto Rican Neighborhoods*. New York: Oxford University Press, 2012.

Rumbaut, Rubén G. "Ages, Life Stages, and Generational Cohorts: Decomposing the Immigrant First and Second Generations in the United States." *International Migration Review* 38 (2004) 11601205.

———. "Pigments of Our Imagination: On the Racialization and Racial Identities of 'Hispanics' and 'Latinos.'" In *How the U.S. Racializes Latinos: White Hegemony and Its Consequences*, edited by Jose A. Cobas et al., 15–36. New York: Routledge, 2016.

Bibliography

Sack, Robert David. *Homo Geographicus: A Framework for Action, Awareness, and Moral Concern.* Baltimore, MD: The Johns Hopkins University Press, 1997.

Salinas, Cristobal, Jr. "The Complexity of the 'X' in Latinx: How Latinx/A/O Students Relate To, Identify With, and Understand the Term Latinx." *Journal of Hispanic Higher Education* 19 (January 2020) 149–68.

Saldaña, Johnny. *The Coding Manual for Qualitative Researchers.* 3rd ed. Los Angeles: SAGE, 2018.

Sánchez, Luis. "Puerto Rico's 79th Municipality?: Identity, Hybridity, and Transnationalism within the Puerto Rican Diaspora in Orlando, Florida." PhD diss., Tallahassee, FL: Florida State University. https://diginole.lib.fsu.edu/islandora/object/fsu:180335/datastream/PDF/view.

Schwartz, Seth J., and Byron L. Zamboanga. "Testing Berry's Model of Acculturation: A Confirmatory Latent Class Approach." *Cultural Diversity and Ethnic Minority Psychology* 14 (2008) 275.

Schwartz, Seth J., et al. "Identity in Emerging Adulthood: Reviewing the Field and Looking Forward." *Emerging Adulthood* 1 (2013) 96–113.

Stavans, Ilan. *The Hispanic Condition: The Power of a People.* 2nd ed. New York: Harper Collins, 2001.

Stets, Jan E., and Peter J. Burke. "Identity Theory and Social Identity Theory." *Social Psychology Quarterly* 63 (2000) 224–37.

Suárez-Ortega, Magdalena. "Performance, Reflexivity, and Learning Through Biographical-Narrative Research." *Qualitative Inquiry* 19 (2013) 189–200.

Tajfel, Henri, and John C. Turner. "An Integrative Theory of Intergroup Conflict." In *The Social Psychology of Intergroup Relations,* edited by William G. Austin and Stephen Worchel, 33:33–47. Monterrey, CA: Brooks/Cole, 1979.

Taylor, Paul, et al. "When Labels Don't Fit: Hispanics and Their Views of Identity." Pew Research Center's *Hispanic Trends Projec* (April 4, 2012). http://www.pewhispanic.org/2012/04/04/when-labels-dont-fit-hispanics-and-their-views-of-identity.

Torre, Carlos Antonio, et al., eds. *The Commuter Nation: Perspectives on Puerto Rican Migration.* Rio Piedras, Puerto Rico: Editorial de la Universidad de Puerto Rico, 1994.

Torres, Vasti. "Familial Influences on the Identity Development of Latino First-Year Students." *Journal of College Student Development* 45 (2004) 457–69.

———. "Validation of a Bicultural Orientation Model for Hispanic College Students." *Journal of College Student Development* 40 (1999) 285–98.

Torres, Vasti, et al. "Identity Development Theories in Student Affairs: Origins, Current Status, and New Approaches." *Journal of College Student Development* 50 (2009) 577–96.

———. *Understanding the Latinx Experience: Developmental and Contextual Influences.* Sterling, VA: Stylus, 2019.

Torres, Vasti, and Rosemary E. Phelps. "Hispanic American Acculturation and Ethnic Identity: A Bi-Cultural Model." *College Student Affairs Journal* 17 (1997) 53–68.

Trudeau, Daniel. "Politics of Belonging in the Construction of Landscapes: Place-Making, Boundary-Drawing and Exclusion." *Cultural Geographies* 13 (2006) 421–43.

Umaña-Taylor, Adriana J., et al. "Ethnic Identity and Self-Esteem of Latino Adolescents: Distinctions among the Latino Populations." *Journal of Adolescent Research* 17 (2002) 303–27.

———. "A Longitudinal Examination of Latino Adolescents' Ethnic Identity, Coping with Discrimination, and Self-Esteem." *The Journal of Early Adolescence* 28 (2008) 16–50.

Urciuoli, Bonnie. *Exposing Prejudice: Puerto Rican Experiences of Language, Race, and Class*. Long Grove: IL, Waveland, 2013.

"U.S. Census Bureau QuickFacts: United States." https://www.census.gov/quickfacts/fact/table/US/PST045218.

Vega, Bernardo. "Memoirs of Bernardo Vega: A Contribution to the History of the Puerto Rican Community in New York." In *Hispanic New York: A Source Book*, edited by Claudio Iván Remeseira, 71–106. New York: Columbia University Press, 2010.

Williams, Chelsea Derlan, et al. "A Lifespan Model of Ethnic-Racial Identity." *Research in Human Development, A Lifespan Approach to Ethnic-Racial Identity Development: Theory and Applications*, 17 (2020) 99–129.

Wood, Susan Carlson. "Do Latino Covenant Churches Need to Be Bilingual." *The Covenant Quarterly* 58 (2000) 45–58.

Yang, Fenggang, and Helen Rose Ebaugh. "Religion and Ethnicity among New Immigrants: The Impact of Majority/Minority Status in Home and Host Countries." *Journal for the Scientific Study of Religion* 40 (2001) 367–78.

Yip, Tiffany. "Ethnic Identity in Everyday Life: The Influence of Identity Development Status." *Child Development* 85 (2014) 205–19.

Index

Page numbers followed by *t* refer to a table on that page. Page numbers followed by an "n" and another number refer to a footnote on that page.

acculturation, 16–17, 157, 159–61, 163
adobo seasoning, 91
Advent, 71, 125
affiliate ethnic identity, 34
African-Americans, 29, 50, 92, 98, 164
age, 9–10, 61, 153–55. *See also* generational differences
Agosto, Efraín, 128
Alegría, Ricardo E., 47
altar calls, 105–6
American assimilated households, 66, 97
American Sociological Association (ASA), 26–27
American-identified individuals, 160, 161
Andrés (research participant), 72, 84, 88, 112, 116–17
Angel (research participant)
    childhood memories of, 69, 70–71, 72, 74
    estrangement and racism experienced by, 93–94, 96, 105
    evangelism by, 115
    on love and service, 112
    on personal relationship with Jesus, 79–80
Anglo orientation, 19*t*, 28, 134, 163
Anglo-American congregations (AACs)
    corporate approach of, 104–5, 119, 120–21

cultural barriers in, 89, 96, 97, 132, 134, 135
hindrances to belonging in, 104–8, 138–40
increasing inclusivity in, 144
individualistic focus of, 75–76, 101, 108
lack of family sense in, 102
racism in, 68, 106–7, 112, 120, 121, 138–39
reasons second-generation Puerto Ricans remain in, 109
in research population and selection, 9, 59, 60, 61, 153–55
Anicama, Catherine, 36
Anthony, Marc, 93
Araujo Dawson, Beverly, 30
Arce, Carlos H., 17, 33, 156–58
ascription, 44
assimilated households, 66, 97
assimilation, 157–58
Axel (research participant), 74, 80, 88, 100, 113

Baltimore, 76
Banton, Michael, 13–14, 25–26, 27–28
Barreto, Amílcar Antonio, 48, 50
El Barrio (Harlem neighborhood), 39–40
Barth, Frederik, 44
Belmonte-Stephens, Armida, 6

Index

belonging
    amongst other second- and third-generation Latino/a(s), 52
    church in, 99–109, 134, 135, 137–41
    comunidad in, 139, 140–43, 144
    cultural identity in, 90–92, 94–99, 131, 132–35, 141, 144
    in ethnic and racial identity theories and models, 15, 16, 32–33
    place in (*see* geographical belonging)
    Spanish language identity in, 49
bendición (blessing), 73–74, 124
Bernal, Martha E., 27
biases, 64–65, 85. *See also* racism
Bible
    ethnic identity and justice in, 52–53, 56, 85, 128, 136–37
    Great Commandment in, 53, 79n7
    Great Commission in, 82–83n9
    in spiritual disciplines, 55, 75, 84–85
Bicultural Orientation Model (BOM), 17–18, 163–64
biculturalism
    in belonging, 98–99, 133–34
    in the Bible, 53, 56, 136–37
    in content-oriented Latino/a(s) ethnic identity models, 17–18, 160–64
    in Lifetime Model of Latinx Ethnic Identity Development, 19t, 20–21, 23–24, 28, 134
    See also negotiating and strategizing belonging
Black Americans, 29, 50, 92, 98, 164
blessings, 73–74, 124
Boone, Herman, 78
borderlands of meaning-making, 18, 19t, 20, 21
Boston, 78, 90, 130–31
Brubaker, Rogers, 43
Bryan (research participant)
    childhood memories of, 67, 68, 75, 85
    estrangement and racism experienced by, 92, 104–6, 112, 120–21
budgets, 104–5
Byrd, Christy M., 36

Cajiga, Luis Germán, 69
Calzada, Esther J., 36
Camacho Escobar, Joann Marie, 50–51
Candelo, Natalia, 161
Carmen (research participant), 74, 79, 89–90, 101, 110–11, 115
Carol (research participant)
    on Bible study, 85
    childhood memories of, 70, 74–75, 77
    church belonging experienced by, 103
    code-switching by, 95–96
    college memories of, 90
    evangelism by, 116
    racism experienced by, 78
Catholics, 8, 55–56, 73
Census (United States), 13, 26–27, 43
Chafetz, Janet Saltzman, 161
character, 98
Chen, Carolyn, 3, 4, 137
Chicago, 42–43, 104
Chicanismo, 17, 156–58
Chicano Ethnicity Model, 17, 158–60
Chicano identity, 17, 156–60
Christian beliefs and values
    comunidad and, 123–26, 139, 140–43, 144
    evangelism in (*see* mission)
    faith and hope in, 55, 125, 141
    hospitality in, 73, 77–78, 118, 125–26, 141
    inclusivity in, 47
    justice in, 52–53, 80–81, 89–90, 106–7, 128, 130
    love in (*see* love)
    in meaning-making, 127–29
    outward- vs. inward-bound, 110–14
    spiritual disciplines in, 55, 75, 84–85
    See also theologies of Latino/a(s) ethnic identity
Christlikeness, 98, 133
Christmas season celebrations, 70–72, 124, 125, 143
church planting, 55, 100, 104–5
churches
    belonging in, 99–109, 134, 135, 137–41
    childhood memories from, 67–68, 72, 74–75

Index

corporate approach of, 104–5, 119, 120–21
cultural barriers in, 89, 96, 97, 132, 134, 135
discipleship in, 75–76, 118–19
in evangelism, 115, 116–21, 137, 138–40
as family, 68, 70–71, 93, 101–4, 140
generational differences in, 54, 86
increasing inclusivity in, 144
participation opportunities in, 100–102, 117–21, 137–40, 144
racism in, 68, 106–7, 112, 120, 121, 138–39
in research population and selection, 9, 59, 60, 61, 153–55
"silent exodus" in, 86
worship services in, 68, 105–6, 118, 124
See also Anglo-American congregations (AACs); Latino/a(s) congregations
civic participation, 161
See also social justice
code-switching, 94–97, 98, 132–33
coding, 62–64
colonialism, 44, 46–47, 120, 139
communications ministry, 101–2, 118
compassion, 113
comunidad, 123–26, 139, 140–43, 144
Conde-Frazier, Elizabeth, 14–15, 52
content-oriented Latino/a(s) ethnic identity models
background on, 4–6, 10, 17–18
Bicultural Orientation Model as, 17–18, 163–64
Chicano Ethnicity Model as, 17, 158–60
comunidad and, 126
Mexican-American to Chicanismo Model as, 17, 156–58
Multidimensional Model as, 17, 160–62
potential for exchange with process-oriented models, 23
Racial Identity Orientation Model as, 18, 27, 164–66

context, 21, 22, 32, 35–36, 46
continuous meaning-making, 19*t*, 20, 21, 35, 127–29, 143
Conzen, Kathleen Neils, 30–31
Côté, James E., 22
COVID-19 pandemic, 9, 60, 61, 78, 102, 103
credentials, 120–21, 139
Crespo, Orlando, 3–4, 48, 51–53, 134
critical moments, 19–20, 19*t*
See also dissonance
Cross, William E., 164
Crystal (research participant), 74
cuisine, 71, 91, 92, 125, 130–31
cultural awareness, 159, 160
cultural enclaves, 39–40, 41, 42, 67, 90–91, 130–31
cultural identity
in acculturation, 16–17, 157, 159–61, 163
in belonging, 90–92, 94–99, 131, 132–35, 141, 144
in the Bible, 53, 56, 136–37
Christian values and, 70–77, 141
comunidad in, 123–26, 139, 140–43, 144
in content-oriented ethnic identity models (*see* content-oriented Latino/a(s) ethnic identity models)
in cultural enclaves, 39–40, 41, 42, 90–91, 130–31
in evangelism, 83, 143
family in, 29–30, 48, 66–69, 159, 160
festivities in, 46–47, 70–72, 124, 125, 143
in Lifetime Model of Latinx Ethnic Identity Development, 19*t*, 20–21, 23–24, 28, 134
in multicultural environments, 91–92, 111, 121, 131
Puerto Rico's political status in, 41–42, 50–51
in racial socialization, 28–30, 32
Spanish language in, 47–51, 95, 97, 132–33, 161, 162
See also Latino/a(s) ethnic identity

Index

cultural racialization (racial socialization), 28–30, 32, 33

data collection and analysis, 62–64
de La Torre, Miguel A., 125
Denton, Rachel Ann, 8–9, 39, 41, 49
Díaz-Comas, Lillian, 157
discipleship, 75–76, 118–19
discrimination. *See* racism
dissonance, 19–20, 19t, 34–35, 127, 129, 143
Diversi, Marcelo, 35–36
diversity, 91–92, 111, 121, 131, 144
domestic violence, 78, 119, 127, 138
Domínguez-Rosado, Brenda, 49
Dominican-Americans, 29
double inheritances, 73, 126

Ebaugh, Helen Rose, 161
Ecklund, Elaine H., 161
ego identity theory, 16, 23
Ejesi, Kisa, 36
El Paso, 78
Elaborative coding, 64
Elizondo, Virgilio, 54–56, 136–37
emic, 26, 28
enclaves, 39–40, 41, 42, 67, 90–91, 130–31
English immigrants, 31
English language, 48, 49, 50, 58, 95, 159
English-speaking Latino/a(s) congregations (ELCs)
    belonging in, 100, 102–4, 134, 135, 138, 140–41
    exodus from Spanish-speaking congregations into, 86
    as family, 102–4, 140
    outreach ministries in, 119–20
    in research population and selection, 9, 59, 60, 61, 153–55
    spiritual disciplines in, 84–85
ERI (Lifespan Model of Ethnic-Racial Identity), 36
Eric (research participant), 84, 105, 114
Erickson, Erik H., 16, 22
Escobar, Samuel, 128, 139
Esteban (research participant), 68, 70, 75

Esther, Queen of Persia, 53
estrangement, 92–94, 104–8, 131, 138–40
ethnic and racial identity theories, 15–17
ethnic enclaves, 39–40, 41, 42, 67, 90–91, 130–31
ethnic identity. *See* Latino/a(s) ethnic identity; Latino/a(s) ethnic identity models (LEIMs)
ethnic loyalty, 159, 160
"ethnicity" concept, 27–28, 30–34, 36, 43–46
ethno-religious identity, 3–5, 6, 21, 46–47. *See also* Christian beliefs and values; churches; theologies of Latino/a(s) ethnic identity
etic, 26, 27–28
evangelism. *See* mission
Excel, 62, 64

faith, 55, 141
family
    in Christmas season celebrations, 70–71, 124, 125
    churches as, 68, 70–71, 93, 101–4, 140
    comunidad and, 125–26
    in cultural identity, 29–30, 48, 66–69, 159, 160
    in evangelism, 82–83, 135–36
    in Latino/a(s) ethnic identity models, 22, 29–30, 34, 159, 160
    in multicultural environments, 91–92, 131
    as "number one ministry", 76, 112
    religious upbringings from, 67–68, 74–75, 124
    in Spanish language identity, 48
Felix-Ortiz, María, 17, 24, 160–62
Ferdman, Bernardo, 18, 27, 164–66
Fernández, María Teresa, 67n1
Ferré, Luis A., 50
Fiestas de Santiago Apóstol (Festival of the Apostle James), 46–47
fifth-generation Latino/a(s), 49, 160
Fine, Mark A., 35–36
first-generation Latino/a(s), 3, 6, 9, 48, 54, 67
five-finger rule, 115

Index

Flores-González, Nilda, 49–50
Flores-Hughes, Grace, 13
Florida
    cultural belonging in, 91
    lack of cultural enclaves in, 40
    Latino/a(s) congregations in, 67–68, 120
    Puerto Rican ethnoracial identity in, 38–39
    in research populations, 61, 153, 154, 163
food, 71, 91, 92, 125, 130–31
forgiveness, 78–79, 103–4, 127–28, 141
fourth-generation Latino/a(s), 49, 159
Freeman, Melissa, 63, 65
friendships
    evangelism in, 82, 115–16, 135–36
    in geographical belonging, 38, 91–93, 131, 132
    love and service in, 112–13
    in strategizing and negotiating cultural identity, 94, 97

Galilee, 56, 136–37
Gallegos, Plácida, 18, 27, 164–66
Gautier, María Pabón, 36
Geertz, Clifford, 31
gender, 14, 61, 153–55, 162
generational differences
    in churches, 54, 86
    in Latino/a(s) ethnic and racial identity, 25, 52, 159, 160
    in Spanish language proficiency, 48–50, 52
    See also specific Latino/a(s) generations
geographical belonging
    barriers to, 92–94
    Christian beliefs in, 88–90, 129–32
    church participation in, 137–38, 143
    in cultural enclaves, 39–40, 41, 42, 67, 90–91, 130–31
    as future research area, 35–36, 145
    in multicultural environments, 91–92, 111, 131
    prior research on, 37–43
Georgia, 163

Gerber, David E., 30–31
Glazer, Nathan, 31, 32
God
    ethnic and racial equality before, 47
    in evangelism, 83, 88
    in justice, 52–53, 90
    relationship with, 79–80, 84–85, 113–14
    in spiritual disciplines, 55, 84–85
grace, 111–12
Grace (research participant), 78, 93, 107, 111–12, 116
Gracias a Dios (Thank God), 124
Great Commandment, 53, 79, 134
Great Commission, 62, 82, 114–17, 130. *See also* mission
Grosfoguel, Ramón, 44
Gustavo (research participant)
    childhood memories of, 73, 77, 80–81, 82–83
    on discipleship, 119
    estrangement and racism experienced by, 96, 106, 107
    geographical belonging experienced by, 91–92
    on love and service, 112

Harlem, 39–40
Harris, Max, 46–47
Helms, Janet A., 32
Hernández, Carlos I., 4
Hernández, Ebelia, 18, 20, 28, 35, 123, 164
Hernández Colón, Rafael, 51
Herskovits, Melville J., 16
high-level bicultural individuals, 160, 161
"Hispanic" label, 12–14, 25, 45. *See also* Latino/a(s) ethnic identity
Hispanic orientation, 163
hope, 55, 125, 141
horizontal dimension of race, 25–26
hospitality, 72–73, 77–78, 118, 125–26, 141, 143
Houston, 82
Hughes, Diane, 29–30
Humacao, 72
humility, 111, 141

Index

iceberg illustration, 116
Illinois
    church planting in, 104–5
    geographical belonging in, 42–43, 88, 92
    in research population and selection, 8, 60, 61, 153, 154, 155
In Vivo coding, 64
Indiana, 8, 60, 61, 70, 154
individualism, 76, 101, 108
interview methodology, 57–59, 62, 147–52
inward-bound Christian values, 113–14
Ishmael (research participant), 91, 116, 118

James (research participant), 75–76, 88–89, 106–8, 114, 118, 121
Jao, Gregg, 6
Javier (research participant)
    in church leadership roles, 118
    evangelism by, 111, 119–20
    on family and church family, 76, 103
    on relationship with God, 114
    on strategizing and negotiating cultural identity, 94–95
Jessica (research participant)
    bicultural identity of, 99
    childhood memories of, 67, 68
    church belonging experienced by, 68, 108
    on evangelism, 83, 120
    on Puerto Rican hospitality, 73
    on Three Kings Day, 70
Jesus
    as advocate, 81, 128
    compassion of, 113
    Galilean identity of, 56, 136–37
    Great Commandment of, 53, 79, 134
    in Great Commission, 82–83n9
    relationship with, 79–80, 113–14
    salvation through, 82, 129–30
Jeung, Russell, 3, 4, 137
jibaritos, 69
Jiménez, Tomás R., 34
Joanna (research participant), 69, 81, 84–85, 102, 117, 118

journalism, 81, 97, 128
Juan (research participant), 103–4
Julio (research participant), 78, 98, 115
justice, 52–53, 80–81, 89–90, 106–7, 128, 130

Keefe, Susan E., 17, 33, 158–60
Kenosha, 88–89
Kiang, Lisa, 36
Kim, Jean, 164
KKK (Ku Klux Klan), 68, 127
Knight, George P., 23, 27

Landale, Nancy S., 43, 45–46
language
    in Anglo-American congregations, 106, 132
    generational differences in, 47–50, 52
    in Latino/a(s) ethnic identity models, 159, 161, 162
    in Puerto Rico, 48, 50–51
    in research interviews, 58
    in strategizing and negotiating cultural identity, 94, 95, 96, 97, 132–33
"Latino" label, 12–14
Latino/a(s) congregations
    belonging in, 100, 102–4, 134, 135, 138, 140–41
    childhood memories from, 67–68, 72, 124
    discipleship in, 75–76
    as family, 68, 70–71, 93, 102–4, 140
    outreach ministries in, 119–20
    in research population and selection, 9, 59, 60, 61, 153–55
    "silent exodus" in, 86
    spiritual disciplines in, 84–85
    worship services in, 68, 105–6, 118, 124
    See also English-speaking Latino/a(s) congregations (ELCs); Spanish-speaking Latino/a(s) congregations
Latino/a(s) ethnic identity
    in ethnic and racial identity theories, 15–17

Index

language identity in (*see* language)
Latino, Latinx, and Hispanic labels in, 12–15, 25, 45
religious identity in, 3–5, 6, 21, 46–47 (*see also* Christian beliefs and values; Latino/a(s) congregations)
theologies of, 51–56, 134, 136–37, 141
See also Dominican-Americans; Mexican-Americans; Puerto Ricans
Latino/a(s) ethnic identity models (LEIMs)
background on, 2–3, 4–6, 10, 17–18
content-oriented models as (*see* content-oriented Latino/a(s) ethnic identity models)
"ethnicity" concept in, 27–28, 30–34, 36
interdisciplinary approach to, 145
Lifespan Model of Latinx Ethnic Identity Development as (*see* Lifespan Model of Latinx Ethnic Identity Development (LMLEID))
race in (*see* race)
religious identity and, 3, 5, 21, 126, 127, 131–32
self-awareness and well-being in, 34–36, 129, 157–58
specific national backgrounds and, 5–6, 21
Latino/a(s) month (*el mes de la Latinidad*), 68
Latino-identified orientation, 160, 161, 165
Latino-integrated orientation, 165
"Latinx" label, 14–15
Lebrón, Lolita, 81
Lee, Andrew Y., 52
Leeman, Jennifer, 49
Levine, Charles, 22
Lifespan Model of Ethnic-Racial Identity (ERI), 36
Lifespan Model of Latinx Ethnic Identity Development (LMLEID)
background on, 18–24, 19*t*
biculturalism in, 19*t*, 20–21, 23–24, 28, 134

Elaborative coding for, 64
meaning-making in, 19*t*, 20, 21, 35, 127–29, 143
race and racism in, 19–20, 21, 28
Linnaeus, Carl, 25
Linton, Ralph, 16
little devils (*vejigantes*), 47
Lluch, Jaime Gerardo, 44–45
Loíza, 46–47
looping, 18, 19*t*, 21, 23, 50, 129
López Santiago, Angel 'Monxo', 37–38, 39–40, 41, 42, 132
love
  in churches, 100, 103–4, 108, 141
  in evangelism, 83
  in Great Commandment, 53, 79, 134
  overview of Puerto Rican and Christian belief in, 77–80, 114
  as response to injustice, 78–79, 127–28
  in service, 100, 112–13
low-level bicultural individuals, 161–62

Marginal Orientation, 163–64
Marks, Amy, 36
Martí, Gerardo, 4
Martínez, Juan Francisco, 52, 54–55, 125, 141
Martínez, Sylvia, 18, 20, 28, 35, 123, 164
Martinez-Fuentes, Stefanie, 36
Maryland, 76
Massachusetts, 61, 78, 90, 130–31, 154, 155
matutinos (*parrandas*), 71, 72, 124, 125
Maxwell, Joseph A., 64
meaning-making, 19*t*, 20, 21, 35, 127–29, 143
Medianía, 46–47
Meeus, Wim, 22–23
memory, 65, 86
Memphis, 89–90
el mes de la Latinidad (Latino/a(s) month), 68
mestizaje, 164
mestizo theology, 55–56, 136–37
Metro-Orlando area, 38–39, 40, 41, 90, 91, 130–31

Index

Mexican-American to Chicanismo Model, 17, 156–58
Mexican-Americans, 13, 17, 22, 156–60, 162
Mexico border, 111–12, 116, 128. *See also* undocumented immigrants
micro-aggressions. *See* racism
Microsoft Excel, 62, 64
migration, theology of, 10, 11
Mildred (research participant), 71, 82, 92–93, 105, 118–19
minoritized groups, 16–17
missiology, 51–56, 135–41, 143–46
mission
    church participation and, 115, 116–21, 137, 138–40
    in geographical belonging, 88–90, 129–30
    individual understandings of, 114–17, 135–37
    in Latino/a(s) ethnic identity, 55
    outward- vs. inward-bound Christian values and, 110–14
    relational nature of, 82–83, 88, 111, 115–16, 130, 135–36, 143–44
    theology of migration in, 10, 11
mission trips, 115, 117
Moore, Margarette, 39, 40–41, 42
Morales, Ed, 52
Mordecai (biblical figure), 53
Moses, 52–53
Moynihan, Daniel Patrick, 31, 32
multiculturalism, 91–92, 93, 111, 121, 131, 144
Multidimensional Model, 17, 160–62
Muñoz Marín, Luis, 50
music, 68, 71, 72, 100, 118, 124
Myers, Hector, 17, 160–62

Narrative coding, 63
nationality, 25, 31. *See also* political identity
Las Navidades (Christmas season celebrations), 70–72, 124, 125, 143
Navy (United States), 43
negotiating and strategizing belonging, 94–97, 132–33

Nelly (research participant), 55, 84, 103–4, 113, 114
New Jersey
    cultural enclaves in, 67
    Latino/a(s) congregations in, 82–83
    multiculturalism in, 80–81, 91–92
    in research population and selection, 61, 153, 154
New Year, 72
New York
    geographical belonging in, 37–38, 39–40, 41, 92, 93
    in research population and selection, 61, 155
Newcomb, Michael D., 17, 160–62
Nieves-Squires, Sarah, 48–49, 50
Noche Buena (Christmas Eve), 70, 124
NVivo, 62–64

Ocampo, Katherine A., 27
Office of Management and Budget, 13
Ohio, 67
Ong, Anthony D., 32, 33, 34
Operación Serenidad (Operation Serenity), 50
Orlando, 38–39, 40, 41, 90, 91, 130–31
Oropesa, R. S., 43, 45–46
Ortiz, Manuel, 53–54, 140
outreach ministries, 78, 119–20, 138
outward-bound Christian values, 110–13

Padilla, Amado E., 17, 33, 158–60
parrandas (*matutinos*), 71, 72
pasteles, 71
Paul, the Apostle, 53
pedir la bendición (asking for blessing), 73–74, 124
Peña, Milagros, 4
Pew Research, 14, 47
Phelps, Rosemary E., 17, 163–64
Phinney, Jean S., 23, 24, 31–32, 33, 34
Phoebe (research participant), 121
political activism, 161
    See also social justice
political identity, 41–42, 44–45, 50–51
post-secondary education, 9–10, 60, 82, 90, 162

Index

prayer, 75, 84, 102, 114
process-oriented ethnic identity models
    definition of, 10
    Lifespan Model of Ethnic-Racial Identity as, 36
    Lifespan Model of Latinx Ethnic Identity Development as (*see* Lifespan Model of Latinx Ethnic Identity Development (LMLEID))
    non-linear proposals for, 22–23
proclamation. *See* mission
professional identity, 98
Protestant denominations, 8, 145, 153–55
Puerto Rican Day parade, 90
Puerto Rican nationalism, 81
Puerto Ricans
    racial self-identification in, 43
    religious demographics of, 3, 8
    in United States demography, 3
    See also second-generation Puerto Ricans (SGPRs)
Puerto Rico
    ethnic and racial identity in, 5, 44–46
    ethno-religious identity in, 46–47
    hospitality in, 72, 73
    language identity in, 48, 50–51
    political status of, 5, 41, 42
    Puerto Rican diaspora's connection to, 43, 67, 91, 97, 99
puertorriqueñidad (Puerto Ricanness), 43, 50

qualitative research. *See* research methodology
Quintana, Stephen M., 32, 36
Quiros, Laura, 30

race
    definitions of, 25–27, 28
    ethnicity and, 27–28, 30, 32, 33, 36, 43–46
    in Lifetime Model of Latinx Ethnic Identity Development, 21, 28
    in Puerto Rican identity, 43–46, 132, 133
    in Racial Identity Orientation Model, 18, 27, 164–66
    socialization by, 28–30, 32, 33
    in theologies of Latino/a(s) ethnic identity, 51–56
    US government's categories for, 13–14, 26–27
racial and ethnic identity theories, 15–17. *See also* Latino/a(s) ethnic identity models (LEIMs)
racial constancy, 27
Racial Identity Orientation Model, 18, 27, 164–66
racial socialization, 28–30, 32, 33
racialized religion, 4
racism
    in Anglo-American congregations, 68, 106–7, 112, 120, 121, 138–39
    Christian faith in responding to, 68, 78–79, 81, 127–28
    geographical belonging and, 88–89, 91–92, 93–94
    in Lifetime Model of Latinx Ethnic Identity Development, 19–20, 21, 28
    parental preparation for, 29–30
    in strategizing and negotiating cultural identity, 96
    See also social justice
Ramón (research participant), 72, 74, 77–78, 79, 111, 118
Raquel (research participant), 74, 92, 98, 112–13, 116
Redfield, Robert, 16
Regatta Columbus (1992), 51
relationships
    in churches, 75–76, 101, 118–20
    evangelism in, 82–83, 88, 111, 115–16, 130, 135–36, 143–44
    in geographical belonging, 38, 91–93, 130, 131, 132
    with God/Jesus, 79–80, 84–85, 113–14
    love and service in, 112–13
    in Puerto Rican Christian beliefs, 79–80
    in strategizing and negotiating cultural identity, 94, 97
    See also comunidad; family; friendships

Index

religious identity, 3–5, 6, 21, 46–47. *See also* Christian beliefs and values; churches; theologies of Latino/a(s) ethnic identity
Remember the Titans (film), 78
research methodology, 57–65
    data collection and analysis in, 62–64
    interview methodology in, 57–59, 62, 147–52
    limitations of, 8–10, 86, 144–46
    research locations in, 8–9, 60, 61, 153–55
    research population and selection in, 8–10, 59–61, 153–55
    research questions in, 7–8
    validity in, 64–65
respect, 108
Rodríguez, Daniel A., 139
Rogers, Leoandra Onnie, 36
Roman Catholics, 8, 55–56, 73
Rúa, Mérida, 42–43
Rumbaut, Ruben G., 25, 28, 46

Sack, Robert, 38
Saldaña, Johnny, 63–64
Salinas, Cristobal, Jr., 14
salsa music, 68
salvation, 82–83, 88, 129–30. *See also* mission
Sánchez, Luis, 8–9, 38–39, 40, 41, 61
Sandy (research participant), 103
Santiago, the Apostle, 46–47
Schwartz, Seth J., 23
Scriptures. *See* Bible
Scull, Nicholas C., 32
second-generation Latino/a(s)
    in churches, 53–54, 140
    differences based on country of origin, 144–45
    as generational support network, 52
    in Latino/a(s) ethnic identity models, 6, 162, 163
    in *mestizo* theology, 55–56, 136
    racial self-identification in, 25
    Spanish and Spanglish usage by, 49–50, 52
second-generation Puerto Ricans (SGPRs)
    belonging experienced by (*see* belonging)
    cultural identity in (*see* cultural identity)
    definition of, 9
    methodology for research on (*see* research methodology)
    religious demographics of, 3 (*see also* Christian beliefs and values; churches; mission)
self-ascription, 44
self-awareness, 34–36, 157–58
self-esteem, 15, 34, 35, 36, 129
self-hatred, 158
service, 100–102, 112–13, 116–20, 137
Seville's World Fair (1992), 51
silent exodus, 86
social identity theory, 15–16
social justice, 52–53, 80–81, 89–90, 106–7, 128, 130
socialization, racial, 28–30, 32, 33
socialization model, 22
socioeconomic status, 31, 50, 104
Sofía (research participant), 69, 101–2, 112, 113–14, 118
Sonia (research participant)
    childhood memories of, 67, 71, 72–73, 75
    college memories of, 82
    on evangelism, 115
    on strategizing and negotiating cultural identity, 96–97
South End (Boston neighborhood), 90
Spanglish, 52
Spanish language
    in Anglo-American congregations, 106
    in cultural identity, 47–51, 95, 97, 132–33, 161, 162
    in research interviews, 58
Spanish-speaking Latino/a(s) congregations, 9, 67, 68, 86, 105
spiritual disciplines, 55, 75, 84–85
Stavans, Ilan, 47–48

Index

strategizing and negotiating belonging, 94–97, 132–33
Structural coding, 63
Syracuse University, 39, 40

Tajfel, Henri, 15
T. C. High School, 78
Tennessee, 61, 89–90, 154
Texas, 61, 78, 82, 153, 163
theologies of Latino/a(s) ethnic identity, 51–56, 134, 136–37, 141
theology of migration, 10, 11
third-generation Latino/a(s), 3, 49, 50, 52, 53–54, 159
Three Kings Day (*Los Tres Santos Reyes*), 70, 124
Torres, Vasti, 17, 18, 20, 28, 35, 123, 163–64
triangulation, 65
Tuitt, Nicole R., 36
Turner, John C., 15

Umaña-Taylor, Adriana J., 35–36
undocumented immigrants, 80–81, 128. *See also* Mexico border
United States Census, 13, 26–27, 43
United States Navy, 43

validity of research, 64–65
Values coding, 63
Vanessa (research participant), 111
Vega, Bernardo, 37–38, 39–40, 41, 42, 132
vejigantes (little devils), 47

vertical dimension of race, 25, 26
Victoria (research participant)
  childhood memories of, 67–68, 70, 71
  church belonging experienced by, 67–68, 102–3
  geographical belonging experienced by, 90–91
  on Puerto Rican hospitality, 72
  as worship leader, 118
Vieques, 43
Virginia, 61, 78, 154

Washington, 88
Waukegan, 88, 130
well-being, 34–36, 129, 158
Wendy (research participant), 78, 111, 119
White, Lauren, 36
White Americans. *See* Anglo-American congregations (AACs)
White-identified Latino/a(s), 165
Whitesell, Nancy, 36
Williams, Chelsea Derlan, 36
Wisconsin
  Anglo-American congregations in, 75–76, 89
  racism and estrangement in, 88–89, 91
  in research population and selection, 61, 153, 154
Wisemen, 70
women's ministries, 78, 119, 127, 138
worship services, 68, 105–6, 118, 124

Zoom, 61, 62

www.ingramcontent.com/pod-product-compliance
Lightning Source LLC
Chambersburg PA
CBHW051739230426
43670CB00012B/2083